Hitler's
Boy
Soldiers

Hitler's Boy Soldiers

How My Father's Generation Was Trained to Kill and Sent to Die for Germany

HELENE MUNSON

THE EXPERIMENT

NEW YORK

The Experiment, LLC
220 East 23rd Street, Suite 600
New York, NY 10010-4658
theexperimentpublishing.com

THE EXPERIMENT and its colophon are registered trademarks of The Experiment, LLC. Many of the designations used by manufacturers and sellers to distinguish their products are claimed as trademarks. Where those designations appear in this book and The Experiment was aware of a trademark claim, the designations have been capitalized.

The Experiment's books are available at special discounts when purchased in bulk for premiums and sales promotions as well as for fund-raising or educational use. For details, contact us at info@theexperimentpublishing.com.

Library of Congress Cataloging-in-Publication Data available upon request

ISBN 978-1-61519-859-7
Ebook ISBN 978-1-61519-860-3

Jacket design by Beth Bugler
Cover photograph by Corbis Historical via Getty Images
Text design by Jack Dunnington
Author photograph by Janet Picinich

Manufactured in the United States of America

First printing May 2022
10 9 8 7 6 5 4 3 2 1

If you tell a lie big enough and keep repeating it, people will eventually come to believe it.

— Joseph Goebbels

Thou shalt not take vengeance, nor bear any grudge against the children of thy people.

—The Torah, Leviticus 19:18

Hamburg

Bremen ◉

Salzwedel

Hanover

Biederitz

Ro

Falkenberg/Elst

Dortmund

Essen

Düsseldorf

Leipzig

Germany

Cologne

Karlovy Vary

Frankfurt

Nuremberg

Stuttgart

Hans's journey from the Eastern Front back home to
Bremen in 1945

The author's journey from Berlin to Závada in 2013

Munich

CONTENTS

INTRODUCTION: *Závada Revisited* 1

1. The Wrong Time to Die 13

2. Traveling to Another Country 25

3. The Vanished Boarding School 37

4. Not a Napola 51

5. Castle Birdsong 65

6. Schooled by Barbarians 81

7. The Flag Is More Than Death 93

8. Franz and the Flak 107

9. Glasses and Mineral Water 125

10. Barrack Blues 135

11. Dresden and Departures 151

12. Arriving in Sudetenland 161

13. The Battle for Zawada 181

14. Saved by a Grenade 201

15. *Germanskis* on the Run 211

16. A Long Way Home 231

EPILOGUE: *The Back-to-Front File* 247

AFTERWORD: *The Glass Cabinet* 259

APPENDIX 1: *List of Locations* 271

APPENDIX 2: *List of Abbreviations and Glossary* 275

NOTES 279

BIBLIOGRAPHY 285

IMAGE CREDITS 291

ACKNOWLEDGMENTS 293

INDEX 295

ABOUT THE AUTHOR 310

ZÁVADA REVISITED

S OME OF US HAVE family members who had fascinating lives that inspire us; some of us have relatives whose lives were memorable, but troubling to contemplate. I had both in my father, who was known as Dr. Hans Dunker—a PhD in history, ambassador for the Federal Republic of Germany, family man, and dedicated church alderman. But he was also one of Hitler's boy soldiers and saw violence and evil that no child should witness, let alone be party to. The dark days of his childhood left him unable to talk about them. Instead, he bequeathed to me his boxes of carefully collected documents and the diary he had written of his days during the Second World War.

After my father's death in 2005, I banished the document boxes into the basement of my apartment in Berlin Kreuzberg, unable to face whatever they contained. What could have been so important that my father had kept those papers, transporting them from country to country as his diplomatic career required him to move around the world?

Six years later, I attended a course at Oxford Brookes University focusing on armed conflicts and children in war-torn countries such as the Democratic Republic of the Congo (DRC) or Afghanistan, making me realize the importance of my father's eyewitness account as a child soldier.

But the boxes contained much more: albums of sepia-colored photos; expired IDs from countries that no longer exist; letters written on translucent, thin airmail paper; and once urgent telegrams. A second diary had been written when he attended Feldafing, an elite Nazi school.

As I unpacked the containers, the story unfolded. Singled out as an extremely gifted child at age nine, my father Hans was separated from his parents, who lived as German expats in South America. In the misguided belief that a German boarding school would best serve their son's potential, his parents inadvertently turned him over to an elite Nazi educational system so controversial and inhumane that, until recently, postwar Germany has worked hard to keep it secret. When the school sent him into active combat at age seventeen, he was already accustomed to seeing death. He and his classmates had been shooting down enemy planes since they were fifteen years old. But what happened in a small eastern village just before the end of the war would devastate and cripple him.

Hans's poignant account, starting in early spring 1945, details how he and his school friends, badly trained, with neither enough ammunition nor sufficient food rations, were sent to the front wearing makeshift uniforms—at a time when the war was already lost.

Originally, I intended to publish the war diary on its own as a warning to a world still sending children into battles, oblivious to the true cost to society—not just to the underage soldiers, but to their families and future generations. After working

Hilde, Hans's mother, promoting Olympia typewriters, as Hans's father, Heinz, is building up a dealership for German equipment in South America while their son is sent to boarding school in Germany.

on the diary—translating it, researching its historical context, and interviewing eyewitnesses to substantiate its accounts—my work felt incomplete. I needed a deeper emotional connection to understand what had really happened to my father, leaving him with a post-traumatic stress disorder that had affected our family for decades.

On the first page of my father's yellowed and brittle diary was one word: *Zawada*.

I discovered that Zawada was a little village with great significance for him. Eventually I located it after cross-referencing the name with surrounding towns mentioned in the diary and determining that the German *Zawada* was now the Czech *Závada*, spelled with a *v* instead of a *w*. I ruled out several other villages with the same name in Poland, since I knew that my father had fought in what is now the Czech Republic but until 1993 was part of Czechoslovakia, in an area Sudeten Germans had inhabited since the Middle Ages. Using a place-name dictionary published by displaced Sudeten Germans, I reconstructed his route from a pre–Second World War map of the area.

In his old age, my father could have returned to Zawada, once West Germans were allowed to travel into the former communist states after 1990, when the Cold War ended. But my mother told me he had refused. They had only traveled as far as Pirna, a town located between Dresden and Germany's border with the Czech Republic. By the time I read the diary, he was dead. I felt obliged to complete the journey for him. After translating the village's Czech website, I sent an email in English to Závada's mayor.

The mayor's English-speaking assistant, Andrea Lorkova, sent me a kind reply and invited me to visit. In March 2013, I started out from Berlin and headed toward Dresden on the autobahn, rebuilt with several lanes after Germany's reunification in 1990. The new highway system once again connected the two parts of Germany. I followed my father's original route from Berlin; his cattle train had stopped on the outskirts of the city on the way to the Eastern Front.

When I first read the diary, the place names Hans mentioned meant nothing to me. For my generation of West Germans, the areas south and east of Berlin were blank parts of the map, hidden behind the Iron Curtain. Now these places appeared before my eyes. The weather was just as cold and unpleasant as it must have been when my father was deployed in the spring of 1945, with snow flurries and a still-frozen ground. After a two-hour drive, I reached Dresden and enjoyed a stroll through its carefully rebuilt historic city center, the city once more a magnet for culture and art.

Dresden was in total ruins when Hans traveled through. When the Allies dropped a record number of bombs on the city in 1945, Dresden was overflowing with thousands of desperate refugees. Among them, hundreds of children were killed.

After Dresden, my route narrowed to a single lane, involving hairpin curves over mountain ranges and winding through farming villages with speed restrictions. I stopped at the small city of Pirna, sixteen miles south of Dresden, where Hans had stayed in a hospital for several weeks. The kindness of Pirna's inhabitants, who had shared their own meager rations with the injured boy soldiers, left a lasting impression on him. I passed the turn to the small town of Bad Gottleuba, where my father spent another month in a sanatorium, recuperating from his injuries. I decided not to stop, as I wanted to reach the Czech Republic before dark. The drive took me through "the Switzerland of Saxony," with its dramatic mountain ranges and deep forests. In the fading light, I drove through the valley of the River Elbe, with its spooky, bizarre rock formations— just as Hans had described it.

I spent the first night in the Czech border town of Děčín, once known as the Sudeten German town of Tetschen. I chose to stay at the Hotel Faust, an image of the demon Mephisto gracing its entrance hall. Goethe's play of the same name as the hotel had been my father's favorite. He carried the book with him during his whole ordeal.

The next day, I drove over a mountain range through several villages in which the famous Bohemian crystal is still produced. Glistening chandeliers could be seen in small shop windows that advertised outlet sales. I passed several antique shops and decided to stop at one. Many items had German writing on them—a first aid kit, kitchen utensils, and toys. I found some Karl May books in German and imagined that a little boy, just like my father, must have once considered them among his most cherished possessions. Photo albums had been torn apart, and the images were sold by the piece. Presumably these things, which still filled the entire antique shop from floor to ceiling, had belonged to the 3.5 million Sudeten Germans who had to leave everything behind when they were driven out by the Czech population at the end of the war. I picked up a heavy, rusty, black metal helmet with hardened brown leather straps. The store clerk informed me it was German. I wondered what had happened to the man who had once worn it. The items were quite inexpensive, and I would have liked a souvenir of this trip, but every piece had a sad story to tell, and I wanted none of it.

The next day, I noticed a large gray concrete bunker by the roadside. I stopped the car and walked around it. Here was some tangible evidence of the war I had come to rediscover. The bunker's interior was accessible, but I was hesitant to walk into the dark, cavernous space without a flashlight.

A German first aid kit in a tin box in a Bohemian antique store.

As I continued along the road, I saw many more bunkers. Soon, I did not bother to stop. I later learned that more than ten thousand still exist. Originally, I assumed that the German Army had built them, but learned that, instead, the Czechoslovak government had constructed them between 1935 and 1938 to defend its people against the Germans. In a tragic irony, the 1938 Munich Agreement turned the situation around. By granting Hitler the Czechoslovak areas settled by ethnic Germans as protectorates, those lines of defense fell into German hands.

I arrived in Závada shortly after lunch, exhilarated to have made it to the place I had imagined so many times while reading my father's diary. Looking at a few remaining older buildings, I realized that my father would have seen them too. In the middle of the village stood a small, pink church and, next to it, a stone crucifix. A German inscription on the stone base, dated 1898, used the original German spelling of the village name: *Zawada*. It felt strange standing at the spot where fighting took place. I stood where my father had stood, separated by sixty-eight years, almost to the day.

Vintage German postcard of the small church in Závada.

Andrea Lorkova, whom I had corresponded with, met me in the village square and took me to the mayor's office. Jan Stacha, a handsome man of sixty-two, with striking blue eyes, straw-blond hair, and a light complexion, received me warmly.

He made a lighthearted joke about himself looking very German. Andrea brought coffee and cake. Our meeting was emotional, with all of us talking about how the Second World War had affected our families. While my father was brought to fight in

Base of stone cross next to the church of Závada with a Protestant Sudeten German inscription from 1898.

this village, the *Wehrmacht* (the armed forces of Nazi Germany) had drafted Jan's father and uncle away from Závada to fight at the opposite end of the Reich. Only women and children were left behind; they either hid in their cellars or fled to relatives in Ostrava, 15 miles away, which was perceived to be safer but was also besieged toward the end of the war, as Hans had noted in his diary.

Jan Stacha (right) and Andrea Lorkova (left), the mayors of Závada, in 2013.

Jan retrieved a map of the village and produced the official village chronicle. For generations, each mayor had recorded village events as a historical record for his successors. Jan read the entries for the days my father was there, April 17–20, 1945, and Andrea translated. Although the chronicle addressed the loss of civilian life and contained an exact count of the remaining livestock, no combat details were included.

I asked many questions: "Where did the old manor house stand?" "Where was the village well?"

Jan was astonished at my knowledge of the village, based entirely on the diary. He confirmed what I had suspected: Hans's account is the only known eyewitness record of those fateful days in Závada. In this diary entry, Hans recounted the day he was wounded, writing about himself in second person:

> In the morning of the third day the commander gave us some recognition for sticking it out in this windy corner, and the announcement that the general attack of the Russians was imminent. The remaining parts of our platoons had been significantly decimated, and our defense became weaker . . . After one hour under heavy drumfire, you had a weird urge to stand up. At great pains, the faithful Wenzel managed to keep you down. . . . The gaunt König carried you back. You had been hit.

The battle ended with the total annihilation of his army division, but my father did not write about that. Combat ended for him when he was wounded. I wanted to leave a copy of my father's account in Závada, so I had brought photocopies of the diary and its English translation for the village archive.

I spoke to Jan and Andrea about my father, his school friend Karl who died in the battle, and the other boys from his school class at Feldafing—Gerd, Georg, Albert, and Dieter—whose fates were unknown to me. Nor did I know what happened to the other men who had fought alongside my father, or their bodies— Wenzel, old Martenson, König, the shepherd Hans, and platoon leader Hoffmann. I asked Jan where the German soldiers were buried. He told me that both armies retreated without being able to carry their dead. The few villagers who had been hiding in their cellars came out and were overwhelmed by death. They counted the bodies of ninety-eight German soldiers and eighty Russian soldiers that lay scattered all over the village. The townspeople dumped the bodies, regardless of nationality, in ditches in the street or in holes they dug in their backyards. Nobody bothered to ask who they were or mark the sites. But Jan recounted one incident that Andrea translated: "One woman retrieved personal documents from the body of the dead German she found in her yard. After the war was over, she mailed them back to his wife in Germany."

In February 1948, Czechoslovakia came under Russian influence, and the remains of the Russian soldiers that could be retrieved with the help of villagers were given a proper burial—but not the German bodies.

I told Jan that I was sorry for all that happened, and I was sure my father had felt the same way. Jan and I both expressed our regrets that my father hadn't made the trip back to Závada. He might have been less reluctant to face his painful memories once again had he known what a kind reception awaited him. To my apologies, Jan responded, "The past cannot be undone, but we can try to make the future better."

I spent the rest of the afternoon with Andrea at a bunker we identified based on my father's description and some calculations on the map. This was where Hans was taken after he was hit by pieces of a grenade. The bunker, a very large structure, sat abandoned in a stretch of woods still visibly streaked with now-overgrown trenches. Like my experience in the town center, I felt an odd sensation standing in the silent forest that, in 1945, had been covered with abandoned military paraphernalia, dead men, and wounded soldiers waiting for first aid and contemplating their fates.

No hotels or guesthouses existed in Závada, but as we returned from our afternoon excursion, Andrea kindly offered me her daughter's room. In the evening, we talked about war, peace, and the future of our children. We did not know it at the time, but two years later, Andrea would replace Jan Stacha as the mayor of Závada.

I told Andrea that I wanted to have a prayer said for the German boy soldiers in the little pink church. Our family had been Lutheran for many generations. While religion had not been a major part of my life, it had been very important for my father, who served as a church elder in Rheinbach, the town where I grew up, for many years.

The next day was Good Friday. Heavy snowflakes were falling when Andrea and I stopped at the priest's house across the street from the church in the neighboring village of Bohuslavice. Závada's church had no clergyman of its own.

The nameplate announced that the priest's name was Kazimir Buba. The blond young man who opened the door was dressed stylishly in a checkered flannel shirt and jeans, looking more like a hipster than a clergyman. Andrea explained my request in Czech, and he asked us in. He said that he spoke a few words of German but preferred for Andrea to continue to translate from my English to Czech. He ushered us into a room with a large, round table and bay windows that looked out onto a tranquil lake. It felt like the kind of room where many people had already comfortably poured out their hearts.

I talked about the six boys from Feldafing School and that my father's friend Karl Hacker's body was somewhere out there in the ground of Závada. Andrea translated, and Kazimir Buba listened. I wrote down the names of the six boys and placed the list folded with some Czech koruna banknotes on the table. I had learned from my days of visiting places of worship in the Ukraine that it is customary that a request for prayers be accompanied by a small personal sacrifice. Kazimir Buba reached into a drawer to issue me a receipt for my church donation. I told him that I did not care for a piece of paper. All I wanted from him was a promise that he would pray for the six Feldafing boys the next time he was holding a prayer session at the little pink church in Závada.

From my bag I pulled out six red candles with tin covers and asked him if there was a way to light them. He looked straight at me and promised he would pray for the young soldiers. Seeing the anguish in my eyes, he asked me politely if I would like to see the Bohuslavice church next door. Not sure why he was suggesting it, I nodded. We crossed the street, and just before the church entrance, he stopped in front of a memorial to the village's local soldiers and war victims.

My eyes wandered over the marble slate and I started reading: "Postulka, Alois, born 1928, died 1945 . . . Kotzur, Hans, born 1936, died 1945." The children of this village had also been senselessly slaughtered in those last weeks of war. Pastor Buba motioned me to place my six candles next to the ones already in front of the memorial. Andrea took a candle from my hands and, as we struggled to light it in the snowy wind, she said, "This one is for your father."

The priest folded his hands and spoke a prayer in Czech. When he saw my tears, he began to recite the Lord's Prayer in German. I joined in, and when he could not remember the last few lines in German, I completed them. This prayer was the one I had not spoken with my father at his deathbed and wished I had. I was moved to see candles for my father and his friends lit and placed underneath a memorial for Second World War soldiers. And I realized that this small ceremony was probably the first and only act of commemoration for this group of German boy soldiers who were now only remembered in the pages of my father's diary.

1

—

THE WRONG TIME TO DIE

T HE GROUNDS AROUND THE Rudolf Virchow Hospital in Berlin, where my father spent his last days, were elaborately landscaped. The architect, Ludwig Hoffmann, had envisioned a hospital surrounded by gardens to promote patients' healing. When it was inaugurated in 1906 by Kaiser Wilhelm II, the layout was considered the most innovative and advanced facility in all of Europe. By 2005, the trees had grown tall and gnarly, providing shade on a warm July day. Twittering songbirds perched up high in the branches, adding to the sense of tranquility evoked by the lush, green vegetation and the cut-grass–infused smell of summer. Partially moss-covered stone benches and some marble heads on pedestals, depicting forgotten pioneers of medical history, were spread all over the property.

I pushed my father's wheelchair over a gravel path and parked it next to a bench, on which I sat. It was an odd feeling to see my once statuesque father so small and fragile. The flimsy hospital gown covered by a bathrobe was an open acknowledgment that he was a man too sick to dress up to go out in public. His now-thin calves were naked. A pair of my mother's hand-knitted socks covered his feet, stuck in a pair of felt slippers. I looked away. As a little girl I remembered him dressed in a tuxedo or morning coat attending official functions, wearing the medals he had been awarded during his diplomatic missions. The most striking one was a large gold star hanging on a broad white-and-blue ribbon. The color picked up the bright blue of his eyes. How hard we laughed when my mother told us that when they had been presented at the Court of St. James's, Her Royal Highness Princess Margaret accidentally addressed him as His Excellency the Ambassador, when he had only been the first secretary at the German Embassy.

My relationship with my father had been difficult. At times I had resented him. But he had always been there, sometimes domineering and imposing, at other times teaching me about literature and art. I was not ready to see him die. I banned the thought of death from my mind. It felt much safer. Two agile, brown squirrels chased each other playfully across the grass. It seemed very much like the wrong time of year to be dying.

In contrast to me, my father was not in denial of his situation. He had been diagnosed with pancreatic cancer two months earlier and was rapidly declining. He sensed that he did not have much time left. An urgency to tell me about himself seemed to overcome him, as he struggled for words in deciding what to say first. Unable to remember what he had already told me in the past, he decided on a recap of his life:

I was born in 1927, in Concepción in the South of Chile. My parents were Heinz and Hilde, who had left Germany after the First World War to escape the chaos of the Weimar Republic. My father, Heinz, had an uncle in Chile, which must have inspired him to emigrate. My mother, Hilde, was always up for an adventure, having spent her childhood in colonial Burma.

His tone softened as he started to reflect:

> You know, my parents, your grandparents, never stayed in one place very long. My earliest memories are from living in Peru. Did you know that I spent my elementary school years in Miraflores in Lima? I was so happy there! My parents must have enjoyed their carefree expatriate lives in South America. I was a cute, flaxen-headed young boy, and they called me *Hansito*, which in Spanish means "Little Hans." All my parents' housekeepers fussed over me. I guess in the Latin culture all young children are indulged.

Hansito (Little Hans) during his happy childhood in Chile on vacation in 1933 with his parents, Heinz and Hilde, in the foothills of the Andes.

A shadow came over his face as he continued:

> But all that changed for me when my parents visited Germany in 1937. They left me there to get a "proper" German education. I was only nine years old, and Germany was a foreign country to me. There were so many rules to follow! I was terribly homesick, and had I known that I would not see my parents and my brother again for over ten years, I would have probably despaired. But your great aunt, Auntie Tali, my father's sister, took me under her wing. We visited places in Bremen that would have made any child happy. There were delicious meals of *Labskaus* in the *Ratskeller*, hot chocolate and cake at the *Meierei*, and a whole series of Karl May and Doctor Ulebuhle adventure books at the bookstore in the Böttchergasse.

Hans at the train station in 1937, leaving for Feldafing School.

Sinking deeper into the chair, he remembered Auntie Tali:

> Auntie was a spinster, like so many women of her generation. Not enough men had come home from the First World War. I became the child she never had. She doted on me when I was staying with her in Bremen. I was particularly excited when paddling with her in the folding Klepper canoe on the River Weser. I learned how to use the 8mm cine camera she had given me. Later in the war, I filmed the planes that we boys had shot down when we were in the Flak.

16

He paused for a moment; then he recounted his earlier experience of arriving in Bremen: "At first, I was supposed to stay with my mother's parents, Johann and Marie. They owned a grand, old house on the Göbenstrasse in Bremen. They lived on the same street as Paul von Lettow-Vorbeck."

"Who was he?" I interrupted.

"You don't remember him from your school history lessons?" he asked, somewhat irritated.

"No, we were never told about him. There are lots of things that we were not taught," I responded somewhat defiantly.

"He was to the Germans what Cecil Rhodes was to the British: a hero during Germany's brief, ill-fated, colonial aspirations," he explained, assuming correctly that I had at least heard of Rhodes. Returning to his original story, he continued:

My mother's parents were old-school and felt that, according to the educational maxims of the time, children were to be seen, not heard. Grandfather Johann had been the German consul in British colonial Burma. Grandmother Marie had been a grand dame in the Rangoon expat society. She raised my mother Hilde and her other two daughters with the help of fifteen servants. My grandparents were nice enough but had little patience with a young boy. So, I went into the care of my father's family, more precisely Auntie Tali. She was a teacher herself and had convinced my parents that it would be best for me if I were to attend a first-rate government school with other children instead of living with my aging, inattentive grandparents. The school she suggested was special. Only the best and the brightest Aryan boys were accepted. It was she who convinced my parents that by attending Feldafing boarding school, I would be guaranteed a bright future in Germany, or as an *Auslandsdeutscher* if I chose to return to South America.

Hans in Feldafing School uniform saying goodbye to his father, who is leaving for South America. Hans wouldn't see his father again for more than a decade. He is flanked by his grandparents, August and Martha, who would take over his care together with Auntie Tali.

His mood changed to brooding. Almost to himself he mused, "How differently might my life have turned out if I had returned with them to Peru."

My father looked cold. He was so thin; I spread a blanket over him. For a while we sat next to each other in silence. The sun was lower now, and the frolicking squirrels had been replaced by dark shadows growing longer and longer. I wheeled him back into the building.

The next day, I arrived earlier at the hospital to catch more of the warm afternoon sun. I asked an orderly to bring a wheelchair, and as two men in white uniforms tried to lift my father into it, he grimaced in pain. With a tired movement of the hand, he asked to be returned to his bed. I sat down next to the bed expecting him to continue his story from the day before. But he stared into space saying nothing. Suddenly he grabbed my wrist and pulled me toward him. Looking straight at me, he asked urgently, "You have read *Zawada*, haven't you?"

About a year earlier my father had visited and placed a cloth-covered diary on my living room coffee table. It had the word *Zawada* written on it.

"Maybe you'd like to read the diary I wrote when I was a school-boy and they sent us into combat on the Eastern Front?" he had suggested.

The months went by and I had picked it up only once, reading a random passage in an earlier chapter:

> Marching in a row toward the dark woods, the moon is protecting
> its shining brightness with a thin veil of clouds in the middle of
> a deep, dark, fairy-tale-like blue. Every small leaf of the trees
> appearing a coal black, which longingly reaches toward the light,
> defends itself against the yellow paleness with which the lower
> part of the horizon is gradually being filled . . . pours itself against
> the magnificently displayed cloud art!

Impatiently skipping passages, I continued:

> Unstoppable and unforgiving, a golden wall of light pushes
> itself over the celestial sphere. Bonded with purplish, reddish,
> yellowish, and at last saturated, penetrating gold, the untiring
> cloud group continues its play of lines, circles, vortexes,
> silhouettes, and veils: form and emblem at the same time! In its
> eternal purity the vessel of the blue celestial sphere is holding
> all together in its holy circle. And the small group of humans
> continues to stride through the silent, still landscape of mounts.
> The earth is always ready; she can change in an instant in the
> most amazing ways. There, a ruby red flash through the tangled
> brambles! But the view is soon hindered by the dark shadows
> of the woods. The way leads below a heather heath. The tips of
> the heather bushes are radiating on top of crests. . . . The blue
> has almost vanished. . . . The eternal announcement of light has
> happened.

I had put the book down in disgust. The language was over the top; the description of a sunrise was overwritten. Occasionally, he had used such language in real life. I resented him for it and put distance between us. It would take me years to understand that this language was something he had learned at school. It had been a tool to mold the boys' emotions so that they could be exploited for a supposedly higher cause. If I had cared enough to read further, I would have found out that the diary contained the most heartbreaking story I would ever read, told in his own words. It was only the opening chapters that were written like a school essay gone wrong.

When my father visited again a few months later, he noticed that the diary was still in the same spot where he had left it, now covered with a thin layer of dust. He said nothing. He quietly put it back in his bag. I had the uneasy feeling that I might have missed out on something important. My father had retired and was making attempts to spend more time with us, his children. Most of his adult life he had been preoccupied by his postings as a German diplomat, organizing international conferences, liaising between government officials, and, most importantly to him, helping Namibia gain independence without bloodshed. According to his own definition, it had been his duty to contribute toward repairing Germany's damaged image in the world. He had been very serious about his work and had rarely found the time to attend high school graduations or other milestone events in the lives of his children. But now I was an adult myself and it was me who was too busy to spend time with him. Recently divorced and a single parent, I was in charge of a house in postunification East Berlin that, after years of communist negligence, needed to be renovated from cellar to roof. It was only after I found out how ill he was that I made time. Now seeing his slight silhouette in a mass of white starched sheets and pillows, I did not have the heart to tell him that I had not read the diary and lied, "Yes, I read most of it."

He scanned my face. I was embarrassed and wanted to avoid his gaze. Not knowing the story, I tried to look as neutral as possible. He let go of my wrist, looking into space again. Then returning to the moment, he said, "Never mind!" trying to hide his disappointment. With some solemnness he added, "After I am gone, I would like you to safeguard the family documents and *Zawada*, the diary. You are my eldest, I have always relied on you. I don't expect you to read them now, just keep them."

Having already failed him once, I promised, giving his hand a gentle squeeze, not realizing what a heavy burden I was taking on.

In the days that followed, my father deteriorated rapidly. Most days he seemed to be dozing or maybe he was unconscious; I could not tell the difference. He woke up only occasionally and would say something. Once he begged, "Please don't leave me alone here!" The place he was referring to was a room with gray linoleum floors and icy white, rough fiber wallpaper. Like a revolving door, hospital personnel filed in and out all day, each one performing their task on schedule with much efficiency, from checking his pulse to mopping the floor; their timetables were always out of sync with the patient's needs. It felt like the wrong place to die. I tried to spend as many days next to his bed as I could, usually reading the book I had brought to read to him.

One day I left it at home and, being bored, searched for alternative reading material. The pickings in the nearby visitors' room were slim: a few abandoned magazines of *Der Onkologe* ("The Oncologist") and a dog-eared copy of the German medieval romance *Parsifal* by Wolfram von Eschenbach. There was nothing I could do about the cancerous growths inside my father, so I did not want to read magazine articles about treatments that had not helped him. I decided on *Parsifal*. It was the kind of old-fashioned German literature that would have been read in school in my father's days. Much of the Nazi symbolism was borrowed from the regalia of medieval knights. In my own school days, we had read different books, such as Alfred Döblin's 1929 expressionist novel *Berlin Al-exanderplatz*, following a protagonist who, amid the hardships and deprivation of Germany's interwar years, struggles unsuccessfully to stay a decent man. Even though the *Parsifal* book was a trans-lation from the unreadable Middle High German (spoken in the High Middle Ages) to contemporary language, the reading was slow going. Eventually, though, the story captivated me: Parsifal, a naïve youth full of curiosity, has been wrongly instructed by his elders never to ask unnecessary questions. As he travels to become a knight, he meets Anfortas, the lord of a castle who has been injured in a wrongful fight. The wound festers and never heals. To give him relief from his pain, the tip of the lance of Christ is dipped into it. Heeding the advice given to him, Parsifal watches the ritual in silence. Only after he leaves does he find out that he is the only one who could have relieved the man's pain by asking one simple question: "What ails you, my lord?" After that, Parsifal has to go through years of trials and tribulations to eventually redeem himself for his initial error.

The following day, my father was transferred to the palliative care ward. The doctors had informed me that nothing more could be done for him. Patterned curtains and a few pieces of bright-ly upholstered furniture decorated the room to make it look less institutional. By now my mother had arrived, and we took turns sitting next to his bedside. My younger brother brought his three children; my daughter had returned from a vacation with her father and played with her cousins. They painted pictures for their *Opa* that he would never see.

The older of my two brothers stayed away, as he and my father had fallen out. He had always been interested in military history, ever since he and his friends had found some Second World War paraphernalia on forgotten battlefields in the Eifel, a mountain range in Germany. But anything related to the Second World War and the Nazis could provoke an outburst of rage in my father.

I had one such experience when I brought a box of books into the house that was given to me by a neighbor whose husband had died. On top was a book with a swastika. My father screamed at me to take that filth into the garage and dispose of it. I knew better than to challenge him.

The palliative care unit had a Protestant minister on staff who came around daily. One day he asked us if we wanted to pray with him. I declined, thinking there would still be plenty of time for such things. I was wrong. Unaware that it would be his last day, I knelt next to my father's bed to stuff the stiff, white sheets back under the mattress resting on the metal frame. Suddenly I felt his hand on my head, gently stroking my hair. Awaking only for a moment he said, "You are taking care of everything. Who is taking care of you?"

A lump formed in my throat as I fought back tears. This difficult, at times harsh, man had loved me after all, and I had failed him by not bothering to find out what had made him into the person we had known.

We buried him in Bremen next to Auntie Tali. We ate *Labskaus* in the *Ratskeller* in his memory. After, I picked up the boxes of family documents from my parents' house just as I had promised. It would take me another six years before I could finally bring myself to read his diary, while on a sabbatical in India.

2

TRAVELING TO
ANOTHER COUNTRY

T HERE WAS MUCH ANTICIPATION. Hanging on to their treasured belongings, people were waiting in line for the counter
to open, to check in for their flight from Berlin to Mumbai.
Women wore colorful saris or modest, dark burkas; men were piling
plastic suitcases high on airport trolleys; and children were clinging
to their parents and their favorite stuffed animals.

Waiting, I pulled out my own treasure: a copy of my father's diary,
Zawada. After all the passengers had located their seat numbers and
I was snugly shoehorned into my space with a black belt strapped
across my midriff, I began reading my father's account of traveling to
the Eastern Front:

> I am still sitting in a café in Berlin, a city wet with rain and ready to
> fight, where the coffee-drinking people look at me in amazement.
> They are probably wondering why such a young guy like me is
> still sitting here in civilian clothes. I have been in three cinemas, in
> which I enjoyed a little bit of everything, to recover from waiting for
> three hours on the train platforms of the Lehrter railroad station,
> overcrowded with thousands of people.

I paused, thinking of today's Berlin. Where there had once been the
sprawling, majestic nineteenth-century train station, only three arches

remain, standing forlorn in the middle of a small park, where locals walk their dogs. Nothing reminds park-goers of the thousands of travelers who once passed through the place every day. In the last days of the war, millions of refugees were crowding its platforms. In 1945, both my parents passed through these arches within days of each other, my twelve-year-old mother traveling west to flee the approaching Russian Army, and my seventeen-year-old soldier father on a suicide mission to the Eastern Front. I continued reading:

> Children were almost squeezed to death. Mothers turned into
> hyenas out of an instinct of self-preservation and to protect their
> offspring. It somehow happened that I did not make it onto that
> train. I have not much hope, that even in the SFR [special priority
> train for people going to the front] I will get a standing spot. I met a
> comrade by the name of Rüffer who told me that our friend Hacker
> will also be in our party.

Yes, that sounded like my father. He had been fond of the Hacker family, whom we had visited in Nuremberg many times in the 1960s and 1970s when I was a child. It took me years to figure out that the family I had known belonged to the younger brother of the classmate Karl Hacker my father was referring to.

My father's decision to kill time between train departures by seeing as many movies as possible was consistent with his lifelong love of films, his favorite form of escape from reality. On that day, the atmosphere must have been desperate in overcrowded Berlin. In early spring 1945, streams of displaced people and refugees from the eastern German states, fleeing the wrath of the Russian Army, were passing through the city. The Allied forces were in the process of conquering Germany; Auschwitz had already been liberated, but beleaguered Berlin would hold out for a couple more months. Hans and his schoolmates were still being sent into combat even though the war was already lost to all but the Nazi elites, who were increasingly turning against their own people, desperately holding on to power at the expense of the civilian population. It was the time when the *Volkssturm*, an army of civilians, was mobilized, and every grandfather who could still walk and all schoolboys tall enough to hold a gun were sent into last-minute war massacres. But while there was already a serious shortage of everything, especially food, Joseph Goebbels's film propaganda machine was still going strong.

Hans saw the movie *Kolberg*, a grand-scale movie epic in color, a novelty at the time, depicting the resistance of a tiny Prussian town

"A fighter for the Third Reich" from Deutschland erwacht.

against the siege of Napoleon's grand armies. The subject matter was not coincidental. It was meant to encourage the population to believe in the *Endsieg*, the final victory against all odds. Even though the reports from the front by returning, injured soldiers were more than discouraging, the official line was that those were only temporary setbacks and Germany's victory was imminent. Believing otherwise was considered treason. In the final months of the war, anybody suspected of being a traitor was court-martialed and usually shot on the spot, a fate that my mother's seventeen-year-old brother, Ludwig, only narrowly escaped.

Kolberg opened in Berlin in January 1945 and ran under the constant threat of air raids until the fall of the city in May. I have never seen it, as it has been under lock and key in German film archives since 1945, considered a dangerous propaganda tool. Only snippets of it can be found on YouTube.

I continued reading the diary. Hans's tone changed dramatically in the entry written a few weeks later, during his stay in the barracks where he and several classmates were receiving a hastily contrived basic training. Here, the diary took on the form of letters addressed to his beloved Auntie Tali:

> You see, my writing has become as rough as my hand, which nowadays is only accustomed to clean, scrub, and polish my gun. In this regard we are spared nothing. I just found the last piece of candy in the corner of my locker and ate it with great delight. We have given up everything civilian. Right now, I am trying to direct that last bit of my remaining tenderness toward my gun, which has already revealed its age-acquired quirks and peculiarities to me.
>
> Yes, you're right in noticing, these letters are reminiscent of those I wrote in second or third grade. The numbness that I am experiencing at the moment appears to be hard to overcome. But we know that the time in this feared and infamous base camp for the recruits is a time when every German has to prove himself. Right now, for me there is only stand to attention, marching, cleaning, sleeping, and . . . the barracks.
>
> We are still far from starving. Sometimes we get two warm meals a day. Our communal hope to get time off to go outside has been repeatedly squashed. Not even taking the oath will help us. There are people here who have not been outside the barracks for 6 months. For now I am, and will stay, an infantryman! Yet even if I only had bloody stumps for legs, at heart one still remains a tank grenadier. The training starts with the basics again. Why? We are pushing the rock of Sisyphus from the first training weeks uphill again. Yes, right now everything is coming at me at once, it all seems to become confused, doubtful, and falling apart. One is only functioning. Against that one has to try to maintain one's own, personal, clear goals. I am muddling through. One has responsibilities—up to this day my platoon leader does not know me by name. To the contrary, one feels that it was all a giant betrayal, the party membership, the questionnaire, everything is probably already in the wastepaper basket.

I stopped reading; words had been crossed out after the diary had been completed. At first I could not figure out what they had been, but then I remembered an incident in the early 1990s in Rio de Janeiro, which had involved the local chapter of the B'nai B'rith, the oldest international Jewish organization, coming to my father's aid after a media campaign was mounted against him in the Brazilian press.

The crossed-out words had been *Partei Mitgliedsantrag* (party application), and Hans was very wrong about it being lost in a wastepaper basket. But how could he have applied to become a member of the National Socialist German Workers' Party (NSDAP)? Until 1975, the age of majority in Germany to vote and join a political party was twenty-one years. Anybody younger was part of the Hitler Youth. I picked up the diary again:

> One is only supposed to be a mass as a part of even greater masses, second-class, cheap substitute, cannon fodder without a feeling of community or pride. Yes, it seems to me that my life's purpose has already been carefully planned for me and I am trying now to fulfill it. I am here, to fulfill my obligations as a voluntary recruit, but I have to totally change a large part of my worldview. Any kind of ambition around here is dangerous. The more you can crawl into yourself and withdraw, the better. There is almost no connection to the surrounding world anymore, at least not an emotional one. Recently there was a moment of lightness during a march through the heather, which made it possible to overcome the present surrounding circumstances for a moment.

At the beginning of the passage, he is still referring to his aunt in the second person. By the end of the passage, he is using the second and even the third person when referring to himself, skillfully using pronouns to put some distance between himself and his experiences. He had started to realize that he was now far away from his cozy boarding school where they had been shielded from what was going on in the rest of Germany. Out there was another country, and it was rough.

I had arrived in another country as well. From Mumbai, I took a regional flight to the south Indian capital city of Kochi, in Kerala, famous for its Ayurveda, the ancient Indian art of healing the mind along with the body. I had come to undergo a whole course of treatment known as *panchakarma*, which culminates in purging oneself of mental and physical toxins that cause imbalances to the *doshas*, the life energy that needs to remain balanced in order to avoid sickness.

During the monsoon season the humidity in this lovely historic town was stifling. The oppressiveness of the stained mosquito net hanging over the bed, together with the humid, mold-infused air, was not conducive to falling asleep in my hostel room. For part of the night, I stayed up reading my father's diary in the dim light of a bare bulb hanging from the ceiling. Page by page, the story unfolded. The boys' bond becomes stronger as they are sent with a medley of mercenaries into an uncertain fate. I read:

> Rushed departure atmosphere, aggravation, hurry, and inconsiderateness. So, at the end of the insane training, you find yourself for a few minutes in the dirty, stale-smelling, cold room, which in the past weeks has only given you a few hours of rest each day. Really, the end is near. Whatever thugs could be rounded up in Europe seemed to be enjoying an undeserved honor here in these merciless barrack blocks. The honor to be treated and respected as soldiers who are supposed to fight for their fatherland. Like shadows, a thousand pictures of the vicious training program pass through your mind. You are almost unable to stay awake even for a few minutes on the worn-flat mattress without remembering it. One has become indifferent to the many experiences of an inhumane existence, which is not worth being recorded.

The sense of despair and betrayal were palpable in those lines. I started to understand why my father had not trusted the motives of other people for the rest of his life. In hindsight he might have wished he had not trusted his teachers. The boys were young and naive, but at least they had each other and tried to make the most of it. Hans wrote:

Nevertheless, it was an opportunity to experience beautiful moments in nature, in the heather and in the forest: the experience of friendship, to be together and walk next to each other. A ring has been forged around those who oppose the arbitrariness of destiny with their common firm will. And you felt that you could belong to the community of the living and the dead whose circle keeps you in their middle and leads you toward your goals.

Finally, in the early morning hours, I fell asleep and woke up exhausted and depressed. Why was it so hard to read this diary? Why had I left it untouched for years? As a West German of my generation, I always knew that we Germans had started two world wars and killed millions in the Holocaust. I had attended school in in the 1960s and '70s. In our history lessons, we had been shown the films of the concentration camps over and over, with images of emaciated figures with shaved heads. We had learned that the Holocaust had been the worst crime against humanity ever and that we as Germans were collectively responsible for it. There was no question about it. But reading about the plight of Germans in the diary added another facet that I could not easily reconcile with that narrative. The boys were being sent into combat on the ferocious Eastern Front as though it was a school trip, with desperate refugees on the train platforms, mothers fearing for the lives of their children; I could not help but pity them. But we had been the perpetrators, we deserved what we got.

31

I pulled myself together and went about my tourist agenda. My plan for the morning was to visit the last historic and oldest synagogue in India, in the Mattancherry part of town. I had never been inside a synagogue. Many ethnic and religious groups had lived peacefully side by side for centuries in this once famous spice-trading town. There had been a substantial Jewish community and a large Jewish cemetery was nearby. Now the sole remaining Jewish family in Kochi had become the self-appointed guardians of this unique place.

Tower of the synagogue in Kochi, India.

A woman in a headscarf and three-quarter-length skirt sold me an entrance ticket. A man wearing a yarmulke carefully checked my bag and locked it up before allowing me inside. It was a small, intimate structure with a white bell tower. The interior's most attractive feature was an abundance of crystal chandeliers. It was a peaceful place, but it was not grand. Surely there had been dozens of such small synagogues all over Germany, but I had never seen one. Only after my return from India would I find out that a very similar structure had once stood in Rheinbach, the town where I had grown up. It had been located across from the movie theater where we children had gone to watch Saturday matinees. Why had it taken until 2011 for the town of Rheinbach to erect a modest memorial plaque at the site of the synagogue? Why had my generation never asked if there had been a synagogue in our town? It seemed that our parents had sent us the unspoken message that those questions were better not asked.

What had possessed Germans to stand by idly when those sparkling chandeliers were trashed in what became known as Kristallnacht (the Night of Broken Glass)? But had they? I remembered one of the few anecdotes that my mother had shared about her own father, a middle-school teacher. In front of his students, he had vented his disgust over the barbarism of burning the synagogue in Mülheim, his hometown, and he had almost lost his job because of it. I made a mental note to call her and ask about the details.

There was so much more to know about those years, but it had never occurred to me to ask my father any of those questions while he was still alive. My generation had accepted our parents' silence. What we knew, we had learned in school. But we had sensed that there was another reality. The dad of one of my Rheinbach classmates had only one arm. The father of another one was never at home; he spent most of his time alone with his dog in the woods under the pretense of hunting, but never returned with any prey. My father was a rageaholic with a large, ugly scar on his leg. They had grown up in a time when boys did not cry and the term "post-traumatic stress disorder" had not been invented.

My heart and head felt heavy. Aimlessly I walked around the picturesque Kochi streets and saw a barbershop. A pretty young girl with waist-length, shiny black hair was the sole attendant. Overcome by a desire to clear my head, literally, I entered, telling her, "I would like you to shave my head."

"What?" she asked in disbelief. "Why? In India we women are so proud of our hair." But she obliged and opened my braids to brush out my long, chocolate-color hair. Reaching for the scissors, she asked, "Are you sure?"

"Please, take one last photo with my camera before you start cutting," I requested, feeling sentimental for a moment. But I was sure; giving up my hair seemed right. I felt sad, and having one's head shaved has been a mourning ritual for millennia.

"Save the strands carefully," I urged her and explained, "I will mail them to a British charity that makes wigs for girls with cancer."

When she finished, I looked in the mirror. I did not recognize myself. I felt vulnerable and a sense of shame, no longer having my hair to give me an identity. The black-and-white images of women with shaved heads in prison uniforms, behind barbed wire, looking all the same, flashed through my mind. They had been the victims of atrocious treatments. I had brought this upon myself, voluntarily and by choice. Humiliated, I looked away and wrapped my new nakedness self-consciously in a scarf.

Outside, the daily monsoon downpour had cleared the air. I stopped in a tea shop in the historic part of town. I sat at a table and after ordering some oversweet Indian tea, took out the diary and started reading again:

> I have reported to you at length about these events. I have to confess, the reality is much worse. Once accepted thoughts and rules are churned around in the poor, empty brain again and again. By obsessing over them, they become disjointed, empty, stale, and unbelievable. I want this condition to be recorded and hope for better times.

I looked up. A man of sturdy stature, in his early sixties with graying hair and a friendly, jovial smile, entered and sat at a table across from me. We were the only guests. Under a pretext, he started a casual conversation with me. After a few pleasantries, he remarked, "With your headscarf and conservative outfit, you look just like an Orthodox Jewish woman." I was wearing a knee-length tunic with wrist-length sleeves over loose trousers. On my first trip to India twenty years earlier I had learned my lesson. All through Delhi's Red Fort, several teenage Indian boys had trailed me, commenting on my tightly jeans-clad backside, with words that I did not understand and gestures that needed no translation.

Chaim had started to talk to me, to find out whether there were other Orthodox Jews in this town besides the guardians of the

34

synagogue. He explained, "I am visiting from southern California and am staying with the only Jewish family in town. They are my friends."

I felt grateful. Chaim, being Jewish, had a personal understanding of the Holocaust and the suffering that had gone with it. He was the perfect person for me to talk to about the thoughts that had weighed heavily on me all day. I told him my father's story. The boys had been teenagers and had suffered so much. I showed Chaim the diary.

We debated the complicated questions of guilt and innocence. Who was a perpetrator? Who was a victim? The answers were neither black nor white; there were way too many shades of gray. We talked at length about the suffering of children during war. Had the boys in the diary not suffered? Did they not have a right to feel that there was forgiveness for the sins of their forefathers? In the end, Chaim asked a question to which there seemed no answer: "Who would be able to forgive them? Would it be God, their fellow man, or survivors of the Holocaust?"

For a split second it occurred to me that the worst of it was that my father had not forgiven himself. He had died with the sense of guilt, and that guilt had become my inheritance. I felt responsible, despite the fact that I had been born in the late 1950s, years after it all happened. I wondered if the next generation of German children would feel transgenerational guilt as well. A thought formed in my mind. The story of these terrible events had to be told and be made public. The story had to be treated not like a dirty secret but rather as part of a horrific past that had to be confronted and learned from, to ensure that it would never repeat itself.

Maybe this was not about forgiveness—some things were too horrible to ever be forgiven—but about redemption. I remembered that Richard von Weizsäcker, a former German president, had once said, "The secret of redemption lies in remembrance."

As Chaim left the café, he turned around once more and said,

"Tell your father when you see him, to let go of it." It was too late for that; my father was already dead. It was kind of him to want to make me feel better, but it was not that easy. I answered with a grateful smile.

3

—

THE VANISHED
BOARDING SCHOOL

A
FTER MY RETURN FROM India, I was determined to make up for a whole lifetime of not asking about my father's youth under the Nazis. I was curious about his school days. How had they shaped him? I knew that he had attended a boarding school that he had referred to as "Feldafing," named after the affluent community on the shores of picturesque Lake Starnberg in Bavaria.

My research told me that Feldafing, to this day, is a quaint, little village with roughly 4,500 inhabitants, located about twenty miles south of Munich. The construction of a railroad line in 1864 made it accessible from Bavaria's capital. Aristocrats and wealthy industrialists started to vacation there in the summer, building luxurious villas close to the lakeside. In contrast to the heavily bombed Ruhr area, where my mother grew up, Feldafing's villas survived the war mostly intact.

Today, Feldafing is an exclusive resort that promotes itself as a wealthy retirement community and a traditional tourism destination with a long history. The Kaiserin Elisabeth Hotel advertises that Empress Elisabeth, nicknamed "Sissi," the beloved wife of the Austro-Hungarian Emperor Franz Josef, used to stay there. Just like Princess Diana, she was a tragically romantic figure. It was also the place where Adolf Hitler stayed once, on a visit to the village.

However, he never set foot in the school, because to him it was the *Röhm Schule*, originally founded by his former *Sturmabteilung* (SA) chief and later adversary, Ernst Röhm, in 1934. The same year, the SA, an early Nazi paramilitary wing that helped Hitler rise to power at the beginning of the war, fell out of favor with the Führer. But this information is absent from the tourism website. History has been edited to fit the village's current self-image.

On a road trip to Munich with the aim of visiting nearby "Mad King" Ludwig's castle, *Neuschwanstein*, I decided to take a small detour to see the village for myself. Was it still as beautiful as my father had described it in his school diary? At Feldafing station, little had changed since the days Hans had arrived. It was a picturesque, historic, Tudor-style brick structure from the second half of the nineteenth century. Similar train stations can be found all over Germany, but many of them are now defunct and have been converted into restaurants. The one in Feldafing stood forlorn in the middle of an overgrown stretch of land, just outside town. I got out of the car and walked across the abandoned railroad tracks. It was late summer. Insects buzzed in the tall, dry-smelling grass. What an odd sensation to stand in the same place where my father—a shy, ten-year-old boy whose first school language had been Spanish— must have arrived seventy-five years ago. I wondered if his Auntie Tali had accompanied him on the roughly ten-hour train trip from Bremen, or if he had traveled alone, entrusted to older members of the Hitler Youth as was common practice at the time.

Driving into Feldafing village, I stopped several times to ask where I could find the old boarding school. The school's full name had been *Reichsschule der NSDAP Feldafing*. I was keen to see the old mansions I had read about, especially since one of them, named Villino, had once housed the literary Nobel Prize–winner Thomas Mann while he was writing his book *Magic Mountain* in the early 1920s. But everyone I asked stared blankly at me or told me, "No idea what you're talking about."

Finally, at the town hall, a reluctant clerk informed me, "The old boarding school is now used as the barracks for a telecommunication unit of the *Bundeswehr* [the German Army]." With a stern voice, he added, "There is nothing for you to see there."

A short distance outside the village, I spotted the entrance to the military facility. The whole area was closed to the public, fenced in and surrounded by barbed wire. The setting was idyllic. The lake was in walking distance, and one could go swimming. But it was disappointing to have come all this way only to be prevented from going anywhere near the buildings. So, I had to resort to the internet to see old photos. The villas were magnificent, each of them unique, and several decorated with art nouveau details. Although I had not seen any mountains, the area had poetically been called *Villenkolonie am Höhenberg* (the Colony of Villas at the High Mountain). Starting in 1898, twenty grand mansions had been built on the site. The most famous but modest structure was Villino, the country house that had belonged to Thomas Mann's Jewish father-in-law. In 1937, the NSDAP bought out the original owners and turned the buildings into a school. It appears that the Jewish owners were actually paid, but it is not clear if they were fairly compensated. The stylish residences were then renamed after Nazi heroes, for example the "Horst-Wessel-Haus." Villino was converted into the caretaker's abode.

I wondered how my father had ended up in such a place. How had the family even known about it? Generations of our family were from northern Germany, and this was in deepest Bavaria. As far as I knew, nobody in the family was a member of the NSDAP, although I had my doubts about Auntie Tali. When I visited Hans's parents, my grandparents, in the 1970s, they were living in Brazil. I noticed that they had no interest in politics, neither South American nor German.

In 1937, they lived in Peru and had come to Germany for a visit. It seems the idea for their visit had come from my father's aunt who was a teacher in Bremen. At the time, attending lectures and work-shops that trained teachers how to instill ideals of National Social-ism into their pupils was mandatory. They were also instructed to identify promising, gifted children, mainly boys, so they could be educated in elite schools. Apparently, Auntie Tali convinced Hans's parents that it would be best for him to be educated in Germany.

Hans must have briefly attended a local school while she handled all the extensive and necessary paperwork to get him accepted into the elite school, which included presenting an *Ahnenpass* (an ances-try passport that certified he was Aryan).

It was a very competitive school, and getting in took some effort. Bremen was located in the NSDAP administrative district of the *Gau Weser-Ems*, which was only allowed to send two, or three de-pending on the source, students each year. Hans also had to pass a battery of physical and academic tests. Parents were only required to pay a small school fee adjusted to income, with most of the bill being footed by the state. Initially, Auntie Tali paid out of her own pocket, but from 1941, all expenses were paid by the state. My grandfather, Heinz, was pleased with those arrangements, especial-ly the financial ones, as he sometimes found himself cash-strapped in between his South American business deals. Hans's mother, Hilde, had found mothering to be overwhelming. Leaving their little Hansito in the hands of such competent educators seemed to be the right thing to do. My father never forgave his father for what he perceived as abandonment. Only on Heinz's deathbed in 1982 were the two reconciled.

Talking to my mother, I discovered that there had been another reason why my father had been accepted. She explained to me:

Only two Feldafing boys came from South America. Your father and Hermann Lundgren, who was from Brazil. His grandfather, an early twentieth-century self-made Brazil-ian millionaire of Scandinavian descent, had recruited a decorated, but impoverished, aristocratic German officer from the First World War as a suitable husband for his daughter. This officer insisted that his son should get a decent education back in Germany. Hermann's looks did not conform to the Aryan norms as his mother was of mixed ancestry, but this was magnanimously overlooked because he was considered a valuable resource for the future Reich. Both boys were considered *Auslandsdeutsche* [expatriate Germans], and they were expected to return overseas one day and spread the Nazi gospel. Both felt discriminated against by other students because of their foreignness, but they did their best to fit in and win a higher place in the class pecking order.

My father had never talked about his time as a soldier, but he shared the occasional benign anecdote from school: "When I first arrived, they called me *'Furzkiste'* [fart box]. The greasy Bavarian sausages and cabbage dishes did not agree with me. I was accustomed to dishes like *Anticuchos de Corazón* [marinated, grilled beef hearts with roasted corn].

Das ist Deutschlands Zukunft

"This is Germany's future."

Drawing from several sources, I was able to find out more about the boarding school. Germany's first golf course had been built in Feldafing in 1926, and the boys learned to play on it. They had access to tennis courts, a yacht harbor, an airfield for hang-gliding planes, and riding lessons. Two school buses drove them to Munich to attend the opera or theater. On winter days, they went to the mountains for skiing lessons. The future Nazi elite were expected to be cultured, educated, and physically fit.

The school had gone through four distinct stages and, like everything in the Third Reich, all of them were short-lived. During its first stage, from 1934 to 1937, the school was run by the SA. There were only four villas in use, and the school was relatively small. As it became integrated into Hitler's system of elite schools, 1937 to 1941 saw the school's heyday, but it lost prestige and fell into decline between 1941 and 1943. Teachers were drafted, and war shortages took their toll on school life, although the boys were still eating well compared to the rest of Germany. From 1943 to May 1945, the school slowly disintegrated as younger and younger age groups were drawn into the war; the older ones sent to combat, the younger ones taken for auxiliary services.

All the students whom I read about felt that the academic standards were good, although there was an emphasis on Nazi-centric history and German heritage. As for languages, English and Latin were taught. Due to their Viking and Anglo-Saxon heritage, the English and Scandinavians were considered Aryan, while Latin was needed to read *De Bello Gallico*, Caesar's account of his military tactics in conquering France.

The interviews conducted by Johannes Leeb and published in the book *Wir waren Hitlers Eliteschüler* ("We Were Hitler's Elite Students") were insightful, although slanted toward the positive. It seemed that only students who had enjoyed their time at school were willing to talk about it. All those interviewed pointed out that the teachers and educators were very different from one another—there was no typical Nazi teacher. Many were outstanding academics, and some even cracked the odd joke about the regime. A minority, mainly those teaching physical education, were hardcore Nazis.

When I mentioned the author's name to my mother, she knew who he was and explained, "In the late 1990s, he tried to interview your father for this book, but your father said no."

Once more I felt clueless about my father's life. He must have been very conflicted. He never did manage to reconcile the horrors of the Nazi regime with the country that had been home to him, nor a school that had provided him with a challenging but superior education. He never found the words to express the feelings that must have come from having the people most dear to him push him, with the best intentions, into an abyss.

While the rest of Germany was already at war, the boys were studying German philosophers like Immanuel Kant and Friedrich Nietzsche, discovering the brilliance of Renaissance paintings by Albrecht Dürer, and marveling at the military accomplishments of Frederick the Great, the eighteenth-century Prussian king. As their works were considered degenerate, Jewish authors such as Karl Marx and non-German writers such as F. Scott Fitzgerald were not included in the curriculum.

The parameters that decided whether an author was considered Aryan or not had been firmly set during the Nazi book-burning campaign in 1933. The boys were discouraged from reading work by writers such as Robert Louis Stevenson and Jack London, substituting instead German authors like self-taught astronomer Bruno Bürgel, and the nineteenth-century German adventurer Karl May. Hans particularly liked the books by Walter Flex, an author forgotten nowadays, who wrote about humanity, friendship, and suffering during the First World War. Hans quoted him often.

I found details of life at Feldafing written by my father in an elegant, green, leather-bound journal, very different from the rough paper quality of the *Zawada* diary. It was dedicated "To my Auntie

Tali, Feldafing, Christmas 1941 from Hans."

Neatly written with a fountain pen in blue ink, it was a detailed chronicle of his life at school. The expensive booklet had nothing in common with an informal schoolboy's composition book. It was a carefully crafted project to impress a student's parents. Several drafts corrected by the teachers must have preceded the final, neatly written copy. I finally understood where my father had learned his overly romanticized use of words that had kept us from speaking the same language. I read a passage in this school journal, shocked at how even innocent-sounding passages could be filled with pro-Nazi propaganda:

> The Feldafing inhabitants were mainly peasants . . . few people knew about the beauty of nature in this area . . . according to the will of our current Brigadeführer [the headmaster had a military rank] the Reich's school is built in the middle . . . of what reminds one of a fairy-tale forest. From the beginning it was conceived that for the boys educated here, it would become a second home.

Leeb's first Feldafing interviewee was Hans Fischach.[1] He was five years older than my father and had attended the school from its early SA days. Fischach was from a traditional Bavarian military family and had always wanted to attend a cadet academy, as his father, grandfather, and great-grandfather had done. He described his experience at Feldafing as "the happiness of my youth." He loved the elitist atmosphere and adored the many different, semi-military school uniforms designed by Lodenfrey, a Munich fashion house that remains prestigious to this day. Fischach describes the details of his gala uniform with its ceremonial sword, the everyday gray uniform, Bavarian leather pants with a brown shirt, tracksuit, ski outfit, short cape, coat, and several matching forage caps decorated with assorted insignia. The only civilian piece of clothing was a bathrobe, brought from home.

After graduating in 1940, there was no question in his mind

that he would join the *Schutzstaffel* (SS). No longer interested in a military career after the war, he instead became a fashion designer for men's clothing in Munich. As far as I could see, there was no critical reflection on the ideological content of his education, just the self-centered notion that his parents could never have given him such a luxurious upbringing otherwise.

The least agreeable but most enthusiastic of Leeb's interviewees was Ernst Esser.[2] At my mother's suggestion, I interviewed Franz Mannhart, a surviving school friend of my father's. According to Franz, two sons of Hermann Esser, a prominent figure in the Nazi Party, had attended the school. Hermann Esser had been an early member of the party who distinguished himself by holding membership number 2. He had also earned himself a reputation for assaulting underage girls and other sexual transgressions. Even Hitler found him unsavory but had once remarked that Esser knew too much to be booted out of the party. In Leeb's interview, his son Ernst Esser said, "I was proud of my time in Feldafing." But the feeling was not mutual. The children of Nazi dignitaries were looked down upon by regular students, who had to undergo rigorous entrance exams in sports and academics to achieve a place at the school. His fellow students did not consider Ernst the sharpest tool in the shed, and he was expelled after middle school. Although it was perhaps reassuring that cronyism did not work in this demanding environment, the merciless selection process was disconcerting. I learned later that there was a whole hierarchy of Nazi schools, and in other locations, the weeding out and harsh treatment of children not

Franz at Feldafing School, 1937.

considered robust enough had resulted in expulsions and sometimes even death.

In another interview, Otto Schuster explained how he entered the school in 1941, around the time that Ernst Esser was let go: "There were always vacated spaces at Feldafing school because the weak ones would not be coached into the next grade but sent back to their old schools."[3] In 1941, my father wrote in his school journal:

> In the years we have been here, one remembers a few students who are no longer here . . . Each class has the right to weed out foreign bodies whose characters are not good enough to make the grade. They can be reported to the educators even if their academics and performance in sport are sufficient. It is the character itself that counts.

Convincing the boys to weed out any individualism seems a ferocious way of promoting survival of the fittest. My father mentioned in his journal several times that in the younger grades, the whole class would gang up on an unpopular pupil and give him a good thrashing. The staff designated such behavior as "roughhousing" and didn't interfere. They often used physical punishment themselves—mainly smacking the boys. One of their favorite pastimes was to subject the pupils to a much-hated game of "masquerade." In fast intervals of three to five minutes, pupils had to change their outfits, with full regalia. If their clothing was not folded at the end, they would be punished by being forced to march throughout the evening. Several students, including Franz Mannhart and my father, recalled:

> A favorite game for our *Erzieher* [a type of teacher] was to harass us boys, or depending on whose view you take, teach us agility and discipline with what we called a *Maskenball*. We had to change our outfits on command in rapid succession, and when we messed up our closets in the process, we were reprimanded and punished.

At Feldafing, Hans practices long throw using a dummy stick grenade instead of a disc in the summer of 1943.

But that was only the beginning of the Darwinian selection process. The boys had to wake up at 5:30 AM and raise the flag, march in unison to start school lessons at 7:00 AM, and undertake five and a half hours of lessons before lunch. This was followed by bedrest and more marching and sports, often with military overtones, in the afternoon. This was the routine every day, except for Sundays when other duties were discharged. One day a week was reserved for outdoor activities only. All boys were trained to handle guns in target practice; in discus throwing, dummy stick grenades replaced the traditional circular disks. Games in the forest were designed to encourage boys to find their way through unfamiliar territory and develop survival skills. Regular athletics were also taught, complete with competitions against other schools. Whoever could not keep up was let go.

In every respect, Otto Schuster's experience at school was very different from Fischach's. His working-class family mistrusted the Nazis and wanted their son to become a miner, just as his father

47

had been. But Schuster turned out to be extraordinarily gifted, and his teachers suggested a transfer to Feldafing, which his father only agreed to as it meant no school fees. It was 1941, the school was already softening its approach, and there was a shortage of teachers, as described by my father in his journal:

> Because of the war, unfortunately our educators keep changing, as they are being drafted. Students from the eighth grade became our squad leaders. To take such leadership positions is a valuable experience for them, but we have lost all discipline. Soon that class will graduate and we will have a new set of students in charge of us.

The practice of substituting adults with children was widespread from 1943. But I was astonished to read that by 1941, there was already a lack of manpower. It was encouraging to learn that my father was allowed to write something mildly critical in his journal, as his educators must have read it before it was sent home, but this entry also foreshadowed the end. In 1943, my father and all the students born between 1926 and 1928 were taken out of school to man the Flak antiaircraft guns so that the older attendants could be sent to the front. In the autumn of 1944, the boys were urged by their teachers to sign up for combat, although they could choose the type of unit in which they wanted to serve.

Franz talks about the curriculum at Feldafing School, which included orientation, survival games, and premilitary training in the forest.

While the boys were fighting on the front, the school, supposedly their second home, unceremoniously disappeared and

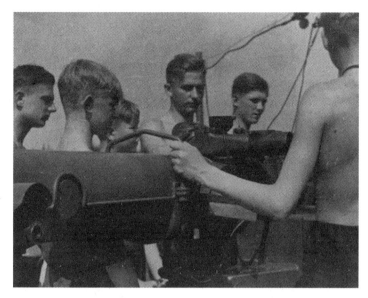

Hans (center) and Feldafing classmates trying to figure out how to shoot with the antiaircraft guns. Shown is the command part of the gun, 1943.

was completely closed by the Allies in 1945. The teachers, who had enthusiastically sent the boys to fight, were not held accountable. Upon their return from war and captivity, the surviving students found themselves barred from higher education until 1949. That hardly seemed fair to me, when *Brigadeführer* Julius Görlitz, their headmaster who had joined the SS in 1937, was cleared of all wrongdoing. In the postwar denazification proceedings, Görlitz was classified as a "follower," the lowest form of Nazi involvement, and no penalties or punishments were ever levied on him.

4

—

NOT A NAPOLA

"**W**HAT ON EARTH IS A NAPOLA?" I asked my mother, dumbfounded. I had studied twentieth-century German history at university and never once heard the term. The nonchalant way in which she had just used the word made it clear that it was something she had known about all her life. She spoke out the abbreviation: *Nationalpolitische Erziehungsanstalt der NSDAP*.

A tongue twister even in German, it translates into the National Political Educational Institutions (officially abbreviated NPEA). The term came up after my mother had pulled out a blue-and-white, cloth-covered album I had never seen before. She had attached a

Hans and Feldafing classmates rowing on Lake Starnberg, 1937.

Hans in his first year at Feldafing in 1937, in a miniature military school uniform with swastika armband.

sticker on the outside: *Feldafing 1937–41.* The inside was made up of heavy, dark-gray paper with white ink lettering on it. I recognized the neat handwriting of Auntie Tali. The first page held a photo of a ten-year-old Hans happily rowing on Lake Starnberg with a few equally young-looking classmates in school uniforms. The caption read: "summer 1937." I turned the page. Sepia-colored pictures, some out of focus, showed a cheery Hans climbing a tree, hiking in the woods, playing with other boys, or gathered around uniform-clad teachers. Of particular interest was a photo of Hans in a miniature military dress uniform, complete with swastika armband, with his grandparents and Auntie Tali. I turned more pages and remarked, "How smart they look in their uniforms, a different one for each activity!"

My mother responded, "Yes of course they do. After all, Feldafing was not a Napola! There was fierce competition between the Feldafing boys, who looked down on other students in the scruffy, common *Hitler Jugend* [Hitler Youth] uniform, and the Napola boys, who retaliated by calling them *Goldfasanen* [golden pheasants]."

"What an odd name! Why were they called that, and what about the Napola?" I asked.

Patiently she explained:

It was a derogatory term. In private, when we felt safe that no officials were listening, we nicknamed the German, high-ranking Nazis officers *Goldfasanen* because their uniforms were brown with gold insignia, reminiscent of the birds' colors. We considered them vain with a superiority complex, and that is how the Napola students felt about Feldafing. To them they were snobs.

It had not really occurred to me previously that Feldafing School might have been the tip of the iceberg of a much greater network of Nazi schools. My curiosity was aroused. Feldafing had been the jewel in the crown of a school system intended to educate the future Nazi elite. It explained why Feldafing put such an emphasis on playing golf and attending the opera—those social skills were needed in the future to connect with elites in other countries.

Once I knew what I was looking for, it was mind-blowing to see how the Nazi educational system unfolded layer by layer. From eyewitness accounts in books and the German media, I pieced their story together.

Fanfares of the Hitler Youth.

Other schools were less luxurious than Feldafing but even more regimented. From the beginning of his rule in 1933, Hitler had advocated a special, separate National Socialist–controlled education system for particularly promising youngsters. This had led to the formation of a hierarchy of elite schools. They had the task of supplying the future Nazi state with reliable and brainwashed party leaders, administrators, law enforcement, and military officers. Some schools were a direct continuation of the Prussian cadet schools, appealing to the older generation's nostalgia for the days of Prussian law and order. In this tradition, there had been elite boarding schools before the time of the Nazis, several reserved for the children of aristocrats. As with everything else in Germany, the Nazis inherited a well-functioning school system that was easily adapted to their own goals.

Suddenly aware of their existence, I asked my mother, "Did you attend such a Napola as well?"

"No, I was at the school where my father was a teacher. We were all in the Hitler Youth though."

There seemed to have been only three Napolas for girls. As they produced no notable graduates, were run only for a short time, and had to change venues due to the war, they are not well known. I found the recollections of Hertha von Bergh, who had attended the girls' Napola in Achern near Baden-Baden. For her, it had been an escape from the academically demanding and stifling atmosphere of the convent school she had previously attended. But regardless of whether girls enjoyed an elite education or not, they all knew their duties toward the Führer.

As my mother recalled:

For Hitler our highest goal in life was to become mothers and serve our husbands, who served the Reich. The *Bund Deutscher Mädchen* [BDM] taught us about such matters. Our neighbor Mrs. Lange had ten children. She received the Gold Mother's Cross, a special medal given to all women who had born the Führer eight children or more.

"What? Your neighbor had sex with Hitler?" I asked, in a lame attempt to be funny.

My mother, only slightly amused, answered matter-of-factly, "Of course not! Every child born in Germany was considered a gift to the Führer. At least, that is what we were told."

Napolas were the most common of the thirty-six elite schools and were considered the lowest in rank. Although one book on the topic mentions forty schools, this figure probably comes from the fact that many of them were in various stages of planning and construction. As with so many other grandiose Nazi projects, these glorious plans were a far cry away from the pathetic reality. The first school was effectively inaugurated on Hitler's birthday, April 20, 1933. The rest were located all over Germany, and a few were in the newly occupied territories. Twenty-three existed by the time the Reich collapsed. Only those that had been superimposed on pre-existing Prussian cadet academies were fully functioning. They were not reinventions, but modified the curriculum to serve Nazi goals, and they ran in parallel to the public school system.

To minimize the influence of their families, pupils were purposefully assigned to schools that were as far away from their homes as possible. Although Napolas were originally considered state schools, they later came under the influence of the SS.

Of all the elite schools, Napolas had the strictest discipline and physical fitness requirements. Hellmuth Karasek, who was born in 1934 and became a well-known German publicist after the war, was interviewed by Johannes Leeb in 1998 and for *Deutschlandfunk* German Radio in 2005. His accounts shed some light on both the selection process and the actual reality of the schools.[1]

As part of a test of courage for the Napola selection process in 1944, he recalls how he and his classmates jumped off a high ladder. Three of them sprained an ankle or broke a leg in the process. Although his family were Sudeten Germans who lived in Brünn, now in the Czech Republic, he was sent some distance away to the Napola Loben in Upper Silesia, as his father considered him a mama's boy who needed toughening up. Being ten years old, he was extremely homesick; he remembered the terror of the boys who were bedwetters. While making their beds at 6:00 AM, they tried desperately to rub their sheets dry because if they were discovered, they could expect draconian punishments. To prepare the boys for combat, the training included more sports than in regular schools. Karasek and other former Napola students all recall daily routines that included a lot of marching and standing to attention, undoubtedly hard on those who did not excel at sports or who enjoyed more intellectual pursuits.

The Napola pupils wore the uniform of the Hitler Youth. From the beginning, *Gleichschaltung* (synchronization) was an important element. Students from less-privileged backgrounds enjoyed wearing the uniforms, as they felt equal to their peers. In a cigarette-card album from 1933, I found photos of youth rallies, with hundreds of young people dressed in identical uniforms standing in disciplined rows.

"The national socialist youth day on October 2nd 1932 in Potsdam" from Deutschland erwacht.

As an example of Napola academics, I read how mathematics was taught: "According to cautious estimates there are three hundred thousand mentally ill persons, epileptics, etc. in nursing homes (each costing Germany four marks a day). How many home loans for young families at one thousand marks each could be given from this money each year?"[2]

This was hardly a mathematics question, but a not-so-subtle preparation for the top-secret extermination program that started in 1939. In some cases, Hitler's superior boys got an inferior education. Parents noticed how badly their boys were taught, and attendance at the schools declined sharply from 1941 onward. Teachers in regular schools were more aggressively solicited for identifying suitable candidates to replace them, while parents were bribed with free school fees.

In the early 1980s, I remember meeting Rüdiger von Wechmar at a diplomatic cocktail party. He, like my father, was somewhat statuesque, bald with graying sideburns, but a few years older. Over the years, my father had worked under him in the Foreign Office in various capacities, and there were many similarities between the two men, except that von Wechmar's career had been far more illustrious. He had served as Germany's first President of the United Nations Security Council from 1977 to 1978. Years later, I would read von Wechmar's eloquent recollections of his time at a Napola, only disclosed after his retirement from public service.

Von Wechmar was descended from an aristocratic family with a long tradition of providing Prussian Army officers.[3] Their boys had always been educated at cadet schools, but at the time he was supposed to enter the Napola Spandau, his uncle was murdered by the SS, making the family question their association with the regime. It was only after Hermann Goering personally intervened and apologized for the error that they went ahead with sending their son to the Napola Spandau.

Like my father's experience in Feldafing, the beginning was tough, as the other boys mistrusted him when he first arrived. He talked about the initiation, tolerated and even encouraged both by educators and the close-knit community of the students. His accounts of teachers and educators were very detailed and, as in Feldafing, not all were hard-core Nazis. Some were conflicted between the goal of educating young people in good faith and the demands to turn their students into mini-Nazis.

As von Wechmar was older than my father, he went to war in 1942. Just like in Feldafing, recruiters for the different military units came by and solicited applications for voluntary conscription. Eager to follow the heroes who were constantly promoted to them, such as General Rommel, pilot Rudel, or U-boat captain Prien, they signed up. Of the thirty-one boys in von Wechmar's class, sixteen were killed.

As well as Napolas, there were the Adolf Hitler Schools (AHS). A small, locally printed brochure that I bought in the town of Pirna, where one of the schools had been housed, summed up their mission statement: "It was a world of giving orders and obeying."[4]

Although the Adolf Hitler Schools shared some common features with Napolas, they had distinctly different goals.[5] They were exclusively boarding schools and, like Napolas, taught middle and high school students. They were intended to raise the new party elite as per Hitler's personal orders and were run directly under the local NSDAP *Gauleiter* (the regional administrative party chief). Only those students

The ruins of the Adolf Hitler School in Pirna prior to its demolition in 2013.

deemed to have leadership potential or who performed exception-
ally well in the Hitler Youth were admitted. The admission ceremonies were conducted every April 20, the Führer's birthday. Later
I discovered that many more sinister things took place on that day.

As the schools were geared toward creating a new generation of
Nazi political leaders, the education focused on awakening each
boy's lust for power. A former student reported that he saw the
school as a miniature Führer state, constantly building him and
his classmates into future rulers of the master race. Those little
flaxen heads were the perfect raw material to be formed into the
alpha males of Hitler's Aryan vision. Another former student,
Harald Grundmann, stated in an interview that the greatest crime
against him and the other children was that compassion was bred
out of them.[6]

Stefan Wunsch, the academic director of an exhibit at the Burg
Vogelsang museum, added, "I think that schools like Feldafing [or
the AHS] represented a promise of advancement—even in the eyes
of some families who had reservations about the Nazis."[7] Wunsch
explained that it was part of the fatal attraction of National Socialism, a perfidious offer to the boys, who were made to feel superior,
singled out from their old friends and schools. They were to absorb
National Socialism "with the heart" and not merely with the mind.
Being given this extraordinary chance appealed to their enthusiasm
and awakened their will to sacrifice themselves.

The plan was that about ten Adolf Hitler Schools would occupy their own grand buildings, but as with everything else, they
were not completed and the students were distributed between
existing locations, including Burg Vogelsang (Castle Birdsong)
near Schleiden, Castle Drachenburg near Königswinter, Castle
Blankenheim near Weimar, and Castle Sonnenstein in Pirna. The
booklet in my possession, a collection of essays from the Pirna
school, dedicated a section to how chaotic life at the school had
been. The school moved from another location in the town of

Plauen before being established in Pirna in 1941, the third year of war. As in Feldafing, educators changed as more and more were drafted. One author also speculated that the chaos was deliberate, to keep everybody off guard.

On a gray, snow-infused late afternoon, I visited the school in Pirna on a side trip on my way to Závada. It was located right behind the infamous site where experiments for the mass T4 extermination project had been pioneered. Called Aktion T4 (Action T4, or the T4 Program), this horrendous program started at the outbreak of the Second World War in September 1939. It used three hundred thousand physically and mentally handicapped Germans, Austrians, and nationals from countries farther east to perfect the gas extermination techniques that were later used in the concentration camps. I knew about it from websites and having watched a bone-chilling documentary on German television.[8]

The cellar of Castle Sonnenstein is now a memorial site for the victims of the Nazi euthanasia facility: mentally and physically disabled German adults and children, initially taken from the institution in Pirna and later from the surrounding areas. The Pirna institute, with the improbably long German name *Königlich Sächsische Heil-und Verpflegungsanstalt*, had been established in 1811. It had been exemplary and forward-thinking in the care of people with disabilities for over one hundred years of its existence. But in 1940, the Nazi regime closed it and used all seven hundred occupants as guinea pigs for their gassing apparatus that was temporarily installed at the nearby castle.

I descended the steps into the museum of horror. Memorial plaques and fresh flowers were placed respectfully where the first victims of the Holocaust had perished. Heartbreaking stories were recounted in leaflets made available to visitors. The place was a monument of mourning and solemn reflection. I spent a minute in silence. But when I saw an exhibit of some buttons, recovered from the victim's ashes, that included a child's button, I broke down;

tears filled my eyes. How would I have coped as a mother if I had placed my child with Down syndrome into the care of this respected institution, to then receive a formal letter from Pirna's mayor informing me that my child had suddenly died of what appeared to be improbable causes?

Walking the short distance to the site of the abandoned buildings of the former Adolf Hitler School in the sprawling, overgrown castle park did little to lift my mood. A casual visitor who hadn't researched the location would never know what they were looking at. All over the former GDR (East Germany), sites can be found that were first occupied by the Nazis and then kept virtually unaltered by the Soviets. After the fall of the Berlin Wall in 1989, they were often left to decay, as they reminded the locals of the two successive totalitarian regimes they had endured. But for the complex in Pirna, there was an additional reason why the locals wanted nothing to do with it.

The buildings of the school were built at different times, connected by now-cracked concrete walkways. The windows were recently smashed, and the plaster was crumbling. Numbers, painted on walls or attached as enameled plates, attested to the

Vandalized cafeteria at the former Adolf Hitler School in Pirna, 2013.

once orderly administration of the premises. Most buildings were boarded up, but I managed to enter a large, graffiti-smeared, utilitarian hall that must have served as a refectory. I imagined little boys lined up in rows, holding out their clean, scrubbed hands for inspection, anxiously observing the rules to avoid being singled out for punishment. Any punishment was usually extended to their classmates as well, a technique devised so that the boys would self-police each other. I imagined their headmaster in front of the hall, dripping with self-importance, ending an inspirational speech with a typical Baldur von Schirach quote, "He who serves our Führer, Adolf Hitler, serves Germany, and he who serves Germany, serves God."

The deteriorating walls smelled unpleasantly moldy and even my extra sweater was not sufficient to keep out the creeping, damp cold. There was something very wrong about this place, a feeling confirmed when I read the brochure. The school had been housed in the very buildings where the seven hundred patients of the old institute had lived and been cared for. After the last child with a disability had been killed, Hitler's golden boys were unceremoniously moved onto the premises. From a 2012 exhibit in Berlin, organized by the foundation *Topographie des Terrors* (Topography of Terror), I had learned that the Third Reich had killed ten thousand German children with disabilities, mainly in such experimental sites as the one in Pirna.[9] Just as they were unhealthily coddling their brightest and most physically able, they were exterminating their most vulnerable. This took even Nazi Darwinism to new heights, creating space for their supposedly superior human material by destroying those who had previously occupied it. The program had been started when the war was already on everybody's mind. Even the Nazis understood that there would be some resistance from the population, so they waited until Germans were preoccupied with their own survival before starting their program of annihilation.

As I left the complex, I noticed a large billboard informing the public that the site was to be used for blocks of luxury row houses. As I am writing this, I am sure that the place captured in my photos no longer exists. I imagine the new occupants parking their BMWs in their driveways before crossing their manicured, green lawns to the front doors of their impeccable new homes. I wonder if they know that the site once housed an extermination center, later used for the large-scale, institutionalized abuse of the youngsters who became their fathers.

5

—

CASTLE BIRDSONG

IN 2016, I DISCOVERED, by accident, that the most impressive Nazi elite educational site, and overall the second-largest structure ever built by the Third Reich, was a mere 29 miles away from Rheinbach, the small town where I had grown up. As children, my father had taken us for hikes all over the surrounding forest areas of the Eifel. In hindsight, I think nature reminded him of the happier days of his school experience. The boys had always been on orientation walks and treasure hunts, which were intended to teach them outdoor survival skills. But for all that we children learned about the Eifel, my father never took us to this specific location, nor did he ever mention it.

It was a Sunday afternoon in 2017, and my mother had asked me to drive her to a nature reserve with a museum on local wildlife called *Burg Vogelsang*—Castle Birdsong. She always loved songbirds, just like her father, the biology teacher. I looked up the website to make sure that the site was accessible for her walker. I read up on the two museums that had been recently inaugurated at the location only to realize that the quaint name did not refer to a bird museum but to the largest Nazi university ever built. I asked my mother whether my father knew of this place.

She replied, "He once pointed out Burg Sonthofen, another such place, when we drove through Bavaria, but he would never go near any of those sites. He never mentioned Burg Vogelsang."

To both my parents' credit, they would not have been able to take us there even if they had wanted to, as it was off-limits to German civilians.

The British Allied forces had seized the location in 1945 for the use of their troops. Later, the Belgian Army occupied and modified the existing structures. The whole complex was finally returned to the German authorities in 2005. Ironically, the Allied occupation protected the site. Had it been accessible to Germans after the war, it would have been vandalized or maybe razed to the ground. But by 2005, enough time had passed. Those who had attended the university were mostly dead. Nevertheless, it still took years before the museum about the Third Reich educational institution was installed. To my knowledge, this is the first museum of its kind anywhere in the world. The title of the exhibit is *Destiny: Master Race. Nazi Order Castles, Both Fascination and Crime.*[1]

I finally visited the gigantic complex on a gray March day in 2020. Towering walls constructed of rough, giant boulders cover an entire mountaintop. But like everything in the Nazi world, they are mere facades. The reinforced concrete skeleton buildings were erected at considerable expense, the labor procured in the poor Eifel region.

The wall of book titles in the museum's gift store came as a shock to me. I had started my research into the subject of the Nazi elite educational system in 2009, but at the time I had to piece the information together from out-of-print books obtained in obscure secondhand bookstores or on dodgy websites. Now everything one might ever want to know was in one place, freely accessible. The catalogue for the exhibition consisted of almost four hundred oversize pages; the sheer weight of this publication was to take up several pounds of my airline luggage allowance. The catalogue carefully listed the war atrocities committed by the university's graduates down to the last detail.

Besides Castle Birdsong, there had been two more *Ordensburgen* (order castles), in other words, pseudo-re-creations of the castles of the orders of the crusading knights of the Middle Ages. They were conceived as a type of Nazi university to educate the future party cadre. The active order castles were Krössinsee in Pomerania, Sonthofen in the German Alps, and Vogelsang in the West Eifel. A fourth one, Marienburg, near the city of Danzig, was never completed. The site of the Marienburg castle had the greatest symbolic meaning. Associated with the Teutonic knights of the thirteenth century, it evoked an association with the crusaders of the Middle Ages.

Architecturally, all these buildings looked like grotesquely oversize medieval castles. The terminology was taken from medieval language interspersed with military terms. Each *Ordensburg* housed about 2,200 *Ordensjunker* (a medieval term for a knight in training). As sources are scant, the exact numbers are not known. The hierarchical structure was strict, going down from the *Burgkommandant* (the castle commander), to the *Ordensburg Stab* (the general staff of the castle), and finally to the instructors and teachers. Directly in charge of the students' everyday life was a hierarchy of group leaders. In addition to being schooled in Nazi ideology, eugenics, and German geography, these students were trained in military tactics. In theory, men in their twenties and early thirties were supposed to earn a three-year degree, one year at each castle, which were strategically placed at the eastern, southern, and western borders of the Reich. There were two short courses in Vogelsang in 1936 and 1937, each about five-hundred-men strong; they lasted about three quarters of a year. The graduates of these two courses were placed in NSDAP functions. Due to a lack of other facilities, three Adolf Hitler Schools, formerly housed in the *Ordensburg Sonthofen*, were placed inside the Birdsong buildings. They were considered feeder schools for recruiting candidates for the *Ordensburgen*.

Medical students lined up on the roll-call square, most of them in uniform, during the symposium of the Reich Specialist Medical Group on September 17, 1937.

The vast majority of students at Adolf Hitler Schools, who were born from the mid-1920s onward, studied at universities in the postwar period. Some became primary-school teachers, university professors, civil servants, engineers, and architects. Although sources vary, the overall academic performance of the schools was comparable to that of regular ones.

In addition to the *Ordensburgen* were the *SS-Junkerschulen* for ongoing education. They held the lowest rank of all institutions. There were four schools in the locations of Bad Tölz, Klagenfurt, Braunschweig, and Prag Drewitz. Ninety percent of their students had only an elementary school education. No academic merit whatsoever was required to enter these universities, but all students had to be male, above 5 feet 8.5 inches (174 cm) in height, and not wear glasses. I assume that a predisposition toward being the schoolyard bully and a fondness for brawls were additional qualifying criteria. They were indoctrinated in pure Nazi ideology and the graduates had only one career choice: to become an officer of the SS. Once the war broke out, even the SS realized that their intellectual capacity did not suffice for leading whole units of soldiers. Starting in 1940, they courted Napola school graduates to attend those universities, with no success.

Children of all Nazi schools had to present an *Ahnenpass* to prove their Aryan lineage. I found Hans's document and that of Auntie Tali in my father's papers. It is a small book where on page after page, ancestors are listed in blue ink, going back as far as the eighteenth century. Next to each entry is a stamp with a swastika.

But why had there been so many different types of elite Nazi educational facilities? The Vogelsang exhibit dedicated one section to an explanation. Ever since writing *Mein Kampf*, Hitler had advocated controlling German youth, but there were many factions in the NSDAP that followed their own agenda. A scramble ensued, each faction trying to gain authority over the national educational system to ensure that the newly educated elite would be loyal to their personal flavor of National Socialism. But none prevailed, and each faction created their own schools.

Bernhard Rust, the minister for *Volksbildung* (education for the people), created the Napola boarding schools, which were most closely modeled on the Prussian cadet institutions. Robert Ley, who held the title of *Reichsorganisationsleiter* der NSDAP (Nazi organizer of the Reich), built the *Ordensburgen* and later the Adolf Hitler Schools. Many schools were housed in preexisting buildings, but Ley built his grotesquely oversize order castles from scratch. Conventions, weddings, and recreational stays for members of Nazi organizations—the site even had an indoor swimming pool—were organized to show off the monstrous buildings to the world and fill them to capacity.

Professor Harald Scholtz, a historian and former pupil, criticized many schools for lacking academic rigor, based on his personal experience. Born in 1930, he attended three Adolf Hitler schools (AHS) in rapid succession. From 1942 to the German capitulation, he attended the AHS schools of Burg Vogelsang,

Finstingen in Alsace-Lorraine, and Erlenbach-Achern not far from Strasbourg. But it is important to remember that in addition to lots of sports, subjects such as art and music were taught, and students learned to play musical instruments.

From the moment the NS-DAP seized power, the whole educational system was altered to fit Nazi ideology, the biggest change being the introduction of social Darwinist principles. But the changes did not satisfy Heinrich Himmler, head of the SS. He felt that the graduates of all those institutions were still not trained ferociously enough for his organization and sub-

Adolf Hitler parades formations of participants on the roll-call square; behind him walk Robert Ley on the left and Richard Manderbach on the right, November 1936.

sequently created the *SS-Junkerschulen*. Among their graduates were a number of concentration camp commanders, with *SS-Junkerschulen*'s output overrepresented on the lists of war criminals in Nuremberg.

In 1931, Hitler had made twenty-five-year-old Baldur von Schirach head of the Hitler Youth. The young aristocrat demanded to oversee everything concerning German youth, including education, but he was pushed aside by more powerful party members. He continued writing soppy, nationalist songs and marched the children entrusted to him around in endless parades, wearing black shorts and brown shirts, until he was replaced in 1940 by the younger, and more forceful, Artur Axmann, who was put in charge of sending Germany's children into war.

So, where did my father's Feldafing school fit in? It had been created in 1934 by Ernst Röhm, the head of the SA paramilitary group. A tough veteran of the First World War, Röhm had been a friend of Hitler's since the early days. But as he grew more powerful, Hitler felt his leadership position threatened and had Röhm murdered during the Night of the Long Knives, a few months after Röhm had inaugurated the school. The school was reorganized by several administrators under the patronage of the NSDAP Reich Chancellery but remained separate from the rest of the Nazi schools. Hitler never liked Feldafing School because it had been inaugurated by Röhm. As Feldafing's ties to the SA were cut shortly after its inauguration, and no other organization in the Reich actively claimed it, the school's director, Julius Görlitz, stepped into the vacuum and developed the curriculum along his own visions of excellence. The school was an oddity among the Nazi schools. It appears that Görlitz single-handedly shaped its status and reputation as the foremost school in the nation, with the most luxurious facilities and the most rigorous academic education. A full range of scholastic subjects, including music and art, were taught.

The curriculum of the *Reichsschule Feldafing* was somewhat comparable to that of a British public school. As evidenced by the attendance of the sons of important Nazi functionaries, it later became the private school for the children of Nazi elite and was considered very exclusive.

Things started to fall into place. There was a photo in my father's album of a school trip to Obersalzberg to the home of Martin Bormann, who at the time was the head of the Chancellery after Rudolf Hess and, therefore, in charge of the school. His son, Martin Adolf Bormann, was three years younger than my father and was sent to Feldafing in 1940. The son recalled how his father had seen to it that while the rest of Germany was already hungry, the boys were still well provided for. He personally reprimanded the kitchen staff, whom he caught stealing the boys' meat rations during an unannounced visit.

Feldafing school was so well run that it became the flagship school whenever the Reich wanted to show off the merits of its educational system. Franz, my father's school friend, recalled, "Foreign visitors were brought to the school, and it was presented as though this was just another ordinary German school. We had to put on performances, and I remember singing for the Ethiopian foreign minister, as I always had a good voice."

Franz later trained as an opera singer. In contrast to other Nazi schools, the teachers at Feldafing had been selected not only for their political convictions but also for their academic merit. Hans's essays of the period, written with eloquence, demonstrated a very high standard of teaching in language and literature. But there was also the bombastic quality in his writing that initially alienated me. Glorifying and artfully describing things to be truly German, whether it was the landscape, one's mother, or a farmhouse, sounded strange to me. I had been raised in an era when one would rather not refer to any Germanness. I gave a copy of my father's diary to Franz, who had explained to me that this style was how they were taught to write. We nonetheless agreed that the first part of the diary sounded somewhat like a school essay gone wrong.

Some aspects of Feldafing were shared with other schools. In Hans's photo album, pictures were taken with the teachers, who like most Nazi youth leaders were quite young themselves and always wore uniforms, never civilian attire. These were party uniforms of the Hitler Youth or the NSDAP. In all Nazi schools a particular emphasis was placed on the role of the *Erzieher*, who was in immediate charge of the boys while at boarding school. Many were trained at the *Reichsjugendakademie*, an institution expressly established to educate and train the future instructors of the various educational party establishments. Being young, most of them had seen Hitler victoriously come to power in their formative years and had nothing with which to compare those experiences. Discipline was an important element, and educators were left in charge of drills.

It seems to me that the Nazi school system was not a success. It was put together at great speed and relied heavily on the preexisting Prussian cadet academies. As soon as the war started, there was a perpetual shortage of teachers, and academic teaching gave way to Wehrertüchtigung (getting fit for the war). Most of the grand plans were never executed; Vogelsang was still a construction site at the end of the war, and other schools existed only on paper.

There are voices who disagree with this assessment. The luxury that surrounded some of the schools made it a heady experience, and some of the pupils interviewed remembered their schooling fondly. Every boy had fantasized about becoming Hitler's "crown prince." What dawned on some too late, however, was that none of it was earned, nor did it belong to them. It was paid for with unquestioning loyalty to the regime and could be withdrawn at any moment. A scene in the film *Napola* illustrates this. The rebellious protagonist is led out of the school director's office in naked humiliation, as even the underpants are part of the Napola uniform, which he no longer deserves to wear.[2]

As for the long-term success of the schools, Artur Axmann defended them in his only public appearance.[3] The leader of the Hitler Youth gave a single interview fifty years after the war, a year before his death. Recorded in 1996, it was made generally available in 2019 on YouTube. When asked about the elite schools, Axmann pointed out that some former students had successful careers in the postwar Federal Republic of Germany, using it as proof that the Nazi educational system had worked. He mentioned Alfred Herrhausen, the former head of the Deutsche Bank, by name. Herrhausen had attended Feldafing and was in the same grade as Hitler's godson. Axmann neglected to mention that Herrhausen was blown up by a bomb in 1989. The case was never solved, but at the time it was considered an act of terrorism by Germany's Red Army faction (RAF). This group was classified by the German authorities as a militant, far left wing, domestic terror organization engaged in bombings, assassinations, kidnappings, bank robberies, and shoot-outs with police from the 1970s to the 1990s. It was composed of grown-up children of Germans who had been young adults during the Third Reich. Even though Herrhausen was younger, technically a war child, his position in the financial world had made him a target. The activities of the RAF were the ultimate rebellion against their parents, whom they considered to be fascist, as most had been old enough to vote when Hitler came into power.

I started to research where other elite students had ended up. The 2013 German documentary *Herrenkinder* ("children of the master race"), gave me further insights.[4] It was interesting that several students—Hellmuth Karasek, Rüdiger von Wechmar, and Theo Sommer—had all worked in journalism. Even my father had started his diplomatic career in the press ministry, as had his friend Franz. Had the educational emphasis on teaching the German language contributed to these professional choices? Sommer, the chief editor of the prestigious newspaper *Die Zeit*, had attended an Adolf Hitler School, and Karasek, who worked for *Der Spiegel*, an influential German magazine, had been at a Napola. In the interviews in which they evaluated their school experiences, they spoke of having learned to survive and how they developed an iron will. Those qualities helped them to rebuild their destroyed country, but also made life difficult in close relationships, as they had been trained to dominate under any circumstances. I could relate to that. As a family, we had always felt that my father was the commander in chief who had to rescue us from difficult situations. Except, in a small town in postwar Germany, life was peaceful and we did not need saving. It seemed that he constantly created small emergencies so that he could solve them. That behavior added a lot of stress to our lives.

About fifteen thousand boys attended Napolas; at least, that was the number I had found in my research. I had unearthed a few dozen eyewitness reports of former students who told similar stories with only a few variations depending on their ages and family backgrounds. But what happened to the other thousands of students?

In 2007, two years after my father's death, a debate arose around the literary Nobel Prize winner Günter Grass, who had volunteered to serve in an SS unit. The controversy showed how touchy the subject of being associated with anything Nazi still was in Germany and the world, sixty-two years after the end of the war. Grass was born in 1927, the same year as my father.

Another media case also caught my attention. The former German cardinal Joseph Ratzinger, also born in 1927, became Pope Benedict XVI in 2005. From the beginning he was criticized for his conservative views. In 2011, a well-known Hollywood actress casually called him a Nazi in public. Bill Donohue, the president of the Catholic League, retaliated by calling her remark "positively obscene." Donohue explained that Ratzinger's conscription into the Nazi Youth was routine for fourteen-year-old German boys and emphasized that he ultimately deserted the movement.

Despite them being the same age, there was a difference between the two cases. Grass had voluntarily signed up to fight at the front at age seventeen, while Ratzinger had been a *Flakhelfer* (an auxiliary antiaircraft gunner), a mandatory assignment for older boys and girls.

But for all the media attention, one element was not addressed: their attendance at Nazi elite schools. As they must have both shown potential as young children, they would have been singled out and aggressively targeted by school recruiters. The system was efficient. They relied on local teachers to supply information on children. Once the children were identified as having potential, the recruiters approached the parents to make them sign the necessary paperwork. Some signed voluntarily, others under duress.

Where had Grass and Ratzinger gone to school? The absence of attendance information was suspicious. If they had not attended Nazi elite schools, it would have been mentioned in their otherwise detailed biographies. Maybe an outsider might not pick up on this lack of information, but to anybody familiar with the Nazi educational system, it was a telltale sign. I found one source that stated Grass had attended the Conradinum High School in Danzig, now called Gdańsk.[5] But when I correlated that with information about the school, I could not confirm it. Grass was mentioned nowhere. As a Nobel Prize winner, he would have been one of the school's most illustrious alumni. Grass had mentioned the school in his book *Cat and Mouse*, and it seems that because of this mention, it had been assumed that he had attended it. I could not find any actual dates.

Grass, while being considered a moral authority who was awarded countless prizes for his critical writings about the Nazi era, only admitted in 2006 to having joined the Waffen-SS as a juvenile fighter, and only after it had become public knowledge anyway.

Like many Germans, I was disappointed by Grass's lack of courage and moral integrity. Grass had not been the only child soldier in the Reich. There were about two hundred thousand to three hundred thousand of them, the largest number ever used by any country. Thousands were slaughtered, and those who returned alive were seriously traumatized for the rest of their lives. Most of them, like my father, never talked about their experiences. Their reasons ranged from shame and guilt to fearing repercussions in their careers or for their families. There was also the fear that making one's own suffering known would have been perceived as a lack of respect for the victims of the Nazi regime.

Grass, on the other hand, had been a professional writer. He had more freedom in his career and some moral authority. If he had faced his past, he would have truly earned the title "conscience of the nation" for which he was so celebrated. By admitting to what he had done as a juvenile, he would have given a whole generation of former German child soldiers, many of whom had fought in SS units as well, the courage to unburden themselves of their heavy stories. But Grass stayed silent and only admitted to it, in a book, after the press had already been informed through other sources.

Grass missed his opportunity to spearhead that at least a decade earlier, when most children of the war had retired from their active careers and were willing to, but did not dare to, talk about their childhoods under the Nazis. It would have helped them work through their remaining trauma and would have given their children, my generation, the opportunity to finally understand what had shaped our—sometimes difficult—fathers while they were still alive.

There was precious little Grass could have done about his time in the 10th SS Panzer Division Frundsberg. It was an accidental assignment. He had not asked for it. In the last months of the war, divisions were randomly put together and though SS in name, they were not comparable to the infamous SS death squads that had become notorious. Grass had only volunteered to fight, as thousands of German boys had done. His was an SS division that was not involved in any atrocities. There was little for him to admit to, but instead of doing so, it seemed that he had tried to obscure the facts.

As for Ratzinger, I found the name of his elementary school but kept searching the internet in vain with a combination of different keywords for his high school. Finally, my internet search yielded an official notice stating that two entries relating to Cardinal Ratzinger had been removed under the "right to be forgotten" court ruling. It was the end of the line for that investigation.

I stepped back and contemplated how I felt about both. I had no respect for Grass for not helping a whole generation of Germans, who had faithfully bought his books, to work through their lingering war trauma while they were still alive. Ratzinger's reticence to speak out on the matter made sense to me, despite my being neither Catholic nor conservative. He had chosen to uphold traditional church law, in a country where the church had failed its members in their time of need. As a child, he had seen everything that had been done to dissolve the moral authority of the churches, and National Socialism had become the new religion. His opposition to contraception and abortion was anachronistic, but in his youth, he had witnessed how the belief in selective human breeding had led to unspeakable crimes, where some children were considered fit to be raised, while others were anni-hilated as newborns.

Almost at the end of the Vogelsang exhibit, a video, running in a loop, attracted my attention. It was an interview with a former Adolf Hitler School pupil named Helmut Morlok.[6] He talked about his time in Vogelsang and kept referring to "the blessing of the late birth."

I listened to his words and felt uneasy. So far, I had felt that the Nazi child soldiers had been victims. They had been brain-washed into accepting Nazi values, been cajoled into signing up as soldiers, often illegally without their parents' consent, sometimes as young as fourteen years old. They had been too young to vote, join a party, or even go, without the company of an adult, to drink beer in a bar. Until 1975, the age of majority in Germany was twenty-one years old.

But had they already been twenty-one years old, what choices would they have made in those desperate times? Would they have saved themselves by killing others? Would they have sacrificed their own lives to save the innocent? The line between being a victim or a perpetrator suddenly felt uncomfortably thin.

6

—

SCHOOLED BY BARBARIANS

I N 2014, LOOKING THROUGH the German history section at the
Harvard Book Store in Cambridge, Massachusetts, I came upon a
book called *School for Barbarians: Education under the Nazis*. It was
a reprint of a book written by Erika Mann, daughter of the German
literary Nobel Prize–winner Thomas Mann.[1] The original was published in the United States in 1938, one year before the outbreak of the
war, selling forty thousand copies in the first three months. The same
year, it was also published in the Netherlands. Erika Mann gave the
American and European public an early view of how the Nazis were
transforming a whole generation of Germans by hijacking the education of the almost ten million children who were entrusted to them. It
is a comprehensive, carefully researched description of the physical and
emotional enslavement of children and the gagging of their parents.
When Mann published her book, the destruction of the political opposition, the churches, and the family structures was almost complete.

The famous Harvard Book Store has supplied the intellectual community with important books since 1932. To this day, it is
considered a reliable source of relevant writings. I wondered if the
book had been sold in the store when it first came out? How had
the Harvard academics reacted when they read it? It gave those who
were interested a candid view of what was happening to Germany's

youngsters. Militarizing their education was a warning sign, fore-shadowing events to come.

Had Mann's book been published in Germany in 1938, it would have been a one-way ticket to a concentration camp or at least a work camp. A first German edition was finally published in 1986 under the somewhat less provocative title *Ten Million Children: The Education of the Youth in the Third Reich*. Mann's book appears carefully researched, but some of her quotes sounded so bizarre by today's standards that it seemed to me as if she had overstated the facts. Her 1986 German publisher must have felt the same way and obliged her readers by adding a whole fact-checking chapter confirming that her research was indeed legitimate and that she had quoted her sources accurately.

The book gave a graphic impression of how German children lived at the time. Among the interesting tidbits of her book is the origin story of the Nazi *Horst Wessel* hymn, outlawed in Germany to this day. Wessel plagiarized the melody, and his own original text for the song "Hold the Flag High" was full of orthographic mistakes. Every child had to pay homage to this Nazi martyr killed by a communist, when in fact he was killed in a private dispute by a fellow pimp, who only coincidentally had connections to the Communist Party. He is not an isolated case. Many of the Nazis' heroes presented to the children as role models had unsavory pasts that had been sanitized by the time they reached the schoolyards.

The most frequently quoted passage in Mann's book is her es-timate of every German child having to say, "Heil Hitler!" from 50 to 150 times a day, which was required by law. Friends on the way to school had to say, "Heil Hitler!" to one another, and lessons in school were opened and closed with it. It was mandatory for all—the shop assistants, postmen, and train conductors. Buildings with a *Blockwart* (a caretaker) had a Nazi guardian on the premis-es. He would report any family that did not follow the guidelines. Parents had to greet their children coming home from school with "Heil Hitler!" or they could be denounced and lose custody of their

The author's uncle, Ludwig, coming home from school in his Hitler Youth uniform, cuddling his baby sister, Erika, Hans's future wife. Their sister, Marlene, is only in preschool and not expected to wear a uniform yet. All children grew up surrounded by uniforms.

children. Again, I felt that losing custody over one's children for not shouting "Heil Hitler" seemed extreme, but I established that such a law actually existed.

A scene in Taika Waititi's hilariously funny but bittersweet film *Jojo Rabbit*, about a confused boy trying to make sense of the world, presents a persiflage of Gestapo men engaged in endless rounds of "Heil Hitler."[2]

I asked around. I could not imagine my grandmother—in between cooking, washing, cleaning, and gardening—dropping everything, standing to attention, raising her right arm, and shouting "Heil Hitler" any time one of her four children left the house or came home. I asked my mother. She responded, with some indignation, "No, we did not greet each other with 'Heil Hitler.'" They had lived in a house on the outskirts of the town of Mülheim, across from an old timber-framed farmhouse. The family of farmers had not shouted "Heil Hitler" at each other either, before feeding the pigs in the morning or milking the cows in the evening. Nor had they reported anybody for not doing so.

From when I was young, I remember our kindly, elderly neighbor Mrs. Scriba who had come as a refugee from Thuringia. She once told us children, before we knew what she was talking about, "We hated all that stuff, and every time we passed a street parade we would duck into a store, so as not to have to raise our right arms."

But my father's classmate Franz told me a different story: "That is exactly what my mother did! She always greeted me that way. She was a dyed-in-the-wool Nazi. She wondered about the family next door because one could never hear them shout 'Heil Hitler.' She concluded that there was clearly something wrong with them."

When my father arrived as a nine-year-old in Germany, he did not know that there had been a time when Germans had greeted one another with "Good morning" just like the *Buenos días* in the country he had come from. Whether he was greeted the same way every time he came home on vacations to Auntie Tali is among the many questions that I did not know to ask either of them while they were still alive. I could not imagine it.

As a child, I had known Auntie as a no-nonsense and, to some extent, even cynical person. She believed in education and academic excellence and detested any lack of intellectual rigor. If Auntie Tali had joined the NSDAP, it would have been an act of opportunism to secure her own job as a teacher and to get her favorite nephew a privileged education for very little money. I remember her always looking for a good deal. But there was no such thing as "free" with the NSDAP, despite the assurances otherwise. I do not know if she ever realized what a Faustian bargain she had struck.

In her book, Mann perceptively pointed out that *Heil* in German means salvation. It is applied to relations between man and God in the context of eternal salvation. The choice of the word had not been random. It cemented the idea that Hitler was to be presented as having messianic powers. To enforce this superhuman impression, Hitler carefully controlled his images that went into circulation. They show him strong and kind while greeting children or gently petting fawns, but never looking tired, bored, or picking his nose.

There was one more historic connection that occurred to me. *Heil Dir im Siegerkranz* ("Hail you in the victor's crown") was the pompous and nationalistic (by today's standards) hymn that had honored Emperor Wilhelm I, who at the time was still revered by Germans as the unifier of the nation. His incompetent grandson, Emperor Wilhelm II, had plunged Germany into the First World War and its disastrous aftermath. But by aligning his greeting with that of the old emperor, Hitler was indirectly viewed as the true heir to Emperor Wilhelm I.

Even the youngest wore uniforms; no child was exempt—a cousin of Hans, Wilhelm Hoffmeyer, in 1935.

Another powerful historical link and message to the children was the use of uniforms. Heinrich Böll, another German literary Nobel Prize winner, wrote in disgust about the day when he and all of Cologne's schoolchildren had to line the streets in honor of Goering who, during his three hours in the town, changed his uniform four times.[3]

Mann observed that men wearing uniforms, such as those worn by the men of the SS, the *Freiwilliger Arbeitsdienst* (Volunteer Labor Service), and the *Wehrmacht* soldiers, were an everyday sight for the children. It came naturally for the children to wear uniforms as well. This is confirmed by Hans's photo album from the years 1937–40. It shows him both in school at Feldafing and on vacation in Bremen, Mardorf, and the seaside. He is always dressed in a uniform, although there are different ones depending on the activity. Even in a casual family holiday photo on the beach with his grandparents, he is in uniform. For the boarding school kids, their pajamas and underwear were up to Nazi code as well. I wondered if my father had owned any civilian clothes. Franz showed me one of his photos that felt grotesque: a sweetly smiling ten-year-old boy dressed up in a miniature Nazi soldier's uniform with a swastika armband. Mann could have added that the German fascination with uniforms extended back several generations. Even if the children did not have daily visual exposure to them, their parents' respect for military attire would have rubbed off on them.

Hans on vacation with his maternal grandparents, the old Consul and his wife, Marie, wearing his dress uniform even at the beach.

Emperor Wilhelm II had adored uniforms, and what he lacked as a ruler he made up with fanciful parades that had the character of dress rehearsals. During his reign, in 1906, a poor shoemaker with a prison record for a petty crime was denied working papers, leaving him without employment and penniless. In his desperation he bought the shabby, used uniform of an army captain. Dressed in it, he commanded a whole unit of soldiers and occupied the town hall of the Berlin district of Köpenick. There he had his own working papers issued and stole the petty cash box. An odd event that has always captured my imagination, the story of the Captain of Köpenick foreshadowed the disaster of Germany's unholy fascination with uniforms.

The event also shows that prior to the First and Second World Wars, Germans were accustomed to respect a uniform, and its wearer was not required to present any proof of legitimacy beyond his attire. Even a criminal could command soldiers, as long as he wore a uniform. In post–Second World War Germany, three movies have been made about this event. Unfortunately, at the time the incident was considered merely amusing.

A couple of decades after the Köpenick incident, the emerging Nazi Party fully exploited this German weakness. It realized that as long as every German was wearing some kind of uniform, associated with a set of duties and privileges, it was easy to control the country as a whole, including children.

But the most powerful visual tool was the red flag with the black swastika in its center. Mann explained that not a week passed without an occasion on which families were given one reason or another to hang out the flag from their windows. When my father was on school break, he stayed with Auntie and his grandparents in Bremen. Since the late Middle Ages, an impressive, thirty-foot-high statue known as the "Roland" had been the iconic guard in the marketplace of the city and today, the beloved figure is part of a UNESCO World Heritage site. In 1933, the local NSDAP city administration attached a swastika emblem over the shield of the stone knight. Hitler was declared an honorary citizen. To celebrate that event, a cassette containing

Germans were accustomed to associate uniforms with authority, as the Captain of Köpenick incident showed. Heinz, Hans's father, in a uniform in 1918.

Nazi propaganda was cemented into the sculpture, but decades later it was discovered that the artisans had secretly hidden genuine documents in it as well.[4] Until the end of the war, Hans never saw Roland without a swastika. Flags and emblems of the Führer were all over town and displayed on the many occasions for celebration that the Nazis had created. Only the older children had a faint recollection of life prior to the National Socialists; the younger ones were born into it and had never known anything else.

Jews were exempt from these events. Not being considered Germans, they had no national events. German children often heard them being referred to singularly as "the Jew," even when discussing several people or the whole Jewish population. It was a tool used to minimize their individuality as human beings. The same was done to other groups of people. The fear of "the Russian," a giant menace coming from the east, was instilled in the minds of German children as though they were bogeymen or body snatchers. In his diary, Hans refers to the Russian Army in that manner. The image of "the enemy" was systematically cultivated in the children's minds.

Besides flags, signs with slogans were hung from buildings, thanking the Führer for providing work on roads, barracks, and sports fields, all paid for by the state. These slogans were so deeply engrained in the children that when I interviewed my father's eighty-five-year-old classmate Franz, he still used those phrases from his childhood, but now with irony and bitterness. He would tell me about the things that had happened to them as children and if it was particularly bad, he closed his story with a sentence that sounded like a refrain: ". . . and this is what we have to thank our dear Führer for."

Originally, membership in the Hitler Youth was voluntary, as was joining the sister organization *Bund Deutscher Mädel* (BDM)—the League of German Girls. The boys were divided into the *Jungvolk* (young people aged ten to fourteen) and the *Hitlerjugend* (fourteen- to eighteen-year-olds). The girls had the *Jungmädelbund* (ten- to fourteen-year-olds), the *Mädelbund* (fourteen- to seventeen-year-olds), and an additional BDM work association called "Believe and Beauty" for those aged between seventeen and twenty-one, presumably to give them some finishing touches for their future as Aryan broodmares. The social pressure to join was high, and those whose parents did not allow them to join suffered a great deal from social exclusion.

By 1939, about 90 percent of children classified as Aryan belonged to Nazi youth groups, and it became compulsory to attend Hitler Youth events. There was a well-organized hierarchy. An uncle told me:

> We little ones were called *Pimpfe* [slightly derogatory, colloquial word for boy]. We hated that term, which made us eager to become a *Jungmann* [old-fashioned word for young man]. When we turned fourteen, we were finally promoted to full members of the HJ [Hitler Youth]. Each step was accompanied by celebrations, badges, and uniforms designed to make us feel special. The older children who had already paid their dues were in charge of us younger children. There was very little adult supervision. If we felt we were picked on too much, we could look forward to dishing it out to the youngest ones later. Most activities were physical and adventurous. It was great to be out in nature and not feel alone in those preteen years. But not all of us escaped from these activities physically or emotionally unscathed. There were lots of bloody, scraped knees and elbows. Tears were only shed in private, because shy and gentle children were told to toughen up. Rough-and-tumble boys were at an advantage. We didn't know it at the time, but they were getting us ready to be soldiers.

He added, "I still hear Hitler screaming in one of his speeches, 'Everything soft and weak has to be taken out of the German youth.'"

I thought about it. Most parents at the time had gone through the humiliations of the First World War as teenagers and had struggled through the economic upheavals of the 1920s. Wishing for their children to be raised strong and independent might not have sounded all that bad, before they understood the real meaning of the words.

As a child I had lived in Liberia, so when I heard the story of Hans-Jürgen Massaquoi, I was immediately interested. Born in 1926 to a German mother and a Liberian diplomat from a prominent family, he grew up with his mother in Hamburg as an African German. In a German TV interview with the reporter Guido Knopp, he stated: "I would have given up a limb if it would have gotten me an HJ uniform. I was so unhappy not to be allowed to join the Hitler Youth. There was a chart hung up in my classroom with a star next to each child's name who had joined the HJ. After some weeks, only my name had no star."

From his biography, one learns that he kept applying to the Hitler Youth and later to the more prestigious army units, only to be rejected. Despite his academic promise, he was forced into an apprenticeship instead of having access to higher education. Ironically, it kept him safe: Apprentices were considered essential workers and drafted last.

How did Massaquoi survive Nazi persecution? There was no law for the annihilation of Black people, as there were too few of them to pass a separate law. He suffered ridicule and discrimination but was not deported, as most things were done to the letter of the Nazi laws. After the war, Massaquoi, being denied his German roots, went on to celebrate his African roots in New York by becoming chief editor of the African American magazine *Ebony*. A two-part German film was made about his life, based on his memoirs.

Hearing Massaquoi speak on camera was strange. He identified so much more with Germany than I did myself. As the child of a German diplomat, I had been raised abroad, in Liberia, Brazil, and England. I had never felt totally at home in Germany. There was an odd difference between us. He wanted to be German, while

I was uneasy being German. What childhood experiences create one's national identity? The Mann family had left Germany in 1933 and had become American citizens, but Thomas Mann and his children were forced to leave again in 1952 after being targeted by McCarthyism. What made a person a citizen of a country? Being law-abiding was clearly not enough. Was it one's uncritical loyalty to the regime in power?

In the 1938 introduction to Erika Mann's book by Thomas Mann, he wholeheartedly endorsed his daughter's book and warned the world about the impending disaster that was to befall Germany if it continued to educate its children in such a cruel, mindless way. He presaged that the consequences would be dire. It was a timely and urgent warning, but one that went unheard.

7

THE FLAG IS MORE THAN DEATH

A BERLIN FRIEND RECOMMENDED THAT I pay a visit to the "Book and Bunker Town" of Wünsdorf, about an hour south of Berlin. The town's claim to fame is that it offers tours of sinister and moldy but highly impressive bunkers, which, like everything in the Nazi world, were built on a gigantic scale. One bunker, under thick slabs of concrete, housed the infamous Russian map collection, assembled by the *Wehrmacht* under Nazi intelligence officer Reinhard Gehlen, that later would become important to the Americans navigating the Cold War. There was also an array of other army buildings, constructed by the Nazis and extensively used by the Russians after the war. From the day the Nazis took power until the fall of the Berlin Wall, Wünsdorf and the surrounding areas—with ghostly, abandoned buildings littering the forests—was a forbidden zone, off-limits to civilians.

My interest was in the village itself, where several antiquarian bookshops offered hundreds of obscure and out-of-print books for sale. Many were the remnants of the prolific output of the publishing presses of the GDR (the former German Democratic Republic of East Germany), mostly tinged by Moscow's communist ideology. There were East German editions of Russian classics and lots of East and West German books long discarded in other parts of Germany.

A Nazi bunker camouflaged as a house is part of a sprawling complex close to the former no-go area of Wünsdorf.

For my research it turned out to be a treasure trove. The largest store was staffed by a heavyset man in a polyester tracksuit, clearly an "Ossie" (from East Germany). He only needed to take one look at me to know that I was a "Wessie." The wall had come down more than twenty years ago, but Germans still knew who came from the West and who was from the East. Wünsdorf was Ossie territory.

I asked him if he had any books on Nazi education and boy soldiers. He nodded and traipsed to the back of the store. I followed him, trying to avoid tripping over piles of publications stacked in disorderly chaos on the floor. He pulled three books from a dusty top shelf and presented them to me with a triumphant smile, waiting for my reaction. He had given me three different books with almost identical titles: *The Flag Is More Than Death*.

The books were by different authors. One was a hardcover with a dust jacket from 1989 with the subtitle *The Sacrificed Youth*. The next one was a paperback from 1980 with the subtitle *Songs from the Times of the Nazis*. The third one, a somber, dark, cloth-covered

94

hardback from 1958, had the subtitle *Novel of a Betrayed Generation*.

Waiting impatiently for my response, the man started to hum a melody. I looked at him in bewilderment. He realized that I was not understanding what he was trying to communicate, so he added words to the song:

Our flag flies in front of us . . .
We march for Hitler through night and hardship.

Skipping parts, he went on, accentuating the last line:

Yes, the flag is more than death!

I still did not get it, and asked him, somewhat irritated about the unsolicited artistic performance, "What is that song?"

He looked amazed as he explained, "It's the official hymn of the Hitler Youth, composed by the youth leader Baldur von Schirach himself. Didn't they teach you anything in the West?"

"Certainly not Nazi stuff," I replied defensively.

"Ah, that's why you are now hanging out here, to make up for what they never taught you," he teased me, with what we Wessies consider an in-your-face Ossie directness, addressing me with a familiar *du* instead of the polite *sie*, another East-West distinction. In the communist state of the GDR, everybody had been a *Genosse* (a Comrade). The use of the formal *sie* implied a form of class distinction that was considered another tool of the Western imperialists to reinforce capitalist values.

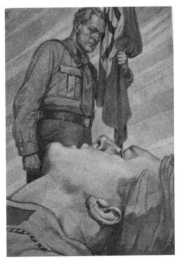

"There is no other thanks but to promise to continue to fight for the Germany that he died for."

95

To change the subject, I observed the obvious, "They must have used this line in their book titles, because it became so engrained on the minds of a whole generation of German children."

"Now you are getting it." He smiled, somewhat condescendingly.

An expression of superiority seemed to come over his face. Here I was, the Wessie, coming to him, the Ossie, and he could impress me with his detailed historical knowledge. Usually it was the other way around. After reunification, West German consultants and government officials had efficiently closed ailing Eastern factories, disrupting what had been a way of life for a whole generation of East Germans and leaving them with a resentment toward the perceived West German arrogance. The German press had labeled this as a worrisome phenomenon and a fertile breeding ground for right-wing ideologies, as unemployable East German men resented the fact that it had been much easier for their women to move to West Germany to find work, while they were left behind.

"Enjoy yourself. I need to return to the cash register."

He made a sweeping gesture toward rows of bookshelves. There was a book for everything I could possibly want to know about the Nazi educational system and young soldiers fighting in the Second World War. One book was absent: Hitler's *Mein Kampf*, first published in 1925. I had never seen a copy, but I knew that it had contained Hitler's blueprint for gaining access to and exploiting the enthusiasm of German youth. I had been raised with the belief that this was the most horrible book ever written, so handling an actual copy would have felt uncomfortable.

Before the Nazi takeover, German newlyweds were given a copy of the Bible. After Hitler's ascent, it became mandatory to present couples with a copy of *Mein Kampf* on their wedding day. It made Hitler, who always sported an image of frugality, a millionaire, as it kept his book in print. Apparently, by 1945, twelve million copies had been produced.

I bought a whole stack of books, and while the attendant was bagging them, I noticed a children's book, *Der Rattenfänger von Hameln*—literally translated as "The Rat Catcher of the City of Hamelin" but known throughout the English-speaking world as "The Pied Piper." I picked it up and read the introduction. The German medieval legend was foretelling the fate of children under the Nazis. Hitler, who was scorned as an artist in his native Austria just like the piper, neither recognized nor paid for his talent, made it his business to seduce the young and abduct them from their parents using irresistible melodies.

Two origins of the legend were put forward. The first one connects it to the Children's Crusade of 1212. Children, young and ill-equipped, ventured over the Alps to fight and free the Holy Land, where their elders, heavily armed knights, had failed. The second theory was more plausible, with a strange, random connection to my story. A local historian from Hamelin had advanced the theory that their young ones were recruited in the twelfth and thirteenth century by agents of the House of *Přemyslovci*, a Czech royal dynasty looking for skilled German settlers for their lands.

A professor of onomatology had traced the family names from Hamelin to northern Moravia. It happened to be the area my father wrote about on his way to the front, Troppau and Olmütz.

I returned the fairy-tale book to the counter, focusing on the less speculative but disturbing literature I had just acquired. Just in case I needed to get in touch again, I asked the talkative attendant for his name, which I started to write down on one of the shop's business cards. "No, no," he interrupted me. "I know, Mike is an English name . . . it was in protest at our GDR regime that our parents gave us foreign names. But they did not know how to spell them, so it was recorded phonetically as M-a-i-k."

How differently the Ossies had been raised from us, in all aspects of life. Their relationship to the history of the Third Reich was very different from our Western one. The Communist regime

97

had always declared that the Nazis were part of the capitalist system and had nothing to do with the workers' and farmers' state of the GDR. This was why I could still find some Third Reich history books here. Several were published by Bublies, a sketchy right-wing publisher. No self-respecting West German antiquarian would have sold them, but they contained a lot of chilling details on the Third Reich not found elsewhere.

Before picking up my heavy load, I hesitated. My father would have hated for me to take those books home. After I left Maik's store, I retired to a nearby café. I started with Georg Walter Heyer's *The Flag Is More Than Death* book on Nazi children's songs. Leafing through it, I recalled that the philosopher Voltaire, who had once lived in Germany at the invitation of the eighteenth-century Prussian king Frederick the Great, had said, "It is forbidden to kill; therefore, all murderers are punished unless they kill in large numbers and to the sound of trumpets." There had been plenty of trumpets at Nazi events and even more singing. Music was hijacked, and Nazi propaganda slogans were packed into pleasant sounding songs, masked as patriotic hymns.

Once again, the Nazi educators had built upon existing structures. A quarter of a century before they took power, a youth movement called *Wandervogel* (Wandering Birds) had inspired the previous generation of German children to go hiking in the woods and sing songs around campfires. Between 1933 and 1935 the organization was forced to integrate into the Hitler Youth, a move from which it never recovered. Its members had been romantics, and their songs reflected a love for the beauty of their German homeland.

A popular song was "Wild Geese Are Flying through the Night" with lyrics by the well-loved writer Walter Flex. He was a pacifist after witnessing the slaughter in the First World War. Carrying a warning, the song's lyric continued, "be watchful, be watchful, the world is full of murdering."

The author's grandmother, mother of Hans's future wife, Erika, as a carefree youth of the Wandering Bird movement, ca. 1923, which was highjacked and outlawed by the Nazis.

I remember my maternal grandmother, Hildegard, talking fondly of her Wandering Bird days, "We girls were still very restricted in what we were allowed to do, and those back-to-nature events gave us a real sense of freedom. We felt we were part of a new world order, so different from the times of the Kaiser that our parents had been raised in."

There were also the *Pfadfinder* (Germany's Boy Scouts). They had organized events, roughing it out in the woods, and they emphasized leadership in the young. They wore uniforms and had flags. Just like the *Wandervogel* organization, they were outlawed by the Gestapo between 1933 and 1934. The Nazis hijacked ideas from both movements and appropriated the songs of the Wandering Bird movement, whose lyrics were sometimes overloaded and idealistically naïve, but never vicious. Jewish children had been part of both groups, but they were excluded after 1933. At the beginning of the Nazi reign, my grandmother saw her own children

singing the same tunes she knew, but increasingly the Nazis substituted their own songs.

The author Georg Heyer had sung them for a decade as a
child, before he was prematurely taken out of school to start
fighting. They must have echoed in his mind for decades, because he published a song collection in 1980, more than forty
years after he had learned them. The book's introduction was an
accusation from the author against the generation of parents and
educators who allowed the Nazis to utilize the traditional German love of music and song to lead their children onto a path of
annihilation. The songs often had a simple rhythm, suitable for
marching.

The lyrics were crass, but there was a logical progression in
them. It started with songs that helped children to deal with
the pain of separation from their families, such as this example:

> A Hitler man went into the world
> Leaving his little mother at home
> And when the moment of separation came
> He quietly said goodbye to her
> But she said in tears to him,
> "Hitler guardsman, do your duty."[1]

To ensure that the children would see themselves as soldiers, they
sang:

> Youth! Youth!
> We are the soldiers of the future
> Youth! Youth!
> Carry out the future deeds, Führer, we belong to you
> We are your comrades.[2]

To prepare them for death, lyrics such as the following were sung:

Sad sounded their songs
Through the small, still town,
Because they were taking to his grave a Hitler comrade . . .
"You did not fall in vain,"
They swore again and again
Three times rang out the gun salute.
He had stayed faithful to Adolf Hitler.[3]

Darwinist principles were taught in few words:

Away with every weak worker
Only who conquers has the right to live.[4]

Anti-Semitism was covered with even fewer words:

Heads roll, Jews wail
The SA is marching.[5]

The Nazi political ambition to expand into the east and settle it with Germans was cloaked in songs as well:

The wind drives east
So put wife, child, and farmhand
On the wagon and horses
We are hungry for fresh earth
And feel the good wind.[6]

Some lyrics attempted to be poetic:

If a comrade dies the death of a hero
The Alpine roses are blooming red in the snow.[7]

In interviews, former Hitler Youth children say that, especially when they were younger, they did not really understand what their song lyrics meant. The melodies sounded so nice! Most songs contained grand keywords such as homeland, honor, victory, or blood.

Prominently featured was the duty to die for the fatherland. Flags and drums are mentioned frequently. Most lyrics were ridiculously exaggerated, to the extent that, even at the time, the German children's book author Erich Kästner, as a parody, composed a song of his own:

> The women have to crank out children
> A child a year, or face imprisonment
> The state needs humans as canned preserves
> And blood tastes to him like raspberry juice.[8]

He referred to the common propaganda slogan that it was women's holy duty to bear children for the Führer. Not surprisingly, his writing style earned Kästner a place on the list of banned authors and he was labeled a degenerate.

Nazi propaganda was not restricted to songs but included slogans such as "Youth has to lead youth." This was intended to minimize adult interference in education from adults who remembered the days before Hitler. "You are nothing, your people are everything" reinforced the children's willingness to be subjugated toward the common good.

A well-known Napola propaganda film at the time had the title *All of Life Is a Fight!* Referring to *Herrenmenschen* (humans lording over others), a term coined by the philosopher Nietzsche, the Nazis referred to superior humans born to rule. They made it clear to the

Photo taken by Hans of Dittler, who was in charge of the boys during their Flak time. Youth leads youth, 1943 (Hans seemed to have disliked him).

children that, to become one of them, they first had to be continuously broken, but they could console themselves with the thought that one day they would lord it over others.

On a side note, it is interesting that the "Horst Wessel Lied," the anthem of the Nazi Party, was banned and is outlawed in Germany to this day, but Schirach's hymn of the Hitler Youth is accessible. Did the Hitler Youth, with its invitation for children to have themselves killed for the flag, not receive the same amount of scrutiny from the postwar German public? It seemed that West Germany took ownership of Nazi atrocities in the concentration camps but chose to ignore what it had done to its own children.

I had seen interviews on German television with former German boy soldiers. Almost all of them said the same. In the world they were growing up in, most boys had only one concern. They worried that the war would be over too soon, before they were old enough to join, deprived of the chance to become heroes. What they wanted most was to prove to the Führer that they were worthy of him. Those who did not like to fight were shamed for it.

I felt dizzy and ordered a bottle of Apollinaris sparkling water before looking at the next book. It was written by Günter Wagner, another former pupil of my father's Feldafing school, and was published in 1958. The subtitle, *Novel of a Betrayed Generation*, referred to the fact that the children had been lured in by the promise of glory and integrity and had only found deceit and hypocrisy. An interview in the September 10, 1958, edition of the well-known weekly German magazine *Der Spiegel* revealed what Günter Wagner and my father had in common. Günter, born in 1925, was also identified as an extremely gifted child. The director of his elementary school suggested to his parents that Günter should be sent to Feldafing School. His father, a factory foreman, was coerced into sending off his boy with the offer of a full school scholarship. The *S* in the Nazi Party abbreviation NSDAP stood for "Socialist," and it was stressed that any gifted child would be given access to the best education, regardless of the family's financial circumstances.

Twelve years after the war, Günter Wagner, a schoolteacher himself, described his Feldafing experience as an education toward inhumanity. He deconstructed how the National Socialist (NS) state, like all totalitarian states, gradually led its young toward an inhuman ideology without allowing it to affect their conscience. During that process, they thought of themselves as the good ones, not realizing at the time the full monstrosity of the ideology they had bought into. The totalitarian NS state used traditional values such as honor and faithfulness to corrupt children, demanding unselfish service for their own goals.

The author of the last book, Ferdinand Simoneit, like my father, had to fight on the Eastern Front at seventeen years old and was heavily wounded. He recalls attending the Napola in Treskau (today the Polish town Owińska, near Poznań). At Himmler's orders, the children were not evacuated from the path of the approaching Russian Army but ordered to senselessly defend the fortifications of the ancient buildings.

As Ferdinand was sent to the Eastern Front toward the end of the war, he observed, just as my father did, how the rage of the defeated Nazis turned against their own people, shooting war-tired infantry men, convicted on the spot for desertion. That experience is followed by witnessing acts of vengeance by the Russian Army, who drove their tanks over civilian refugees. Returning to his hometown, he was denounced by a German neighbor, and while in a British prisoner-of-war camp, he finally understood the truth about the regime of his once idealized Führer.

As I closed the book, I glimpsed at the back of the dust jacket: "The autobiographical description of the spirit of everyday life at the elite Napola school during the NS period. The fate of young people who, injected with the ideals of the times, broke apart in the horrors of the war." When I had started my research, I had only looked for some background literature to fact-check the information found in my father's diary. Now I was in possession of a whole library that detailed the systematic destruction of a generation of German children by their own elders.

The German journalist Paul Sethe said, "Never has idealism been more abused as in the trust of the German Youth in the 1930s."[9] I had to agree with him.

8

—

FRANZ AND THE FLAK

IT HAD TAKEN ME awhile to track him down. I had been desperate to talk to Franz. My desire to read about the Nazi educational system in books had been more than filled. I needed to talk to a real person. Besides my mother, he was the only person who could fill in the blanks between the pages of my father's diary.

Franz and my father had been at school and in the war together and reconnected in the postwar years. My mother had not been sure if he was still alive. I had run Google searches but eventually had to look through old-fashioned phone books to find his address. He was of the pre-digital generation. When I finally located his number, I called. His wife, Karin, picked up. I started to introduce myself, but she knew immediately who I was and joked, "Last time I saw you was at your baptism in 1958."

We both laughed. Franz was taking a long afternoon nap. Karin explained, "We are now both in our eighties and need to rest more often."

When I called again, he invited me to visit. Even though I mentioned that I had a GPS device, Franz went to great lengths to describe how I could find his home. I thought I heard pride in his voice when, in describing the route, he casually mentioned that his house was just around the corner from that of Hans-Dietrich Genscher.

The name of West Germany's former, longest-serving, postwar foreign minister had been mentioned often in our household. I knew from my father that Genscher was well respected for his efforts to end the Cold War, and years later he had helped the country of Namibia to gain independence, which my father had facilitated while he had been an ambassador in nearby Angola. I had also come across Genscher's name in connection with my research on German child soldiers. He was the same age as my father, born 1927. My father, as my mother had told me, had served under General Ferdinand Schörner, nicknamed "Bloody Ferdinand" for good reason. Toward the end of the war, Schörner gained notoriety for ad hoc executions of young, deserting German soldiers, whom he personally shot.

Genscher, on the other hand, had had the good fortune to serve under General Walther Wenck, commander in chief of the 12th Army. In the last days of the war, Wenck had deliberately ignored commands from General Field Marshal Keitel from headquarters to engage in the doomed battle for Berlin. Instead, he had used the manpower at his disposal to safeguard the passage of thousands of Eastern refugees and even managed to evacuate three thousand wounded soldiers. He considered it his responsibility to deliver his entire unit, which at that point consisted mainly of underage fighters, and surrender to the Americans, instead of leaving them to the wrath of the Russians. In contrast to Bloody Ferdinand, he did not flee himself, but went into American captivity, together with his men. Wenck decided to put his humanitarian duty above his military one. Because of him, Genscher had survived the war, physically and mentally intact, with a positive role model to look up to.

I drove up the hill to the small community of Wachtberg, a hamlet not far from Bonn. The flat-roofed 1960s bungalows, choice real estate at the time, were once the pride of their owners, who had successful careers in the nearby capital. Now, just like them, the structures showed their age, and many gardens were overgrown. The younger generation of politicians and bureaucrats had moved to Berlin after the wall came down in 1989. Wachtberg had turned into a retirement community for my parents' generation, who had politically and physically rebuilt West Germany from its ruins. Today, their grandchildren would not know who Genscher was, unless they had an interest in twentieth-century German history.

Franz and Karin welcomed me warmly. Karin, as is customary for the older German generation, had set the table with her best fine bone china, silver cutlery, and starched cloth napkins. She served coffee and cake. Franz wore a striped dress shirt with a camel-colored blazer and gray wool slacks. His white hair was carefully combed back. Only the felt slippers, in which he shuffled about, were an indication that he had dressed up for the occasion. He was heavyset, and Karin only allowed him a small piece of cake. As my father had been, he was diabetic. It crossed my mind that the Californian author and healer Louise L. Hay had once called diabetes the disease of those who felt deep sorrow and for whom life had lost its sweetness.

I had many questions for Franz. I wanted to know what school had been like for him and my father, and to discover what he could tell me about the time when they were taken out of school to fight.

Franz confirmed what I already knew about Feldafing school and added more details. In his view, the academic education, in contrast to the Napolas and Adolf Hitler Schools, had been excellent, despite the Nazi

Franz while being interviewed by the author.

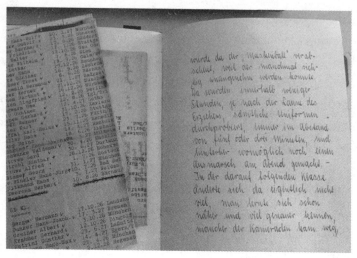

Hans's school diary from Feldafing describing the dreaded masquerade balls, and a class list.

ideology that had been taught to them in more subtle ways. I asked him about the infamous masquerade balls, where educators terrorized boys into changing their outfits in rapid succession, and he replied, "At Feldafing that was considered child's play and rather inconsequential. I came across true chicanery when I joined the army toward the end of the war." With a self-conscious smile he added, "After all I had to be there for the *Endsieg* [the final victory] we had been promised." We both laughed, embarrassed at the thought of how differently things had turned out.

I asked Franz about the book by his Feldafing schoolmate Günter Wagner, which was one of the three *The Flag Is More Than Death* titles, published in 1958. He was not familiar with it but commented, "Some of those early books are not particularly good."

"In what sense?" I asked.

He explained: "They were written to sell and the more horribly the Nazis were described, the greater the number of copies sold. There were lots of things wrong with that terrible regime, but to say that we suffered from abject Nazi cruelty every waking moment of our lives is a distortion. In recent years, historians have tried to take a more balanced view of historical events, but now those who were involved are rapidly disappearing and can no longer speak up. Now the next generation is getting involved."

"What do you mean by that?" I enquired.

"Even those who were not even born when all this happened feel responsible," Franz explained. I leaned forward, listening even more attentively.

I asked, "Do you think that my generation is no longer to blame even though we are Germans and this history is our inheritance?"

"No, it's over! Sippenhaft ended with the fall of the Third Reich," he said firmly.

Sippenhaft translates roughly into "kin liability." It was an ancient medieval German law that was revived by the Nazis. It was dreaded and feared by everybody. Any form of noncompliance to the state could be punished by it. Those who were contemplating any anti-Nazi actions had to take into consideration that even if they were willing to sacrifice their own lives for the cause, it meant potential death or imprisonment for their spouses, parents, and siblings. Even their children were not exempt.

I had read about the most high-profile cases, such as the participants of the assassination attempt on Hitler's life on July 20, 1944. The Hollywood movies about the Stauffenberg group ended with them getting executed or committing suicide. But in reality, the story continued with their relatives. Anyone over fifteen years old was taken to a concentration camp: Stutthof, Buchenwald, or Dachau. Nina, Stauffenberg's wife, was sent to Ravensbrück concentration camp where she gave birth to their fifth child in captivity. Even Count Stauffenberg's sister-in-law was interned, and his mother-in-law died in a concentration camp. The forty-six younger children were collected in the summer of 1944 and brought to a secret, remote location where they were kept in strict isolation and given new names. The youngest child, Dagmar Hansen, was ten days old.

Reichsführer Heinrich Himmler, head of the SS and builder of the concentration camps, had personally ordered this punishment. All were aristocratic, Aryan families with impeccable pedigrees, but that did not protect them from Himmler's vendetta. He had already successfully used it as a tool against the families of army deserters in 1943. In a thundering speech, Himmler proclaimed that Graf Stauffenberg and his like would be wiped out to the last link. But in the chaos of the war's final year, their minders took pity. Some children were quietly released into the care of surviving relatives. The most prominent children were destined for Buchenwald, but the railway line was destroyed before they arrived.

The question of crime and punishment had preoccupied me since starting my research. I asked Franz again, "So you do not think that I have to carry a transgenerational guilt for what the generation of my grandparents did?"

Franz responded thoughtfully:

When the war was over, it was a tremendous task for the Allied forces to run what was called the denazification process. They tried and sentenced the Nazi perpetrators. But to all of us young fighters and the entire generation born after 1919, they extended a youth amnesty, even for Traudl Junge, Hitler's twenty-one-year-old personal secretary. We were not held responsible for what our parents and grandparents had done.

Franz paused for a moment, leaned back in his armchair, and added warily, "If there is more judging to be done, it is not up to men, but to a higher power."

I realized I had exhausted the two octogenarians. We had jumped ahead to some difficult questions to which there were no clearly defined right or wrong answers. I said my goodbyes and was glad to be invited back for another visit.

When I returned a few weeks later, I made it a point to ask Franz about the Flak. He, my father, and their entire school grade had served as antiaircraft gunners. He explained:

In 1943, we were drafted to man the antiaircraft guns, called Flak. It was the end of our regular schooling. All German boys between the ages of fifteen and seventeen were taken out of school. Some headmasters realized that their children might not return in time to graduate from high school, so they rushed them through examinations and presented them with certificates called *Notabitur* [emergency highschool diplomas] sometimes two years earlier than their actual graduation date. After the war, those diplomas were declared invalid. But for us Feldafing boys it made no difference. We had to find other, regular schools anyway, because we could not show our association with a Third Reich school if we ever wanted to get a job or enter university. We called that obtaining a clean *Abitur* [high school diploma]. At the beginning of the Flak time, only pupils from the high schools were drafted, as we were considered more dispensable. Those with only an elementary-school education, who were already in the work force, were exempt at least for a little while longer.

Goering had demanded that 120,000 men were to be freed up on the home front so they could be sent into combat. The only way to get hold of that many warm bodies was to recruit children. The army's callous calculation was to replace seventy able-bodied men with one hundred schoolboys. The order to draft children was not without opposition inside the Nazi leadership. Martin Bormann, probably thinking of his own, tender fourteen-year-old son being safely kept away from the war in Feldafing, was violently opposed to it. But Hitler sided with Goering and signed the decree on January 7, 1943. To the children's parents it was stressed that these occupations were only of an auxiliary nature. But by today's definition the Flak helpers are considered child soldiers.

I thought about the date. Officially, Germany was defeated on May 7, 1945. Various military historians have put forward earlier, de facto dates of when the war was lost, linking them to different German military defeats. To me, the war was lost the day it was decided to use children as soldiers.

When Franz left the room for a few minutes to fetch some papers, Karin added:

Franz at his SS Flak unit in the spring of 1945.

Originally the girls were exempt, but in the following two years they used us as well, but our service was not as systematically organized. In the beginning, they assigned us to lighter tasks, such as operating the searchlights or relaying messages. But later we had to man the Flaks, replacing the boys who were sent to fight at the front. Toward the end of the war, they were running out of girls as well. So younger children were used. Everybody got accustomed to seeing children participate in the war. We used to joke that all baby carriages were about to be confiscated for the war effort, because soon the children born in 1943 would be drafted!

The joke sounded uncomfortable. Toward the end of the war, an entire SS Panzer Tank Division was manned with sixteen- and seventeen-year-old boys from the Hitler Youth brigades. Boys as young as twelve went into military service. These children became famous as defenders in the Battle of Berlin. American men on the Western Front were horrified to fight and kill, and sometimes be killed by, boys who were barely old enough to graduate from elementary school. The Nazi regime rounded up between two hundred thousand and three hundred thousand child soldiers. To this day, it is the largest mobilization of underage combatants by any one country—more than all the countries in the world put together are using today.

When Franz returned, he continued his history lesson:

At the time, our families were not aware that the necessary emergency laws on which the orders of our mobilization were based had already been passed in 1935 and 1938, long before anybody even realized that there would be war. Our teachers were instructed to inform our parents of this compulsory service. We could not stay in school even if our parents asked for it. It became clear that our outdoor sports programs had all been part of a carefully conceived premilitary training program.

Mockingly, he added:

But even the Third Reich had a number of child protection laws in place. For us Flak children, instructions were given not to distribute the daily rations of tobacco and alcohol but to substitute candies. A police order was passed in 1943 that made it illegal for us under the age of eighteen to go to a public establishment after 9:00 PM without adult supervision. So, if we wanted to celebrate shooting down a few pilots with maybe a glass of lemonade in a restaurant after 9:00 PM, we would have to be accompanied by a senior officer or our parents. Even our pay reflected that we were children. Instead of military pay books, we were given pocket money, half a mark per day. Another half mark per day was to be paid directly to our parents after the end of the war. I don't think they ever saw that money.

115

I replied:

> But, I know from my father's diary that once the boys were
> moved to the front, they were given the same rations as the
> adults, tobacco and all. My seventeen-year-old father, Hans,
> with a few weeks of training, was a squad leader at the Rus-
> sian front, with nine men assigned to his command. What
> child protection laws were applied there?

There was one more thing on my mind. When I had mentioned to
an American friend that I was doing research on the subject of Nazi
child soldiering, he flippantly commented, "Yup, our guys never
knew what hit them when they were attacked by crazed German
schoolboys high on speed."

I was stunned. What was he talking about? Having grown up
in Germany, I had never even heard about drug abuse in the *Wehrmacht*. The excessive cocaine use by the megalomaniac Goering was
well known. Hitler, a hypochondriac, had been prescribed everything from methamphetamine to barbiturates, opiates, belladonna,
and even bromide by his physician, Theodor Morell. But that was
all I knew. Why did I need an American to tell me the other part
of the story? Once I started to research the subject, disturbing information came to light.

A drug, produced under the brand name of Pervitin, was handed
out to soldiers. The literary Nobel Prize–winner Heinrich Böll, at
the time a soldier in his early twenties, kept writing home asking
his parents to send more Pervitin.[1] These methamphetamines were
produced by the German company Temmler and are better known
today by their street names of speed and crystal meth. Records
show that the German Army distributed two hundred million Pervitin pills between 1939 and 1945, and it was up to the discretion of
officers to hand them out.[2] Once again it came down to economics.
Had they served their soldiers coffee to keep them awake, it would
have cost them three times as much. The detrimental health side

effects were well known, but the senior medical field officer Otto Ranke at the military medical academy in Berlin summarized the situation, "Obtaining the military goals is the highest priority; the health of the soldier is subordinate to it."[3]

With Pervitin, Germany's young soldiers truly became Hitler's children. Their supposed role model advocated abstinence from tobacco and alcohol but consumed Pervitin and other drugs instead. Authorities not only pushed Pervitin on soldiers but also on civilians, and during the early war years, the drug was available over the counter. It became endemic in German society. For housewives it was available mixed into pralines in boxes of chocolates. Norman Ohler's 2018 bestseller *Blitzed* impressively documents how both the army and the civilian population could only cope during the war by taking state-sanctioned drugs so potent that a drug dealer today would face a stiff prison sentence for peddling them.

I wanted to ask Franz about Pervitin, but it felt disrespectful to ask a man the age of my father whether he had taken drugs, at least by the etiquette rules I had been raised with. Finally, I gathered my courage. "How about Pervitin? Did you take it?"

Franz knew immediately what I was talking about, but if he was astonished about the question, he did not show it. He answered cautiously, "I tried it, but it did not work for me."

It sounded like he did not want to pursue the subject any further, but I insisted, "Did my father take it?"

"I don't know. I don't remember them handing it out when we were working at the Flak, and afterward your father and I were in different military units," he responded, making it clear that the subject was closed for him. Maybe to distract me, he suggested, "Let me show you something."

Franz lifted himself heavily out of his upholstered chair. He walked over to a desk and retrieved the paper he had brought in earlier. It was soft and brittle with small tears around the edges. The typewritten ink was fading. It was dated January 15, 1945, and

was a certification of the verified
shootings of foreign planes by
Franz in his capacity as *Luft-*
waffe Oberhelfer (Air Force Senior Helper).

As far as I could make out, he
had assisted in shooting down six
planes in 1944: three Flying For-
tress IIs, two Liberators, and one
Lancaster. Details were given as
to the witnesses and locations,
but most were so abbreviated
that they made no sense to me.
For each plane he was awarded

Franz's certificate for shooting
down planes.

two points. Franz explained, "It was Goering's idea to award us
boys badges called *Flak Kampfabzeichen* for shooting down planes.
But my total of twelve points was not enough. I had only assisted
and not single-handedly taken them out of the sky."

He added with a touch of sarcasm, "By the time I would have
qualified, they were no longer made out of iron but some kind of
tin."

I calculated. "It must have been just after your fifteenth birth-
days that you and my father killed for the first time."

"Yes, that is about right," replied Franz curtly, not wishing to add
to the subject.

The Flak awards reminded me of Boy Scout badges, except that
they did not involve good deeds like helping old ladies with their
bags—but killing people. My Aunt Marlene had once told me that
her high school sweetheart had been killed while manning a Flak.
But I could not find any separate casualty lists to show how many
children used on the antiaircraft guns had died. There were several
recorded incidents though, where more than a dozen children were
killed, all at once.

I did not remember ever seeing a similar certificate in my father's papers, but I knew that he had used his little 8mm camera for
filming the plane wrecks and the dead pilots. Once, when we were
still children, he showed the movies to a visitor, his second cousin
visiting from Chile. We children were banned from the living room
and told to go to bed. But we caught glimpses of it through the glass
door. As we were falling asleep, we heard the evening ending in a
row. We never saw the visitor again. I asked my mother about the
incident. She recalled that cousin Rudolf's right-wing views, coming from somebody who had never lived in Germany, had seriously
offended my father and that he had told Rudolf never to set foot in
his house again. I knew from other sources that Germans who had
been living in Chile and, for that matter, all over South America
long before the Third Reich, with no firsthand experience of the
physical and mental destruction of the Nazis, had applauded Hitler's law-and-order approach. After the war they had a hard time
letting go of that illusion.

In the years following the incident, the film reels disappeared
before I ever had a chance to see them. I have no clue where they
went, although I am in possession of my father's ancient projector
and a few family films.

In 1943, Franz, Hans and all the Feldafing boys born in 1926,
1927, and 1928 were posted to a Flak unit near Munich, but occasionally they returned to school. Franz told me:

> Some time during the second part of 1944 we were visited
> by Hitler's personal adjutant, General of the Infantry Rudolf
> Schmundt. He gave a passionate speech and tried to convince
> us to join the infantry, where they desperately needed men.
> Karl, Gerd, Georg, and your father were true idealists and
> signed up as volunteers to save the fatherland. I had a more
> down-to-earth approach. I asked to be kept in the Flak. I nev-
> er liked marching, and I had flat feet on top of it. General

Schmundt himself would no longer be around by the time your father started fighting; he died shortly afterward in October 1944, of the delayed effects of the wounds he had sustained on the day of the Stauffenberg attempt on Hitler's life, on July 20, 1944.

In which unit did my father fight? It was a question to which I had not been able to find an answer. I had written to the *Wehrmachtauskunftstelle*, mercifully abbreviated to *WASt*, where Second World War records of individual soldiers were kept. It took almost a year to receive an answer, only to find out that they had no record of my father fighting in any active unit. Hans's *Wehrmacht* file only stated that he had been a Flak soldier. There was something amiss.

I had joined some online Second World War groups to get more information from its members, some of them having very specialized knowledge. It was certain that the Feldafing boys had fought in the *Heeresgruppe Mitte* (Army Group Center) under the command of *Generalfeldmarschall* Ferdinand Schörner and the *1. Panzerarmee* (1st Panzer Army) under General Walter Nehring.

An amateur historian kindly took the time to outline to me that there had been the 78th Sturm Division and the 75th Infantry Division fighting in Upper Silesia before they were sent to Bohemia and then Moravia, finally ending up in the Ostrau (Ostrava) region in April 1945, where the Feldafing boys spent some time according to the diary. The 75th Division was almost totally destroyed, and its remaining members distributed to other divisions. The 78th Sturm Division retreated in conjunction with the 1st Panzer Army to the area of Olmütz, where it was involved in heavy fighting until the last day of the war. Schörner, an overblown, ambitious man who was designated the new commander in chief of the German Army in Hitler's last will, a few days before capitulation, ruthlessly kept his troops fighting until the last moment.

All that information was fascinating to a true Second World War expert, but I still knew nothing about my father's actual unit. Another history buff from an internet forum explained that beyond April 1945 it is hard to establish facts about any units, since anybody who could hold a gun was sent into battle and nobody cared anymore about assigned units. This was echoed in the diary, where Hans stated that they no longer wore any insignia and were reassigned to several units in rapid succession.

The only information I had from the diary was that the Russians had thrown them leaflets with the invitation to surrender, addressed to the 96th Tank Division. I posted more questions on the internet discussion forums. It appeared that there was no 96th Tank Division. I asked Franz, who said, "The Russians probably had their enemy units confused. If Hans wanted to obscure the real one in the diary, he would have not mentioned any name at all."

"So, in which unit did he fight?" I insisted.

He answered, "I do not know, but I think that he and the other boys were sent to the Waffen-SS. I, myself, was in an SS Flak unit."

I felt nauseated; the term "SS" to me invoked images of sadists guarding concentration camp victims as I had seen in many movies. For all my father's shortcomings, I could not see him involved in murder and genocide. As a daughter it had taken me a long time to understand that his sometimes hard shell was hiding an empathetic, compassionate personality, all the traits that Hitler had tried to breed out of the German youth. Later, I would learn about the different

SS men were portrayed as "real men."

branches of the SS. The abbreviation referred to Schutzstaffel, which loosely translates into "protection squad," an innocuous name for a deadly organization. By the time my father went to war, the SS had permeated all aspects of German life, with the Waffen-SS, their armed forces branch, being one of many divisions.

Franz's information left me with a new question. If he had been in the Waffen-SS, why had my father not been tattooed? A tattoo with their blood group was placed on the underside of the left upper arm of every SS soldier. It served to speed up the administration of blood transfusions for the wounded. Franz explained, "The Feldafing boys were only fighting in an SS combat unit in the last few weeks before the end of the war. At that point, their commanders had other problems besides tattooing children. They already knew that many of them would not last long anyway."

I wondered why it had taken me until after his death to find out all this information; why had my father never shared any of it while alive? Franz explained:

It was not safe for us to come forward and publicly speak about our experiences. In a society where after the war everybody claimed that they and their families had been in the resistance, nowhere near the Nazis, we would have been singled out as scapegoats. There was an unspoken agreement to adhere to a collective silence. If we had dared to speak publicly against the former Nazis who had been in charge of our education and who had sent us into war, it would have been to our detriment. Many of them continued to be in charge, and we depended on them as bosses, judges, and police officers. I was only seventeen when the war ended; many were younger. Those of us who survived spoke only among ourselves about the mess the older generation had gotten us into. Your father was particularly affected. When he was in school, I remember him as an athletic, handsome boy. When we reconnected in our twenties, he was severely obese and depressed. Karin and I put him on a diet and tried to build him up again.

Franz paused for a moment and added, "Now many of us are close to death, so we are willing to tell the world what happened from our own perspectives. We no longer have to fear that the information will be used against us personally, our families, or in our careers. But it might be too late."

When I left Franz and Karin for the second time, they walked me to my car, sending me off with warm embraces as though I was a daughter. I sensed that time had run out, and so I had videotaped our conversations. In the following years, I sent them Christmas cards but received no reply.

In 2017, I found out that Franz had died. I remembered our last phone conversation. He had told me, disillusioned, "Nobody wants to hear those old stories anymore."

I disagreed. "The problem is that nobody knows them. I am writing them down, so that what happened to you, my father, and the other children will not be forgotten. There are still child soldiers today. Your stories are a warning that what happens to them today will haunt the next generation of children, long after their wars have ended."

He cleared his throat and said, "I wish you all the best."

9

—

GLASSES AND MINERAL WATER

RANZ'S STATEMENT, THAT MY father had been fighting in an SS unit and that he himself had been in an SS Flak unit, was very disturbing. I did not know that much about the SS, except that it had committed the worst crimes in history. Already emotionally exhausted from researching atrocities, death, and destruction, I realized that if I was to understand my father's war experience, I would have to learn more about the SS. Whole libraries of books exploring every aspect of it were at my disposal, written by prominent historians who had built their academic careers on this topic.

I started with the basics, from the top down. Heinrich Himmler, a main architect of the Holocaust, was head of the SS from 1929 to 1945. His unimpressive stature and fisheyes behind thick glasses did not match the Führer's bombastic attributes. But what he lacked in media appeal he made up for in cruelty and ruthless ambition.

Himmler turned what originally had been a band of ruffians in charge of beer-hall brawls into the most homicidal organization in history. Under the pretext of treason, about two hundred important members of the leadership of the competing SA were unceremoniously murdered, in 1934. While many ordinary Germans were busily cheering Hitler, who was promising them a new, golden age, Himmler and the SS went about, either by persuasion, coercion, or sheer force, incorporating more and more parts of Germany into the SS. This included the police force, parts of the school system, and the military. The public today is primarily familiar with the internal SS units, like the Gestapo, which sent people to the concentration camps; the SS-*Totenkopf Standarten* (skull standards), which guarded and killed them; and the units of the Waffen-SS (armed protection squad) that committed war atrocities, such as the SS-*Leibstandarte Adolf Hitler*, the Führer's personal guard.

But for Germans at the time, there were a multitude of additional administrative, logistical, and medical institutions, all of which were run under the SS flag. The SS even owned and ran companies. One of the many bizarre details that my research yielded was that the SS had acquired several traditional mineral water companies. Himmler, a teetotaler like Hitler, had hoped to substitute beer with cheap mineral water. Alcoholism was not compatible with the rock-hard bodies of the Germanic warriors he was dreaming of. One of these firms, Apollinaris, is owned by Coca-Cola today.

But my research was interested in the units of the Waffen-SS. Before Franz had told me otherwise, I had always assumed that all the Flak divisions had been part of the *Wehrmacht*. Many prominent Germans, including Pope Benedict XVI, had admitted in their adult lives that they had served in the Flak as juveniles. There was nothing they could have done about it; this had been the law since 1943. But until now, I had never heard that there had been *Wehrmacht* and SS Flak units. Technically, that would have made them SS child soldiers.

It made sense that the SS had their own Flak children. After all, they could not just requisition a few from the *Wehrmacht* every time they needed to shoot down a plane or point headlights into the night sky. But whether SS or *Wehrmacht*, it seemed to have made little difference to the jobs of the children. As far as Franz was concerned, he must have been pleased to serve in an SS Flak division. In the later parts of the war, the propaganda machine made sure that every child in the Reich knew that *richtige Kerle* (real men) fought in the SS. For Franz, the future opera singer, who detested marching and crawling through the mud, serving in a Flak unit that was positioned within the SS was the most honorable alternative to the tedium of an infantry regiment.

How committed the boys were to these ideals is reflected in another passage of Hans's diary:

> In our oath we want to show our respect for the gray cloth of our uniforms and the flag, in the knowledge that our still voluntary readiness has found acceptance in the great union and that nothing from the outside will keep us from showing ourselves worthy of it.

The more I read, the more I became confused about the names of both *Wehrmacht* and SS units and their countless subdivisions. Troop strength was another problem, with different sources giving different numbers. I assumed that depending on how fast soldiers were killed and units got replenished, it was a challenge to keep track of accurate figures. At the beginning there had been a conflict between the regular armed forces and the SS. Many *Wehrmacht* officers who had already served in the *Reichswehr* (the armed forces of the Weimar Republic), prior to Hitler renaming it and taking it over, belonged to traditional aristocratic families who had served the country for generations. They resented the ideological fanatics of the SS, who had risen to power overnight on account of their SS and party memberships. But in the later years of the war, as the casualties mounted, units were constantly reorganized and the lines between the *Wehrmacht* and the SS became blurred. Reading different historical interpretations, I had a hard time understanding where the *Wehrmacht* ended and the SS started.

It was also evident in my father's own story. According to Franz, he had served in an SS unit, but I knew from my mother that it had been part of the *Wehrmacht's Heeresgruppe Mitte* (Army Group

Center). Had he said that he had fought in the *Wehrmacht*, he would have been technically correct, although it would have only been half the truth. But he never said anything.

In the early years, there had been a strict separation between both parts of the army. SS men were chosen by more stringent criteria regarding height and physical attributes. They could not wear glasses and had to have perfect teeth. Later, up to six tooth fillings were allowed. Himmler himself would not have qualified.

SS units suffered catastrophic losses early on. Himmler's decision to school the SS youth separately in his *Junkerschulen* and *Ordensburgen* had produced a crop of graduates long on brawn, but short on brains.

Once put in leadership positions, they often lacked the intelligence, education, and foresight to lead successful military operations. By the time the news of the SS men's deaths reached their distraught families on the home front, they had been rewritten as the heroic martyrdom of fearless fighters, rather than the victims of incompetence. The myth was propagated in countless newsreel film clips that were efficiently spread by Goebbels's propaganda machinery.

With the dwindling of ideal SS candidates, standards were relaxed to such an extent that even *Volksdeutsche* (ethnic Germans living outside of Germany) and volunteers from other countries were recruited. By February 1943, roughly eight hundred thousand Germans, together with Romanians, Italians, and Hungarians, had been killed or starved to death in the Battle of Stalingrad alone. Another ninety-one thousand soldiers went into Soviet captivity. At the time, the German news media tried to cover up the disastrous losses. Finally, on January 31, 1943, the German state radio broadcast the somber Adagio movement of Bruckner's Symphony No. 7 in acknowledgment of the defeat. I listened to it and felt overwhelmed by its sadness. The soldiers were put into mass graves in the Soviet Union in places Germans could not visit until the end of the Cold War. In recent years, the *Kriegsgräberfürsorge* (a German charity dedicated to preserving Second World War graves) has unearthed a few hundred skeletons and reburied them. Of the German prisoners sent to Siberia, only about 5 percent finally returned home in 1955–56, having left their families wondering whether they had survived for over twelve years.

The historian Omer Bartov, who analyzed letters written by soldiers who knew that they were not likely to make it out of Stalingrad alive, pointed out that almost all the documents expressed a belief in Germany's ultimate victory and their willingness to fight and die for it, boasting that they were proud to sacrifice themselves for the Führer.[1] This is what I saw reflected in my father's diary, cloaked in his poetic style but with a hint of criticism as it was written in 1945, two years after Stalingrad:

> But the feeling of giving, this overflowing feeling of giving
> yourself away, is close to the soul of us Germans in its eternal
> cycle of feeling and thinking, in the same way that the sense of our
> responsibility does not even stop at the doors of death. . . .

The myth of the Germans through the sacrifice of their dead becomes untouchable and eternal just like the Greeks and the Romans were the carriers of the highest human culture. Clearer than before, the current events show themselves as mistakes, endured with sacrifices and heroism. My father's sentences sounded utterly confused. Somehow, he was trying to make sense of all those senseless deaths by elevating them into a human sacrifice that entitled the Germanic culture to be on par with the revered civilizations of ancient Rome and Greece. He had been taught Latin, and the Romans had referred to the Germanic tribes as barbarians. For him, the time of change had come.

After the Stalingrad fiasco in 1943, three classes of recruits were established. The top class was the original SS category, followed by Germans without those strict qualifying criteria, and thirdly, non-Germans, who did not have to meet any criteria except being able to hold a gun. They had their separate units, but again, as casualties mounted, they were refreshed with people of other ethnicities and abilities with ever lower qualifying criteria.

This is illustrated a year later by the account of a civilian, Dr. Röhrs, relating to my father's SS unit. While recruiting new soldiers in late 1944 in Budapest, he had to substitute for a military doctor. He was presented with a list of once again relaxed standards by which to evaluate potential soldiers. In an argument with the local SS medical chief of staff, Dr. Röhrs responded in disgust, "What other suitability criteria does he want to introduce? . . . If they now want to conduct war with cripples, let the troop leaders themselves take responsibility for it. I, for my part, will not sign off on it."[2]

By 1943, hundreds of thousands of men of twenty-four different nationalities were fighting alongside the soldiers of the Waffen-SS: among them, Hungarians, Croatians, Russians, Italians, Latvians, Estonians, Ukrainians, Belarusians, Albanians, Cossacks, Tartars, Dutch, Belgians, and French. There were also thousands from Finland, Norway, Sweden, Serbia, Armenia, and Switzerland.

Their motivations for joining varied. Those close to Russia assumed that Hitler was a lesser evil than Stalin. In Russia itself there were 1,150,000 *Wolgadeutsche* and *Russlanddeutsche* in the Soviet Union. The *Wolgadeutsche*, descendants of Germans called into the country by the German-born Empress Katherine the Great, were already persecuted by Stalin during the war, and their greatly decimated numbers were deported to remote Siberian regions. The descendants of those who survived were allowed back to Germany from the 1980s onward, when a new law was passed to facilitate their return.

In addition to ethnic German ties, there was also a fair amount of opportunity to cozy up to the Reich, just in case it emerged as the victor of the war. There was even an Indian SS legion with 4,500 men, who were hoping that allegiance would secure them help against British colonialism.

In addition to schoolchildren, the men that who still corralled into fighting in the last months of the war were *Volksdeutsche*. Like the burghers of Hamelin, their families had moved into eastern and southern Europe during the Middle Ages and onward. According to a German census of 1938, about 8.6 million lived outside the eastern borders of the Reich. The majority were *Sudetendeutsche* in Czechoslovakia (3.48 million); *Schlesier* (Silesians) in Poland (1.15 million); Siebenbürgen Germans in Romania (0.75 million); *Ungarndeutsche* in Hungary (0.6 million); *Donauschwaben* and other German groups in Yugoslavia (0.55 million) and Estonia (0.6 million), Lithuania, and Latvia, known to the Germans as Memelland; plus thousands in the free German city of Danzig, today known as the Polish city of Gdańsk.

Some of them had originally welcomed the idea of becoming part of the German Reich, but as the fortunes of the Nazis declined, few were excited to be taken away from home to fight in a war that was almost over and not truly theirs. The German officers complained bitterly about the lack of commitment from these recruits toward the German cause. My father had mentioned a Hungarian fellow soldier. When I read up on these Magyar recruits, the consensus is that the German Army had drafted them indiscriminately. There was resistance in the population. Many of the young men had German-Hungarian mixed ancestry with little allegiance to Germany. In addition, their own political situation at home was precarious.

The last group of recruits Hans mentioned were minor criminals. In a letter to the parents of his classmate Karl in 1946, after the war, he stated:

> The conditions during those last months of the war were absolutely terrible. The physical demands were taxing, but worse was the psychological strain of being thrown together with a mixed bunch of semi-criminals where theft was a commonplace, daily occurrence. It is under these circumstances that we had to fulfill our highest duty at the front.

The prison inmates with more serious convictions, both political and criminal, had already been pressed into service in 1942. They formed the two penal battalions: *Strafdivision* 500 and *Strafdivision* 999. The army, in need of warm bodies, had given them the choice to fight or rot in jail, with the prospect of redeeming themselves in battle. This was illusory, as they were mercilessly assigned tasks that were likely to claim their lives.

I came across several SS foreign units, like the *11. SS-Freiwilligen-Panzergrenadier-Division Nordland* and the *5. SS-Panzer-Division Wiking*. Given the strong anti-German feelings in France, as evidenced in the cruel abuse of young German prisoners just after the war, I was astonished to find out that between 1944 and 1945, the *33. SS-Waffen-Grenadier-Division Charlemagne* consisted mainly of French volunteers. In Vichy France, President Laval had passed a law on July 22, 1943, that allowed French soldiers to fight in the Waffen-SS. Some of them had been trained at the SS *Junkerschule* in Tölz. A French battalion also joined the *18. SS-Freiwilligen-Panzergrenadier-Division Horst Wessel* on July 30, 1944.[3]

Many of those SS units had the prefix *Freiwilligen* (volunteers) which indicated that the majority of their soldiers were non-German recruits from other countries or ethnicities. Had I been more astute, I would have picked up on Hans mentioning a Hungarian.

Had I looked for a Hungarian division of volunteers, I might have discovered his unit. But instead I kept looking along geographical lines for regiments that fought in Moravia and eastern Czechoslovakia, but none of them matched Hans's descriptions. Only after I arrived in the village of Závada did I realize my error. The mayor, Jan Stacha, explained to me that through a fluke of history, this sliver of the province of Silesia had become part of Czechoslovakia, while the majority of the region was part of Poland. The accounts of Second World War troop movements had referred to the region of Silesia as a whole and I had assumed that all of it was in Poland.

Mr. Stacha put me on the phone with a local historian, who recommended Josef Ossadnik's book, *Land Between the Powers*, about this quaint little part of the world. Over the centuries, lodged between Prussia and Austria, the two superpowers at the time, the area had seen much fighting. Finally, I discovered the unit my father had fought in: the *18. SS-Freiwilligen-Panzergrenadier-Division Horst Wessel*.

My first impulse was to find out if my father's unit had committed any war crimes. His division was founded in 1944. By the time my father joined, it was already on its fourth commander in a little over a year. During that time, it had fought in Hungary, Galicia (a name no longer used, referring to the region around the Polish-Ukrainian border), Slovakia, and finally in Silesia, where it was annihilated. None of those battles, which were carefully documented, involved any atrocities. The only thing I found out was that some soldiers who had been reassigned from already dissolved units might have been involved in war crimes in their previous divisions.

The name of "Horst Wessel" was naively chosen against Himmler's advice, in the hope that some of the last remaining SA men, with short memories and no grudges against the SS for having killed their leadership in 1934, might join by appealing to their nostalgia of the times when the SA had ruled supreme, singing the "Horst Wessel" anthem at torchlit marches.

That idea did not work out, and it was converted into a volunteer division for Hungarians. It was one of four divisions totaling about 120,000 Hungarians fighting with the SS. The estimate is that 80,000 were forced into fighting, owing to a contract that Ferenc Szálasi, the dictator of Hungary at the time, had with the Third Reich. He had already achieved notoriety by killing thousands of Jews and Romani people on his own initiative, in addition to aiding the Holocaust in other ways.

But despite the cruelty of forced soldiering put upon them by their own governments in the year and three months of its existence, none in the Horst Wessel Division committed any war crimes. They must have been busy surviving, with inadequate equipment and provisions, while being marched back and forth between confused, pointless battles in an already lost war.

For me, the fact that my father had served in a division that had not been involved in war crimes was essential. It was vital to understanding who he had been and who I had become under his influence. Since the beginning, I had assumed that it was the great shame of having his idealism abused by his own family and educators, by having been taught the wrong ideology and being sent into a lost war under false pretenses that had kept him silent for a lifetime. But if he had been hiding more than that, I was not sure how I would have felt.

10

—

BARRACK BLUES

WHEN I FIRST READ my father's wartime diary while in India, its contents had been alien to me. His overloaded language while he was in the barracks made me switch off; the cheerful, uncritical way in which he and his classmates went into the slaughter astounded me, and the matter-of-fact description of the ferocious combat left me with a sense that I had somehow ended up in the wrong film. It read like the script for a particularly bloody war movie.

The diary was a challenge on several levels. I greatly struggled with the translation from German. For the first time, I realized that what I always liked about English, its conciseness, proved a disadvantage for translating nuanced German words. Finding just the right tone in English was hard. Should I be true to the original text, or should I simplify the writing to what I thought was being said? I decided to stick to the original. My father's use of pronouns was especially disorienting. Hans often substituted the pronoun *you* for *I*. Occasionally he would use the German word *man*, meaning "one," turning the narrator into a third-person observer rather than a participant. It was a sophisticated writing technique that was difficult for me to interpret. But I could not ignore that his writing had an eloquence that made me wonder if a seventeen-year-old high school student today could turn such complicated subjects into literary prose.

It turned out that there were two versions of the diary. I had always known about the typewritten one; it was the account I was working from. But when I went through the boxes of my father's documents once more, I found the small, leather-bound, handwritten journal that he had carried with him. It had clearly been censored, as there were words and sentences cut out. The reason was so that if the soldier got killed, the enemy could not obtain important military clues from his personal writings. Because of the illegible handwriting, I could not tell if it had actually belonged to my father or if he had taken it from a dead comrade. He had used a combination of Latin and *Sütterlin* letters, which at least until 1941 were taught as *Deutsche Volksschrift* (German writing for the people).

I had had no problem reading his earlier Feldafing school diary, as I was the last generation of German schoolchildren that had been taught Prussian *Sütterlin* in the 1960s, but that writing had been carefully supervised by a teacher. The leather war booklet was filled with rushed, unreadable ink scrolls. Had his handwriting changed so much? If yes, a lot must have happened between the days of being a pupil at Feldafing and becoming a fresh recruit in an SS unit.

The cut-out passages in the leather journal made me realize that at least in the beginning of my father's deployment, he could expect a superior officer to read his writings. Maybe it had been safer to use all his school-acquired essay skills to write endlessly about sunsets, the landscapes, and the great German character traits. In the later part of the diary, during the last days of a lost war, he could be quite sure that those in command had more pressing things to do than read schoolboys' essays.

The typewritten version of the diary had been put together in the months following the war, when he was convalescing from a wounded leg. In it, he had combined letters to Auntie Tali with the original diary text, and in the back he had stuck a copy of a letter written to Mr. and Mrs. H, the parents of his friend Karl, who had died in the war. Written after the war, the letter was more candid than the diary. I read:

> In the barracks, humiliating treatment destroyed our ideals of volunteering for a higher calling. We could only meet briefly at the windows, in the staircase, in the cellar, or outdoors in the heather. Those encounters were a ray of light in those difficult days, and we promised to be pillars to one another. We swore to stay true to our highest ideals and perceived duties in the belief of being part of a select group of loving, self-sacrificing human beings. When we thought about the sadness of the last few years, we tried to make sense of the dark and light moments out of which eventually will come a bright future.

The different elements made the typewritten diary seem to be a collection of fragments. Yet, the later sections that cover him arriving at the front, engaging in combat, and being taken into Russian captivity required little clarification. He had found his voice.

In January or February 1945, we know the boys from Feldafing were sent for basic training in a barracks. Using the little information that I had, such as the description of the landscape, I concluded it might have been the Caspari Barracks in Delmenhorst near Bremen.

In the barracks, the boys were thrown together with any live bodies the Reich could get hold of. There was a mixture of all social classes and different nationalities. The boys were in total disbelief. They thought the fact they had been sent to such a place was somehow a giant mistake. Their school code of honor counted for little among men who already knew that survival was based on the practicalities of securing enough calories and not getting killed. All those grand ideals they had been fed amounted to nothing for a *Landser* (an ordinary infantry soldier). They had envisioned marching onto the battlefields accompanied by the sound of the fanfares that they had heard in Leni Riefenstahl's film *Triumph of the Will.*

It also appeared that they had no idea where and to which unit they would be assigned. The uncertainty of it all took its toll on them. After arriving at the barracks, Hans wrote to his substitute mother, Auntie Tali:

> Thank you very much for the bread coupons. You cannot believe what a difference it makes, if one has an extra loaf of whole wheat bread in one's locker. Since daily duty is from 7:15 AM to 10:00 or 11:30 PM and twice a week until two o'clock in the night, it is impossible to get the fatigue out of one's tired limbs. It's not all that bad, because the mind is kind of foggy anyway, but therefore not much help in raising extra energy.

One of the manipulation techniques of the Nazi educational system was to deprive the boys of sleep, a tactic used during their school days and as part of their military training. Students at Napolas, Adolf Hitler Schools, and even Feldafing all reported that they were kept busy from morning to night with no time for personal reflection, with the less hardy students barely keeping up with the strenuous, physical demands. But in the barracks, those schedules were even more grueling. The food coupons sent to Hans by his beloved Auntie meant that she herself was going hungry. As an industrialized nation, Germany was a net food importer, and owing to import embargos and the breakdown of its logistical infrastructure was no longer able to feed its population by the beginning of 1945.

Auntie Tali having lost weight during the war while sending her own bread coupons to her nephew, Hans. She was dealing with the disappearance of her sister, Irene (her body was never found), and caring for her elderly, bombed-out parents.

Among the papers my father had passed on to me were some of his aunt's writings. In a letter from the 1950s, without mentioning specifics, she contemplated the course of her life and concluded that her biggest regret was not having taken care of her body during the war years. She went on to explain that desperate times had required desperate measures. She died unexpectedly in 1972, collapsing at the Bonn railway station in front of me. I had arrived on the train with my two-year-old brother, and she was supposed to pick us up and care for us while our parents were on vacation. It was the first time I ever saw a dead person. I realized that, at the time, she had been about the same age I was now. Auntie had always told us: "I will not live long." But we did not take her seriously. After her death we found that she had prepaid her funeral and she had disbursed her remaining funds to charity. She had not killed herself—it was some kind of heart failure—but maybe her heart had been broken by a world where she had witnessed so much pain and betrayal.

But prior to the war, Hans and Auntie had had many happy times together, with memories that helped him make it through those dark days. He recalled:

> Our daily training ground, which is soaking up our sweat, is the local peat moss patch with tender birches, sandy paths, heather, and a small pine forest. You know, I have always wished for a stay in such natural beauty. The rain and the constantly wet clothing almost do not bother me anymore. On our march to the firing range we passed several huts, with straw-thatched roofs that give the peasants protection from all kinds of weathers. There, it smells like Mardorf. For me this always conjures up the images of our many excursions around the Steinhuder Meer, with our wonderful sailing trips and bicycle tours through the woods or when we were reading "Doctor Ulebuhle" stories together. Do you still remember?

139

The village Mardorf, by the side of the lake Steinhuder Meer, was close to Hannover (Hanover). For vacations, Auntie Tali had taken Hans there, to a farm belonging to relatives. The ancient, black-and-white timber-framed farmhouse had given him a sense of safety and continuity. That part of the family lived remote enough to survive the war, and we carried on visiting those relatives throughout my own childhood. Hans continued:

> By the way, today we were sworn in, kind of a rush, in between the movie screening and before being allowed to finally go outside; it is a non-event.
>
> On this occasion I wrote in my diary:
>
> "Taking the Oath! For us this is only the confirmation of our expressed will and desire."

Hans was referring to the *Führereid* (oath to the leader). Several versions of that oath existed; the SS had a different one from the *Wehrmacht*. Even civil servants had to take one. All were unconditional pledges of allegiance to Adolf Hitler. Over the years it had been drilled into the boys that it was instrumental in making them full Hitler men. They had seen weekly newsreel clips of SS men being sworn in by the Führer himself in grand, festive ceremonies, where they were allowed to touch the *Blutfahne* (blood flag), a holy Nazi reliquary. It was a swastika flag soaked in the blood of one of the sixteen SA men killed in the Beer Hall Putsch in Munich on November 9, 1923. After Hitler got out of Landsberg prison, he had it fitted with a new shaft, silver finial, and dedication sleeves with the names of the Nazi martyrs engraved. The motto associated with it was, "The banner has to stand even if the man falls."

After these long-built-up expectations, it was a big disappointment for the Feldafing boys that such an important event was carelessly administered at the barracks, like an afterthought. But they were determined to give the act meaning, as they had been taught:

It is also an act of becoming conscious that all our stars are showing themselves to be untouchable and sparkling far away from this reality here. Being bound to the universal laws, we happily feel a sense of belonging with the possibility of the active, unlimited deployment of all our personal force. We do not consider ourselves controlled by the disciplinary board of our units, but we feel part of the group of upright people, of our living and dead comrades.

Baldur von Schirach, the Nazi bard of youth indoctrination, would have been proud. Hans had mastered the quintessential Nazi skill of stringing together grand-sounding words. As they believed in their cause with a religious fervor, it is interesting that they considered themselves above the military hierarchy, accountable only to the Führer:

This is how we today become free in our realization that we are leaving everything dirty behind, that has surrounded us so far. This temporary condition we are in is only the means to teach us our tasks. More urgently than ever before, rises the power of our beliefs that even we small beings can serve. All the painful conditions are a reality one can recognize for their unimportance. The will to take responsibility for oneself in the fulfilment of duty becomes a principle to be adhered to at any price. When physical strength is affected by the mental and emotional strain, only the superman happily realizes that he can still go on. Our spirit has to be the prime factor in overcoming the present conditions.

But for all of the enthusiastic determination to view their circumstances as a test to prove themselves worthy of the ultimate goal to serve a higher good, the boys could not gloss over the fact that they were in filthy barracks, with everything lacking, and disillusionment set in:

If one wants to stay a decent human being around here, one has to starve and end up naked. Today on Sunday I committed an essential act of cleanliness. I swapped the Italian shirt, which I had been wearing since the beginning of the five weeks of my conscription, with my undershirt. Since today I was the last of 350 men in the food line, I got a double ration of cabbage, which somehow made up the additional use of calories around here. But today is really my lucky day! For the lectures I succeeded— hurrah: Triumph of the Will—in conquering one of the three chairs that were available for our twelve roommates. Then one was gloating when seeing the dejected mug of a comrade who got 10 days for stealing from comrades (a piece of bread). One was just a fly on the wall, but one had a satisfying feeling that amends had been made for the torments that one had been put through because of the stupidity of this one guy.

"Triumph of the Will" was an ironic reference to Leni Riefenstahl's movie. In the passage about the theft, I understood that my father was referring to group punishment that was levied on all of them until the perpetrator had been identified. A contemporary source complained about the difficulties of recruiting what it terms "motivated and healthy human material" to replenish the "used up" front divisions in the last year of the war. Hans sensed that being seen merely as material was what his stay at the barracks amounted to. But the resilience instilled into the Feldafing boys, with their premilitary training disguised as play, served him well:

One fact I do not want to keep from you is that every grand and wonderful expectation has been destroyed and replaced by the lowest level. Only one thing you shouldn't forget. I am always there for myself and to pick myself up, just like a tumbler toy, ready to leap up again and again!

With petty theft rampant, the Feldafing boys were stunned. Those things were unknown in a school that up to the bitter end had been reasonably well supplied due to the fact that it was attended by sons of NSDAP functionaries, together with those who had been considered the most precious, gifted children in the nation. At Feldafing, any act of disloyalty toward a comrade was as unthinkable as defrauding the Führer himself.

The unhygienic conditions that my father alluded to must have been dismal: stained, worn-through, bedbug-infested mattresses, with large populations of head lice and fleas living on the bodies and belongings of every soldier. Another condition that I could not even imagine was the state of the latrines. Presumably, Hans did not write about them out of embarrassment. The Feldafing boys had lived in villas that had been built by wealthy industrialists with state-of-the-art amenities. Now they shared quarters with men who were accustomed to the most basic living conditions. As children, we had perceived our father as something of a germophobe, making us constantly wash our hands. I wondered if he had acquired this phobia in the barracks or maybe in the months he had spent in a displaced-persons refugee camp. Still writing to Auntie, he continued:

> I want for this condition to be recorded and hope for better times. You had to experience this to find the external yardstick by which to measure responsibility toward humans in the future. Because after this terrible fighting, just like after the First World War, the revolutionary will of the youth will be taken up again, to carry it to the next generation.

As hard as it was to decipher those flowery words, the message was clear. My father had realized the importance of remembrance as a warning to a future he could only envision. His account of these terrible times could have been made public, but he found it hard to do so in the decades after the war, when a country of guilty collaborators shamed its youths in a culture of collective silence. Mentioning the aftermath of the First World War was a reference to the Weimar Republic. Disillusioned by the absolutism of the Kaiser, the post–First World War generation had created a democracy in its purest form. At the time it had failed, but it became the basis of what I was taught about statehood in my 1970s school days. My father's writing attempted to be more poetic:

> It was offered to them [the youth] by the old ones and the German mothers who found fulfilment in the lives of their children. After this war they again will be the fertile ground from which the steeply uprightly growing German plants will spread over the burned earth, which once before had been blooming so hopefully. After all, they are the quiet keepers and transmitters of the great German intellectual ideals and German values, with which the war youth went into battle, and which fortified it.

The German mother as an abstract, primitive fertility goddess was another concept the boys had been taught. One photo in my father's Feldafing album showed them celebrating Mother's Day far away from their families, forming a circle in the woods as though it was an ancient Germanic rite, not a family celebration:

> The purity of this responsibility will only continue if the living ones learn not to vacillate aimlessly between the dark and the bright side of life, but mindfully gather the thrown-about gemstones and tirelessly put them into their treasure trove. From this invisibly collected strength originates the perfection of the circle that the Germans have drawn and that the world will accept as just. The circle will be drawn by blood and by personal fortitude. This is the only way that the people who are looking for unity can grow upward and not be held back by the masses and their mediocrity.

It was almost painful to read how desperately my father was trying to assign a higher purpose to a situation that made no sense.

I realized how strange my translation from German into English sounded and once again I was torn between simplifying the passages or presenting them just as they were:

> Even if the majority of the people cannot find any grasp for their searching fingers, our values are the most likely ones to remain pure and to bring justice to the people in their natural selection. This war has only been able to give the German people back part of their communal consciousness. These people together have too much of a strong personality for the individual to play a role outside his own sphere of influence.

I kept reading the words over and over and was astounded by my father's peculiar wordsmithing, but felt that he was getting lost in trying to make sense of half-cooked Nazi philosophy:

> The grand German character traits offer a view of the world that can only lead a limited group of Germans into the right direction. Even though one had been going to great pains to constantly control the feelings and beliefs down to the last member of the German nation to bring close to him the highest values, the unique opportunity to unify the Indo-Germanic race seems to be lost through arrogance and inflated scholarship which in reality is a certain incompleteness of thought.

The next section was as though Hans was regressing back to writing school essays—maybe seeking refuge in those good old days. I had read the book that he was referring to, *Der Herr Kortüm*. Using a literary analysis, he was trying to make sense of what they had been taught about their role as future leaders in a senseless war:

> We Germans lack objectivity, which is not connected to our known mistakes. I would like to take as an example the figure of Konstanze Schroeder from the novel of Kurt Kluge. She tries to use the natural harmony of her character to become the center

around which others can gather. We have to come to the people who are entrusted to us, not with closed hearts to impose our wills, but with the ability in our hearts to accept their different characters. Maybe we will succeed in finding a way of living together. Those of us Germans who feel the call for leadership have to descend down into the world of even the smallest, most disagreeable groups of people.

The clash between two different groups in the barracks was also reflected in another account that I accessed. In a Konstanz University research paper from 2015, young soldier Robert Jauss describes how in the barracks there were those callously cruel officers and functionaries slavishly beholden to the SS, and the idealistic young ones who put up with the whole thing because it was the means to an end of following their highest calling.[1] The words that he used to describe his lofty ambitions were almost identical to those of my father:

It is from this low level that the state needs to be built up, in that certain points are reached where you have to set limits on some people so as not to endanger the highest. The state of the war today is not just a misfortune of which the current government is guilty, but also the coming together of many forces in history. All these factors together paint a picture of a German destiny that seems to dissolve in chaos. Now clear goals have to be set to overcome all obstacles where mind over matter is the most powerful weapon of all. The Reich today, as in the past, has the burning will to live and to continue its honorable tradition and history. Every one of those written words represents a step further toward the will to live.

In the power struggle of competing strengths, the decision over life and death is taken. Nature is fair and unrelenting; life goes on. Just as we, the still-living witnesses to Germanness, will find out how its fate continues, in the same way the nation might see how, under changed circumstances, the thirst to live will break through.

The passage sounded pretentious, but it answered a question that I heard often: "Why would those young men go into this war?"

The real question was why would they *not* go, when they were totally brainwashed into believing not only that they were superior to the rest of the world but that it was also their holy duty to share that superiority with less fortunate people. For my father, the reality was hard to shut out, especially when the merciless basic military training was conducted during the still-freezing cold and rainy days of early spring:

> Do you still remember, you ask yourself, when the rainy afternoon, heavy with fog, was witnessing your first exercises on the humid, muddy ground? When the humidity made the thin, worn-out clothing stick to your body and you felt nauseated by so much senseless dirt? Do you remember when your profound hatred started to ignite against those who were abusing good will and youthful reliable manpower?

That sentence stayed with me. For all my father's attempts to romanticize the war experience, he was fully aware of the exploitation of child soldiers, the hardships endured by older recruits, and the senseless cruelties dispensed down the Nazi hierarchical structure:

> Where even the old comrades in arms had to run, with their guns in front of them, panting to keep up with the prancing white horse of the shining captain. Who can forget the monotonous, strenuous marches to the firing range, over the cobblestone pavement, with its protruding stones against which one's tired feet banged again and again? Was it not the brutal hunger and the constant cold that motivated the last animal spirits to secretly organize some supplies to alleviate the purposely created shortages at the barracks? There you sneaked off during a rainy night exercise after midnight to a turnip heap and used the side of your gun to break off half frozen slices and devoured them. You

aimed with blanks at the only surviving hare in the entire combed-through heather. Tired and apathetic, you were trotting behind the indifferent lieutenant to espy the imaginary enemy outposts beyond the ridge. When the gray of the morning finally dawned, you felt relieved and warmed up your grimy hands on a crackling fire hidden from sight of the mean superior.

None of that sounded agreeable, but what was the alternative? The boys were too caught up in Nazi ideology to even consider running away. Of those soldiers who did, more than thirty-five thousand were convicted by German military courts in the last months of the war. Some twenty-three thousand were sentenced to death, and at least fifteen thousand were actually executed, with Nazis like Ferdinand Schörner, commander in chief of the units in which the Feldafing would be serving, taking great delight in personally shooting them:

> Wherever you stood, whether it was a frozen forest path or a foxhole, you were capable of the deepest sleep, if you had not been constantly reawakened by a well-meaning warning signal from a comrade or the thin rain. Rarely did you feel a self-conscious clarity in all this senselessness, which seemed to be swallowing you whole, the only happiness being the four hours of sleep, a quarter of the pot filled with the evening soup, and letters from home. But then you felt it again, the pride and the secret satisfaction to be allowed to participate. You did not grow tired of practicing the simple manual steps needed to operate the many weapons and machines, in the opinion that the fatherland can now only be helped by well-trained forces.

The effects of sleep deprivation were recalled by other young soldiers. In an interview with *Deutsche Welle* in 2015, another boy from Bremen, Werner Schleef, explained that for him the end of the war meant that he finally got enough sleep. I thought of my talk with

Franz and was wondering to myself how much of those superhuman efforts at sleep deprivation had been facilitated by Pervitin. My father's desperate efforts to see anything grand and holy in what was happening felt very sad:

> Again, and again you tear yourself out of the desperate emptiness, to write those letters and diary notes, which one day will be the only witness of this time that you have passed through. The strength of nature, how she gives the treasures of a wintery heather landscape, had become a big part of your physical and mental recovery. You did not miss out on any glimpse of a group of pines, a deer, or a catkin, without being thankful for the unfathomable kindness of Mother Nature.
>
> This time also passed; more waking hours spent during the night than the day. You had become a poor sleepwalker between two worlds, where one could no longer fool you about the other. It was the same heather where you stood as a sentry and in your mind were writing the latest letter full of doubt feeling a bitter barb, but nevertheless wrote full of determination and hinting what was becoming bitter reality. It was the cold blue morning of a sleepless exercise night, and one could only dream if one wanted to escape reality because there was already a total disconnectedness between the real world and the me of my dreams.

Despite feeling sorry for the Feldafing boys, I could not help but think how fortunate they had been to be physically fit enough to qualify for military deployment. On July 23, 2020, I read in the news that in Germany a ninety-three-year-old man, identified as Bruno D., had been tried under juvenile law for what he had done seventy-seven years ago. He was sentenced to two years in prison on probation due to his advanced age and demonstrated remorse. The case referred to the time when the seventeen-year-old defendant with a heart condition had been found unfit to undergo the type of military training Hans had undergone, even with the relaxed recruiting criteria of 1944. Instead, he had been sent for several months to work as a security guard at the concentration camp of Stutthof. He was tried for assisting in murder. The defendant confessed and stressed that his assignment to the concentration camp had not been voluntary. He deeply apologized to the survivors and their families.

They experienced what no one should ever have to live through; even those not drafted into the SS went through the worst. In 2006, I saw an interview on German television and cried. The eyewitness, Martin Bergau, now an old man, was fighting back tears himself as he recalled the events. On January 31, 1945, about the same time that the Feldafing boys started their training in the barracks, the sixteen-year-old Hitler Youth was summoned to the major's office in his Pomeranian hometown. He was told to accompany an SS unit and about three thousand mostly young, Jewish women down to the beach of Palmnicken, close to the town of Königsberg, which is now the Russian city of Kaliningrad. In the blistering cold, he was asked to help the SS drive the women into the ocean, so they would die of hypothermia. It was a callous calculation to save on ammunition, which was already running short during the last months of the war. This atrocity only became widely known when Bergau wrote a book: *The Boy from the Amber Coast*. He recounted, "Another Hitler boy from our town refused to carry out the order. An SS officer shot him on the spot. All my life I felt guilty for staying alive."

11

DRESDEN AND DEPARTURES

MY FATHER'S CONTEMPLATIONS FUELED by barrack bore-
dom came to an end. Four Feldafing classmates, Gerd,
Karl, Georg, and my father, Hans, joined by Albert and
Dieter, who were from the same school but not in the same grade,
had become tight-knit friends as they embarked on their long, adven-
turous trip to the Eastern Front. I reread some diary passages:

> It was the fourth time that you were awoken from a restless slumber
> by a commanding whistling, to force the shapeless long packed
> backpack onto your back and to say goodbye to the chaos of the
> barracks one was leaving behind.
>
> Sallow sunlight filled the air when you stood freezing for the
> last time in rank and file in front of the barrack building. From its
> archway the smirking, haggard top sergeant appeared. He wished
> us lots of luck for our journey to the front, which he preferred to
> watch from a distance. One could see that he was happy to have
> cheated us once again out of our daily tobacco ration.

The tobacco rations were an indication that at seventeen years old
they were considered fully grown men. I remembered that the Flak
children had been given candy and vitamin drops:

So, we left through the high, imposing archway, stared at by many arriving civilian newcomers who were now embarking on the trail of suffering we had already been through. The platoon went down to the freight terminal of the small town, where we were loaded up. Who of us many would be returning?

Finding out numbers of how many Nazi child soldiers were killed or wounded proved impossible, as their statistics were not recorded separately from adult casualties, but one source revealed that, of the elite school students, half would not make it home. Sadly, that seemed right. I knew with certainty that two of the four Feldafing classmates had been killed:

You found yourself on an unusually long cattle train, where forty-two comrades tried in vain to stretch out their legs without getting bumped by somebody else.

Whatever hooks were on the ceiling were soon used to hang assault packs, canteens, coats, ammunition belts, and steel helmets. It was quite comfortable in the fresh straw, which was to be our only piece of earth for the foreseeable future. Four comrades lay next to you, busily eating or contentedly sleeping. A small air hole at the back of the wagon was soon to be the cause of endless fighting over whether it should stay open or be closed. You also fell asleep through the rattling, grinding, and rolling of the train that was moving toward the hazy evening. Now it was apparent, we were moving again toward a new, unknown future, where we only had each other.

The relentless clattering and chattering of the morning, which brought us back into consciousness, during the night had taken us away from our familiar surroundings for good. A glimpse through the gap in the cattle car door did not give any information as to our whereabouts. A smooth, cloudy sky was hiding behind rapidly moving trees and shrubs. Sometimes there is a quiet farmhouse surrounded by wintery gray-green fields. Finally, a reference point, we stopped at a train station known to us, which is not that far from our loved ones, whose presence we longed for.

As they would have been already far from Bremen, the town Hans referred to was Hannover, where in peacetime he had changed trains to visit his relatives at the Steinhuder Meer. It must have been a sad sight. The town had already been ruined in an aerial bombardment on the night of October 8, 1943, with 250,000 inhabitants losing their homes. The fire brigades counted about 3,000 detonation bombs, 28,000 phosphorus bombs, and 230,000 stick firebombs. Eyewitnesses reported that the heat had been so intense that people sank into the molten asphalt and got burned up. But the next cities they were to pass through next had experienced worse:

> We are allowed to write last greetings, collect rations, and stretch our stiff, cold limbs by walking on what was left of the platforms recently destroyed by fighter planes. Bashfully the sun came out behind the bales of clouds to softly illuminate a deep, ugly bomb crater. But soon the relentless rolling cast its spell over us again. What is the destination of the journey? Are we coming near to the big city whose borders are already threatened by the enemy? Will we circumvent her to be assigned farther in the southeast?

This is a reference to Berlin in the latter part of March 1945 when the Russian troops were coming close. On March 5, all boys born before 1929, fifteen years and older, were already recruited as soldiers to the front. The remaining Hitler Youth of fourteen years and younger were used to defend the city. Women and the elderly had to build barricades. On March 18, American planes showered the city with twelve thousand tons of bombs. At least eighty thousand people became homeless, and thousands were killed. Even Berlin's beloved mascots, the bears in their small zoo, were killed. The fires raged out of control and one day later, Hitler issued his *Nero Decree*, ordering the destruction of the city and all industrial sites under German control.[1] This scorched earth command was ignored by Albert Speer, architect and Minister of Armaments and War Production, in Berlin. The already minuscule food rations were cut

153

again, but Goebbels's propaganda ministry kept showing escapist movies in between air raids, and Pervitin was dispensed to those who needed something stronger to make it through the day.

Purposefully rerouted around the bombed-out city center, the boys were still in high spirits, unaware that their own unsatisfactory rations were still superior to those of the civilian population. But for the Berliners, the worst was still to come around a month later. War-crazed Russian soldiers descended on the city, unimpeded by Allied forces who had decided to leave the city to them until their carefully staged appearance on July 4, 1945, Independence Day. Hospital statistics and surging abortion rates indicate that at least one hundred thousand German women of all ages were raped, with about ten thousand dying of related injuries or suicide.[2] The anonymous author of the book *Eine Frau in Berlin* ("A Woman in Berlin"), described how she had an affair with a Russian officer so he would station a guard outside her home for protection.[3] In 1950s Germany, she was unable to publish her book. She had chosen to put her life above her honor, which was a shameful reminder to the men who had returned from the battlefields of their own postwar impotence.

But in the spring of 1945, Berlin was still coping with the damage that the bombers of the US Air Force had inflicted. Those Berliners who still believed that there was a God left church to find themselves under a barrage of three thousand tons of bombs between 11:00 AM and 1:00 PM on Sunday, March 18, only a few days before the boys traveled through the region:

> Comfortably we dangled our legs out of the wagon opening and shook the straw out of our trousers and coats. In good spirits, we were watching the landscape passing by, with the first young, green sprouts in the fields. With burning eyes, one was absorbing as much as possible of the friendliness of home. Who will be the ones who in the autumn will take down the harvest

in the German fields? On this moment of your journey you did not dare to answer some questions that were bothering you. You only knew that it was good and necessary to still be allowed to fight for this land.

Hans had good reason to be concerned. At the time, he did not know it, but his loved ones were already in peril. Auntie Tali and her parents, my father's grandparents, August and Martha, had been hiding in air-raid shelters during the 173 air raids endured by the city of Bremen. When they emerged after a particularly fierce attack, they found their house was completely razed to the ground. A photograph shows my disoriented great grandmother holding a small suitcase, standing in front of the towering ruins of the St. Stephani church that had been

Hans's grandmother, Martha, coming out of the bunker after an air raid on Bremen to find her house completely gone and St. Stephani church heavily damaged with only part of the choir gable remaining, winter of 1944–45.

adjacent to her house. Auntie and her parents had to move in with Hans's maternal grandparents, the old Consul and his wife, Marie, who still had their house. But with a shortage of insulin, the diabetic Consul's leg had to be amputated. Hans would never see him again; he did not survive to the end of the war:

> Soon we were surrounded by the well-organized everyday activities of the regions of Brandenburg. The approaching capital announced itself with radio towers, power lines, and broad concrete streets, a multitude of spread-out settlements with little open fields between them. We stopped on a dirty

sidetrack on which probably a lot of troop transports had
stopped before us. Of the warm soup that we had hoped
for, we only saw the empty kettles. The twilight, full of pity,
soon covered up the filthy locale where soldiers were washing
themselves, picking their lice, or fighting with each other. From
the little, round window, the funny faces of Georg and Karl
expressed a quick good night to you and then you crawled
into your little straw corner, bedded on your haversack and
backpack. After the usual struggle for leg space, in the crowded
wagon, finally everybody slept peacefully on the shoes and
knees of their neighbors. A nippy cold woke us in the morning
of our third transport day. Again, we stood on a big rail track,
under a bridge. Behind the labyrinthine fragments and towers,
a larger city appeared. Light frost had covered the crushed
stone gravel that lay between the railway bolts with a hint of
sparkles. Freezing, we got out our rumpled coats and enjoyed
the first pink shimmer coming up behind the silhouettes of ruins
that started to illuminate the clear, blue night sky. Actually, the
many images of this scenery left a more vivid memory in one's
mind than the expressionless wall of the indifferent faces of
surrounding comrades, who shared my fate. Only the sunny,
cheerful looks of my few close friends accompanied those
images.

Hesitatingly and carefully the long train started to move
again over the provisionally repaired tracks, on which a few
industrious gray figures were busily working in the early morning
hours. We approached the silent witness of horrific events; in
the full light of day we rolled through an eerily quiet, dead city:
Dresden. The loud conversation between the comrades gave
way to a paralyzed numbness: one wanted to scream in this
godforsakenness, in this monstrous product of human insanity.
The slow journey finally came to a standstill on a sidetrack of the
huge main station of the former metropolis of Dresden.

The four greediest ones, armed with a tent tarp and a blanket, made their way to the provisions cart right away and grumbled when they only found bread, margarine, and a bit of sausage for the next day. But in astonishment they looked around, as each of their words echoed ghostlike from the hidden iron skeleton of the gigantic train station hall. Here you stood a year ago in the middle of flowing life, rustling, and whistling locomotives, and gaily blabbering and impatiently waiting masses of people, who were scattering toward the entrances and exits of the large train station. Now there was the sound of desperately pounding hammers through the stillness. The ghosts of the thousands of unredeemed, who stood guard underneath these ruins, had taken possession of the nothingness of the surroundings. Constantly hesitating and stopping, our sputtering locomotive made its way through the chaos.

I imagined how Hans had experienced Dresden in the spring of 1944. The royal city of baroque splendor had palaces, churches, theaters, museums, and cultural institutions. For centuries, it left an impression on its visitors. It inspired Beethoven to use Schiller's poem to compose his "Ode to Joy." The list of its honorary citizens read like a Who's Who of German literature, in addition to foreign writers such as Fyodor Dostoevsky and Henrik Ibsen. It had no military installation or heavy industry. Nevertheless, it was chosen by the Allies to be bombed to the ground to demoralize the German civilian population.

The plan worked. By February 1945, Germans were accustomed to hearing about the deaths of their soldiers. But to see their most treasured cultural heritage sites go up in flames was devastating. In addition to Dresden's 630,000 inhabitants, thousands of Eastern refugees were occupying the city. I tried to establish how many people had actually died in the three days of relentless firebombing from February 13 to 15, 1945.

Interestingly, the sources provided figures ranging from 25,000 to 350,000. The high number might have been Nazi propaganda to motivate the last human reserves, which included Hans and his classmates, to seek revenge for killing helpless women and children. But the low estimates seemed equally unrealistic, given the photos of thousands of human cadavers in the streets of Dresden, stacked sky high for burning. Maybe the low figure was meant to put at ease those who in the following decades questioned the ethics of deliberately annihilating such a large civilian target. By the time Hans's train arrived in the middle of March, those bodies had been disposed of, but the rest of the destruction would remain for years. Some of the important heritage buildings were only to be restored in the 1990s with grants from West Germany:

We breathed a sigh of relief when we were finally received by the full murmuring of the River Elbe that should be leading us on our most beautiful part of the journey toward the border. It had become a bright midday. The rapids of the river touched a multitude of light reflections in our dry eyes, which could not get enough of seeing the majestic boulders, which appeared to have been piled high by giant hands at the side of the Elbe. Ascending, high mountain ridges took turns with steep rock faces, over which could be seen bridges like lines, built by humans. It was an effort for us to shake off the dull-colored days in the barracks and relish this little bit of paradise. We enjoyed it very much, and we projected into this beauty our dreams of the past and all our hopes for the future. And again over it all was the blue of the celestial sphere. Barges were swimming unhurriedly in the middle of the stream. A cordial and sympathetic goodbye wave by the Germans staying behind reminded us of the fact of our approaching destiny. Gerd told us a random anecdote of how as a child he almost met an inglorious death when during a holiday excursion a ferry collided with a barge.

I remembered how my father had also told me anecdotes in the hospital garden about his happy memories of paddling on the River Weser. In the 1930s, water hiking on rivers, with lightweight, foldable boats produced by the Klepper company, was a favorite national pastime. A few years later, the company was to supply the Gestapo with water repellent coats made from the same material as their boats. It facilitated the Gestapo's night raids into the homes of unsuspecting families under any weather conditions. It was chilling! Even happy memories were permeated by the regime of horror:

The trip continued with ever-changing images. The sun was starting to set when our train, with an abrupt jolt, came to a sudden stop. Above us sounded the deep, growling buzz of the little silver birds, which in dense swarms high above us at great height were passing to bring death and destruction to an unsuspecting, flourishing city. Our train ducked into the green narrowing of a river valley. Hurried commands, cursing, and scolding drove us up a slope passing a fenced-in garden and a neat little house, which was perched against the side of the slope. The carefully directed trickle of a mountain spring was watering the few spring flowers. Our donkey beater drove us to the upper rim of the lush meadow. There, underneath the deciduous trees and pines, large brown rocks were hidden. Standing on top of them, one had a beautiful view of the River Elbe, the rock formations, the forests, and the sky. There were a few minutes of rest looking at this sunny valley. You had your diary on your knees and wrote thankful words about the experiences and the trust you had in the future. Your heart was bursting with joy. The danger seemed to be over. When we climbed back into the wagons, some of us had stepped on German soil for the last time.

12

—

ARRIVING IN SUDETENLAND

I HAD NEVER KNOWN THOSE places mentioned in the diary exist-ed, nor could I find the locations he mentioned on any contem-porary map. The moment Hans had crossed the border, seeing the last of Saxony disappear, he entered a world that would become off-limits to my generation until 1989.

The borders of the Sudetenland had been redrawn several times during the twentieth century. But until 1945, the German place names, which had existed since the late Middle Ages, had stayed the same. Fortunately, I found a map from 1904, while the area was still part of the Austro-Hungarian Empire. It proved helpful to trace my father's trip through the Czech Sudetenland:

Endlessly long, the train stopped in the first, filthy Czech railroad station, where foreign-looking railroad workers gave us hostile glances, with their brows knit in the middle. Instinctively we were happy not to be alone with those people. The heat of the day was accumulating in the afternoon, and it seemed to release some emotions all around us. Now strange faces were staring at us from everywhere. We wished more and more that the end of this uncertain journey would soon be reached.

As the day waned, black started to spread over the passing landscape. The rock formations were throwing off deep shadows.

When the light was almost gone, we passed the mighty shadow of the ancient Burg Schreckenstein on our left. The pulsating activities of factories nestled on the banks of the river were the last impressions of the day.

From having taken the trip myself, following my father's route, I knew that my father was referring to a castle whose name literally translated into "Castle Horror Stone," called *Hrad Střekov* in Czech. It had belonged to the Bohemian aristocratic Lobkowitz family for four centuries. In 1948, their property was expropriated, and in the 1990s, after the fall of the Berlin Wall, their property was restored. My father had known about it because it was the inspiration for Richard Wagner's opera *Tannhäuser*. The nearby industrial town of Ústí nad Labem, formerly known by its German name Aussig, had been settled by Germans in the thirteenth century, when they were invited into the country by King Ottokar of Bohemia. Under the disastrous 1938 Munich Agreement, the Nazis had seized the town, but in the 1945 Potsdam Conference it was given to Czechoslovakia, which led to the expulsion of its thirty-two thousand German inhabitants. Taking breaks along my own trip, I was stunned to see how many older buildings still had German inscriptions. It was a world I had known nothing about while growing up in West Germany:

We awoke to the rhythm of the wagon rolling along, as warm sunrays reached the disheveled straw bunks of our dusty living quarters. The sun illuminated the cold, bleak landscape with its barren tree branches that looked frozen in time. Now that there were no more distractions to look at, we paid little attention to our surroundings. This lasted until we were chased out of the wagons once more. There was a renewed roaring and droning of airplanes. In groups we dispersed along a little brook with clear, green water. This day did not bring us much additional excitement, although in the distance, bombs could be heard smashing into targets in rapid succession. Soon we were back to our rolling four walls.

In the afternoon we stopped next to a train transporting soldiers directly from Italy. We cursed a lot when we saw the mess tins of our comrades from the front filled high with food. The sight reminded us how hungry we were. We had already realized a while ago that at some point they had stopped treating us like humans, but now we were thinking of it more and more often. We felt that we were totally at the mercy of what was to come. We felt vaguely ashamed of thinking and acting this way but reassured ourselves that the true moment of proving ourselves was still to come.

Having lived most of my life in the UK and USA, I have always seen movies portraying SS soldiers as order-shouting, heel-clicking sadists immune to pain, or as figures to be eliminated as though they were cutouts in a shooting gallery. But those young SS soldiers with their hopes and fears were different. At least the movies had familiarized me with their mode of transport—the same cattle trains that were used to deliver concentration camp inmates to their extermination:

We drove on and saw that a lot of building and war materials were rolling in the same direction as we were, toward the east. All the little Czech freight train stations were congested with transport convoys. Suddenly a hospital train shining with lights came from the opposite direction and soon disappeared around the corner. "Yes, for them it is over," some of us thought out loud, upon seeing some of the bloody bandages that seemed to be bulging out of the openings of the long train. They leaned against the windows of the wagons, injured comrades, tired, indifferent, and somewhat happy to be able to escape.

For rumors, even steel walls are too porous! A lot of false information had accompanied us on this trip. On the evening of this fourth day it was whispered, "Tomorrow we'll have made it, we will arrive."

The next morning, we realized with sadness that we were starting to look less and less like real soldiers. Our transportation arrangements were changing as well, as we noticed through a thick fog that the train had been divided into two parts. Toward each side, two huffing engines were pushing it. They wanted to bring us over a rather steep mountain ridge close to our ultimate destination. When we were in the last bend of this nasty ridge, dense, dark steam clouds started to swirl around us coming from the busily stomping engine. The traveling speed decreased. After a moment of a hopeless standstill, we started to roll backward. We would have probably ended up in the valley if the quick-witted stoker had not jammed his shovel between the wheels.

Trying to do the impossible by getting locomotives to pull way too many wagons up the mighty Carpathian mountainsides was not an isolated event. I came across a similar eyewitness report in what was to become my go-to source for verifying my father's story, a book written by Wilhelm Tieke and Friedrich Rebstock, exclusively about the 18th SS Volunteers Tank Grenadier Division Horst Wessel, with the title *Im letzten Aufgebot* ("In the Last Deployment"). It gave very detailed accounts, complete with hand-drawn maps, of the battles of this ill-fated division before it was completely annihilated. My second source was Ossadnik's book that Jan Stacha had introduced me to. It outlined the history of the Silesian Czech region, which for centuries had been torn apart by the great power conflicts. Once it had been Prussia and Austria. Now the boys found themselves thrown into the Second World War in this remote part of the world:

Finally, carrying our heavy loads, we stood in file in front of our new boss. In the next days we were constantly marching as we kept being reassigned to different units. In long columns we trekked over the leafy hills, to hide ourselves from the curious birds of the east that we were eager to meet. We kept out of site in the damp, mossy park of a big monastery whose white walls we had already seen from a distance.

Although I could not be absolutely certain, it seemed that according to the information from my books, the boys had been assigned to the SS Tank Grenadier Regiment 39, III Battalion under SS Sturmbannführer Josef Schumacher. Despite the unit's name of a tank division, both the books and my father's account mention only one leftover tank. As a consequence, the soldiers were reclassified as infantry men:

> Returning to our encampment, unseemly figures were squatting, lying down, playing cards, or writing. Instinctively they crouched down a bit as they spotted us newcomers. But seeing them gave us a sense of belonging and comfort. When the ringing church bells reminded us of the nearing evening, the remaining field rations were distributed. One pound of margarine, one pound of sausage, four pounds of bread for four days, this provided a mindless diversion to keep us mentally occupied for the rest of the evening.

When the boys arrived to meet their new boss, the *18th SS-Freiwilligen-Panzer-Grenadier-Division Horst Wessel* had just been "burned up" in the area of Ratibor, as the daily troop report in the Tieck book had described it.[1] New recruits were desperately needed, as the Russians were fighting to secure one of their flanks to close in on Berlin. My father recalled:

> The next day, loaded high with backpacks, we were on the move again. Laboriously slow on the dusty country road, the convoy was walking along, on creaky, worn-through shoe soles, toward the friendly mountain village of Tyrn. Whitewashed walls subdivided by small windows encircled a quadrangle yard, which had only one entrance. This was probably not the first time in its history that warriors had appeared here. From the windows, scruffy Sudeten Germans waved us over in a friendly manner. But there was no stepping out of line from our marching column, just a stumbling,

walking forward. The marching was arduous and did not seem to lead to a resting place. Nobody of the superiors seemed to take any special notice of us. It had been that way for most of our trip. Finally, one bumped into the person in front and noticed that the convoy had stopped marching. Tired, exhausted, and apathetically waiting, we were directed to a dirty local restaurant, where we fought over corner spaces to lie down. From the outside the approaching darkness of an unsteady sky was surrounding us. A few soldiers were quenching their thirst at a nearby brook when suddenly blinding magnesium-colored lights appeared, accompanied by rumbling and roaring in the sky. The first night at the front was dreamless.

The next morning brought more reassignments, confusion, and relocations. As a representative of my six friends, I went straight to the officer in charge, to ask him to be immediately deployed to the front, when I heard that we were supposed to be trained some more. The knowing, somewhat mocking smile around the mouth of the commander felt very unsettling when he refused.

To the schoolboys, not being allowed into active combat was the ultimate insult, but it had been an act of kindness by men who were often fathers themselves. They already knew how fast the front was gobbling up young, inexperienced recruits. Every day of delay gave the boys a better chance of making it to the end of the war alive:

Another stretch of daily marching drill began for us. We were singing in a low voice, digging earthwork and training as sappers with antitank mines, sparkplug leads, and concentrated loads. There were field exercises; we were madly rushing around in fogged-up gas masks, which made some older comrades collapse in exhaustion before completing the assignment.

But in hindsight, those days would be remembered as still carefree. In his letter to the parents of his friend Karl, my father had written:

On the 23rd of March our journey to the front had supposedly started. In reality we were only being stationed in a small Sudetendeutschen village to receive further training. We had free hours and used them for great walks in the middle of this lush, typically German landscape with gently rolling hills. Karl felt that it reminded him of his own home. We could not get enough of pointing things out to each other and describing them. Usually we enjoyed the peaceful, colorful landscape with its bright streets, meadows, and fields from our vantage point of the knoll of the small chapel in the center of the village. Karl was delighted about the multitude of paintable motifs. One could even see the Carpathian Mountains beyond the bluish hills in the distance. But what we both loved most was watching the sky. The evening sun, the morning sun, the moon and stars, and different cloud formations compensated us for the gray emptiness of our barrack days. These were precious minutes of personal freedom, being together with a friend, with God, and with the world. It was Easter.

Resting in the Sudetenland.

Easter 1945 fell on Sunday, April 1. Although their Nazi education had made it a point to alienate them from their Christian heritage, the memories of childhoods spent with families who had always celebrated Easter traditions remained:

> With full bellies in the comforting, warm living room of a farm, where a decent, little woman encouraged us with a friendly look to keep helping ourselves to slices of her poppy cake. It was an enchanted afternoon. Karl had called me quietly over to the window so we both could enjoy how the warm glow of clouds lay like a golden carpet over the blue sky. We walked to the end of the village where a blue and yellow Madonna in a small stone hut presided over the lush landscape. There were three carved pieces of wood stuck into the ground, an ancient Easter tradition. To whom were they to bring fertility? I wandered with my friend along the fields under the sparkling stars. The moment was glorious and brought out a lot of emotions, especially in Karl, who was usually so reserved. At the horizon there were the contours of the Carpathian Mountains, which merged into the outlines of clouds illuminated by the moonlight. It was a great play of light and shadows, which made us sentimental, thinking of home. It forged our friendship even closer. Upon our return, the musty smell of the used-up air in the school classroom where we were staying hit us as our comrades lay slumbering, stretched out in the middle of piles of gray cloth and pieces of equipment.

But the next day, reality caught up with them. In the last days of the war, there was an acute shortage of lower-ranked officers who had to go into combat with ordinary foot soldiers. Tieke and Rebstock summed up the conditions the boys were facing:

> The lack of personnel, especially lower-ranking noncommissioned officers, and the improvised accommodation and

training conditions have to be taken into account for a general evaluation. In addition, the equipment, the arms, and the vehicles never were up to the norms established for gear to be issued. But if one takes those shortcomings and defective supply chains into account, the units delivered more than could be expected of them.

My father's observations were more personal:

The pale faces of the noncommissioned officers in the orderly room were finally dragged out from behind their desks to be our platoon leaders at the front. They revealed to us that a special order was to be expected as we congregated on the rain-wet cobblestones in the middle of the village. Volunteers were solicited to immediately fight at the front and join a company. Hurrah, finally things were about to begin! Now the struggle started for the best machine guns, which had arrived bent, jammed, and missing straps but labeled as new from the factory. Most of them were only good enough to be discarded right away. In the night, there was a feverish packing of backpacks and haversacks, where everybody was busy with their own thoughts. Only the haversacks with a few other personal belongings were to be taken along. The large packs that had been hauled all this way were put in storage. None of us ever saw them again. The next morning, we were herded together and loaded onto five trucks. We did not think much about it when the usually severe top sergeant handed each of us a little package with a first aid bandage, accompanied by a self-serving smirk.

Tieke and Rebstock mention the arrival of fresh recruits on April 4. I correlated the place names and compared the dates to be sure that it referred to the delivery that included the Feldafing friends. The daily report in the book stated:

In these days a larger group of Hitler boys, who had already received their premilitary training, volunteers to the Waffen-SS, arrived in Karlsbrunn. The young volunteers first needed to be prepared for hard combat with the Red Army. All available time was used for it.

But the boys felt ready for the long-anticipated moment; little could dampen their enthusiasm. Hans had observed with disdain that the men who were put in charge of their destinies so far had been primarily administrators, not military tacticians, but he failed to make the connection that this lack of leadership experience would result in fatally flawed military commands:

> With full speed we went along on a smooth, even road, parallel to mounds and across plains, through front villages with sloppily hand-painted signs on each corner. We passed many gray figures that occupied the road and moved in the same direction. After some time, it was very uncomfortable to sit on the machine gun boxes. With lots of thudding we went over the progressively worsening roads, passing the ruins of the town of Troppau, which were belching out smoke since the town lay under constant artillery fire.

A bunker of the former HKL (front line) in the Czech Republic.

Finally, with a jolt, the car stopped at a churned-up forest path, which clearly had seen more than one low-flying aircraft attack and was littered with boxes of ammunition. When we got out, we saw a huge green monster in front of us, a camouflaged German tank. Our ninety-man-strong F Company collected itself among the high pine trees. Randomly and quickly, platoons and squads were formed. Every orderly who so far had only been a hero in an office was given a platoon. I became a squad leader and picked my nine men.

My father never explicitly listed the names of the men he chose, but I pieced together that in addition to his schoolmates, he chose at least two older men: a shepherd, also called Hans, and Martenson, a family man. It was a choice that must have been challenging but turned out to be crucial:

I was proud to be allowed to prove myself, in the way I had practiced so many times. It was a very simple allocation of ranks in those terrible, last days. Whoever ran in front became an officer, whoever ran back was shot. At this moment I firmly bonded with my comrades like conspirators. We were still secretly excited about the prospect of action, with a hunger for adventure. All thoughts concerning a soon-to-be-approaching, inevitable German defeat were forgotten now that we stood at the front.

We were informed that the HKL [main combat line, the front line] was 2 kilometers in front of us. We were to be careful until further orders were issued. Five shots were to be loaded and the gun was to be secured. I elected Gerd as my first MG [machine gun] shooter and Hans as my second. Those were strange feelings as I was lying with my men in the long dry grass among the pine trees. In the small spaces between the trees one could see the German and Russian hunters. There was not much time anymore for long thoughts. Everything stayed concentrated on the needs of the moment.

Panje wagons were used to supply the boys at the front, as neither trucks nor gasoline were available.

In the back, behind the lines, the drivers of the supply battalion of sappers were resting with their Panje wagons and shaggy, small horses in roughly put-together wooden shacks. It had made the rounds that those fat, seedy guys had all kinds of delicacies under their tarps, which were desired by us poor, hungry church mice. We had not been given full rations for days, and even the six cigarettes allocated every day were already smoked. But we were proud to resist and stayed hungry that night. But I felt cheated, so I sneaked around an unwatched cart and took an explosive charge. I stuffed it into a handkerchief, because of its easy detonation, and placed it in my uniform jacket. I snuck away with a Panzerfaust [a single-shot warhead], which was to become the only one in our platoon. I was to carry it on many marches, and at the end its head would break off when it hit the ground, without it ever being shot.

How much my father and the Feldafing friends had changed since the days when they had tried reconciling their high ideals with barrack reality! I thought of a quote from the playwright Berthold Brecht: "Grub first, then ethics!"

For now, I hid it in the high grass and looked with ennui at the poor sapper who was walking around, shouting, looking for his Panzerfaust. In the meantime, I went with Hans deeper into the forest to practice shooting, to find out the accuracy of our guns. I had used the strap from the gas-mask canister as a gun strap and attached a knotted rope to the canister. This is how I entered the war: no shoulder epaulettes, rank, insignia, or unit badge, just a gray bundle from which a cocky, light-gray, cloth cap was sticking out on top.

On February 12, two months before the Feldafing boys started fighting, Rebstock had already complained bitterly:

We had received brand-new tanks but only twenty-five grenades per gun and half of a day's allocation in fuel. . . . At midday we passed the sappers and felt sorry for the poor guys who had to haul all their gear by foot and afterward were supposed to attack.[2]

Exhaustion and exposure to the elements was a constant threat for the Feldafing boys, who started to realize that their lives as soldiers was to be 5 percent heroism and 95 percent perseverance and survival, if they were lucky:

It turned evening and the front stayed quiet. One could distinguish clearly between the hammering of the German MGs and the rattling of the Russian grinders. The first grenades were shot and howled over our heads. We were to spend the night in the forest, which turned dripping wet, from a drizzling rain and the humidity of the night. Chilled, we huddled together, resting our heads on our haversacks with the ammunition belt and our canteens next to us, trying to catch some sleep, as we were quite exhausted.

But soon the rain had penetrated uniform and shirt, so lying on the tree twigs became even more uncomfortable.

Impatiently we walked around in circles, longingly waiting for the food cart to appear. Flares illuminated the ghostly forest. During this night I contracted some type of dysentery, which was going to torture me for the next few weeks. It must have been about 1:00 AM when I climbed with my men over large tree trunks toward a path to join a queue of men to receive some tepid, sweetish tea, bread, soup, and four cigarettes each, which was grumpily handed out from a wagon that was illuminated only by a Hindenburg light [a tallow lamp]. When would it finally be daybreak? Time seemed to have turned into an eternity in this sleepless night. When the pale morning dawned, we trotted with three sets of gun ammunition and several thousand shots in our belts, parallel to the road toward a village where a merciful hay barn provided us with several hours of blissful rest. We looked in envy at the well-fed tank drivers who sat on alert in their vehicles. From time to time they threw down tubes of cheese, tins of meat, and packages of bread. They had so much that they could easily part with it, mocking us infantrymen.

Soldiers camp in Sudetenland, 1945.

By the late afternoon we had made it through a number of low-flying aircraft attacks and marched again in a row along the forest line. We passed little earth bunkers, craters, shot-up cars, and empty cartridges toward an unknown destination. Tiger tanks were thundering by, and ambulances were heading in the opposite direction. The approaching night seemed to have awakened life in a village that we passed through. We were in the Hultschiner Ländchen and were moving into the direction of Jägerndorf.

When I arrived in Závada, the mayor Jan Stacha and I exchanged gifts. I brought him a photocopy of my father's original diary and its English translation, and he handed me a bag with tourist souvenirs of the region. I reached in and pulled out a CD with folksongs of the Hlučin region. I understood that it was what my father had called *Hultschiner Ländchen.* It was the name of the entire region, and the relationship between traditional German and Slavic populations was more amiable than in other parts, which might have accounted for them being treated kindly by the civilian population. Jägerndorf was located not far from Fulnek. That daily report of the 18th Division stated:

On April 4th the company was sent to Fulnek to the SS Field Replacement Battalion that had already provided one unit ready to fight to the company of Schuhmacher.

From the passage in the diary, it seemed that the boys were kept in reserve at this location, fending for themselves in the woods. Now all that they had learned from terrain games in the forests around Feldafing came in handy:

Exhausted, we waited at the side of the road in the approaching darkness for new orders, which apparently could not be given right away. Tanks were moving in both directions, horse-drawn vehicles passed. Flares and light umbrellas from the Russian night hunters, with their piercing red phosphor light, seemed to freeze all life for seconds or even minutes. What was this all about? What plans did they have for us as we were slowly deployed toward the front in stages, without having the faintest idea of what was going to happen to us. Suddenly from nowhere the food cart pulled up next to us and handed out some food, which cheered us up a bit. We wanted to sleep, only sleep, nothing else.

It was not a very long march anymore as we reached the slippery, muddy descent toward a pitch-black forest gorge whose contours we could guess by striking up matches. With difficulty we crawled, bumping into each other along the side walls, covered by prickly pine needles, until finally, we throw all guns and equipment into a heap with indifference and fall asleep in a small hollow. But soon the cold woke us up again and we watched for the first daylight with bleary eyes. I will never forget this feeling of longing and hoping for the first ray of light. Carefully a small fire was made to warm stiff hands and toast a slice of bread on a twig until the twig was burned through and one had to fish the charcoaled slice out of the fire. A clear command came:

"Whoever does not want to freeze in the next few nights has to build a bunker. We are staying here behind the HKL [the front line]."

Were we to excavate the heavy earth and the deep-set roots with our fingers? The squad had only one collapsible spade, skillfully lifted from somewhere, but that was not enough to build a home for nine men.

By the evening we were still freezing in the open, on a bit of used-up straw. The next evening, we proudly moved into our new home, which consisted of an excavated hole in the ground, covered with thin trees and woven pine twigs, although all night the rain washed the mud through the crevices. The next morning, we combed through the woods, up to the edge of the village, hungry for the spoils of war. We had nothing and wanted to survive.

The squad had become a close-knit family who had only one concern, which was to keep its cooking pot filled. From somewhere, Gerd had lifted a small stove, a box with coffee substitute, and army soup powder. On the fourth day of our life in the woods, we started to have a routine. The first one who got up lit a long powder stick, which spewed sparks while burning down. It had been taken out of the cartridges we had requisitioned. Then that person took the big, blue cooking pot, hidden underneath a worn-out sack, and followed the greenish-gray water trickle to the end of the gorge. There he filled it with the slimy water from a small pond to make coffee. Soon a cheery fire was burning in the fire hole over which the pot was strung between two trees on a spit, over burning twigs and more powder from the ammunition sticks. That was what we had learned from other soldiers—how to warm our sooty hands. After that, one after another, we visited the outhouse. It consisted of an artfully placed beam between two trees that regularly collapsed.

When personal needs had been attended to, I remembered the goose, the rabbit, and the chicken, which, in the prison of an empty ammunition box, were awaiting their approaching demise. They were the innocent victims of our disappointing evening hunting trips where we had looked for a deer. We were determined to kill and eat one, otherwise the Russians would beat us to it.

This familiar coffee hour was usually followed by ridiculous, mock exercises of attacking and house-to-house fighting, about 400 meters behind the real front, which we perceived to be highly insulting. Usually we crawled on our stomachs, shot into the treetops, or just lay around until lunchtime, which relieved us of these superfluous activities. There was no food provided during the day, so Hans became our kitchen master. Into the well-used pot full of hot water, he threw as many potatoes, plus as much soup powder and salt, as he could get his hands on. Brutally he wrung the neck of some domestic animals. With his

177

rusty pocketknife from when he had been a shepherd, and using his quick fingers, he cut and broke meat pieces out of the cadaver until he was only left with the intestines, which he discarded, of course. No soup had ever tasted better than the ones he prepared for us in those days, with visible, thick layers of yellow fat.

In the evening, I collected the food rations for my men. That evening as a reward for having managed to acquire the well-hidden little stove, I received half a mess tin full of Schnaps liquor which, in order to be fair, I handed out with a tablespoon.

It was a pitch-black night, and I warmed myself on the still-burning little stove while in the light of a suet candle I wrote into my diary. They were words of concern and secret desperation, which stemmed from the fact that our older comrades were so dissatisfied and often unjust, making my life as a squad leader so difficult. As always, I searched my mind for what I might have done wrong and in my desperation was ready to relinquish the leadership role. But then duty called in the shape of the two-hourly control of the posts and I found my way through the trees and was myself again: a soldier! At 1:00 AM, Gerd relieved me, the dear helpful comrade who with his serious voice always stayed faithfully by my side. I forgot to tell him what time to wake up the company and found myself in great agitation when I was shaken awake by my comrades from a deathlike sleep.

The company should have been awake a while ago. I went from bunker to bunker, and as I got ready to have breakfast with my squad, I heard a crackling behind me that paralyzed me for some seconds; the ceiling of our makeshift bunker had caught fire. The water that Dieter and I poured over the flames evaporated. Others joined us, shoveling earth onto the fire so the surrounding woods would not go up in flames. I ran inside and was standing under a shower of sparks and earth clumps. It was high time to get the fog grenades, the egg grenades, the stick grenades, the haversacks, and the ammunition out of there, if the whole place was not to blow up.

It worked, and soon the rescued things were laid out to dry on the forest floor. All available spades were borrowed to search for the remaining personal items in the collapsed bunker. Over the next two days there was a busy hammering, digging, and nailing, and by the evening of the second day a new wood-lined, firmly built bunker was ready for us. With newly acquired straw we felt very comfortable. During the torrential rain that washed down the gorge in the next few days, our bunker resisted, while other bunkers were almost totally washed away.

Then came a beautiful, bright Sunday with the sun shining onto the horror and the madness of human self-destruction. Suddenly at 8:00 AM the firebombing started with the unrelenting attack of twin-engine Martin Bomber planes in groups of 20 to 40. I was with my little group in the familiar bunker, where the ceiling wood was splintering from the weapons fire. I wanted to look outside to see if the Russians were breaking through. But the firing became stronger and stronger and seemed to concentrate on the forest.

Finally, we swarmed out in a loose formation of shooters to the edge of the forest, expecting the enemy to appear any moment. Bewildered, I watched as a corporal pointed a gun at a man who was falling behind while he tried to fasten the hook of his harness.

I was alone with my squad and had lost contact with the platoon. I had Gerd with the MG behind me, and we walked along the asphalt road without finding anybody. It took quite a while before, in the eerie silence of the Sunday, I found the company runner. The enemy had gone by us on our right and left flanks, and we were in danger of being encircled. Seeking cover, we moved along under trees, passing fresh ammunition boxes and guns and the first body, a German infantryman. A horse was lying there with spread-out legs, and a wounded soldier was hobbling back, gently moaning. Close to the edge of destruction, we walked along feeling the breath of death, which had spared us this time.

13

—

THE BATTLE FOR ZAWADA

IN JANUARY 1945, BLOODY Ferdinand Schörner, the newly appointed head of the *Heeresgruppe Mitte* (Army Group Center), was ordered to hold Silesia at all costs. When the Soviets launched their offensive, the Army Group Center was driven back to Czechoslovakia. In March, Schörner, along with the Führer, predicted a Soviet advance into Prague. During the battle to defend Ostrava from the Red Army advance, Schörner had several German officers executed for voicing defeatist opinions. High-level Nazi leaders had many words of praise for Schörner and his methods, which were always aimed at pleasing his superiors, never at protecting those entrusted to him. In recognition, on April 4, 1945, the day that the Feldafing boys arrived at their front unit, he was promoted to field marshal and received the German Army High Command. However, this was just in name, as he continued to lead the Army Group Center, as there was nobody to replace him. In June 1944, the unit had already been decimated from eight hundred thousand to fewer than four hundred thousand men. Fifty-seven thousand were taken prisoner and marched through the streets of Moscow in a triumphal procession. But Hitler ordered the replenishment of the unit with six hundred thousand soldiers, accomplished by lowering the recruiting standards.

It was named the Moravia–Ostrava Offensive Operation by the Russians, which lasted from March 10 to May 6, 1945,[1] and my father found himself in the middle of it:

> I stood with an old platoon leader on a descending forest plain when his face suddenly turned ash white as there was a strange, hacked bellowing in the distance. He rushed toward the bottom of the valley. As soon as we both lay pressed to the ground, a terrible detonation like an avalanche happened. We lay 200 meters away from a crater caused by a Stalin Organ.

My research yielded that the above-mentioned device was the first self-propelled, multiple-shot rocket launcher mass produced by the Soviet Union. My father, like all Germans, had referred to it as a *Stalinorgel* ("Stalin Organ") because it resembled a pipe organ. The first time the *Wehrmacht* had encountered about three thousand of them was at the Battle of Stalingrad in 1942. Its production was inexpensive, and the launch rails were mounted longitudinally on trucks. No equipment for building conventional artillery gun barrels was needed, but it took longer to load than a large gun—and fired less accurately—which was more than compensated for by the

A "Stalin Organ" in the open-air museum of the Seelow Heights close to Berlin.

high-pitched howling sounds of the weapon's motor that added a terrifying psychological warfare effect, frightening the enemy. Russian soldiers called it *Katyusha* ("Little Katie") after a popular song about a girl missing her soldier lover. By the time Hans encountered it in April 1945, the Russian Army were using ten thousand Stalin Organs. But it was only the beginning. The inglorious role they were to play in the regional wars around the world that would follow the Second World War had just begun:

> Thousands of flyers addressed to the 96th Tank division were covering the ground. We realized that it was not German artillery that was flying over our heads. We returned to the gorge, where we had taken up a hedgehog position with arms to defend ourselves all around in a radius of 400 meters. The Russians had taken the forester's house where we had been two days earlier and where we had been dismayed by the senseless acts of vandalism that some German infantrymen had engaged in.
>
> The previous night we slept restlessly in our disheveled bunker. In the early morning we took position in the second line, 300 meters behind the first line at a forest clearing. It was another sunny day, and we lay in our trenches ready to fight. Close to our heads, hand grenades flew through the tree branches to explode against the rock wall of the gorge. At about lunchtime we heard the rattling and clanking of the Russian supply units, but on the German side it stayed shockingly quiet. To the left of us was a lone German Pak [tank destroyer] gun with carefully rationed ammunition, pointing its mouth toward a forest road where a row of pushed together anti-tank obstacles was the last barrier to the expected Russian breakthrough.
>
> This is where, in the high, green grass, leaning on a tree trunk, I spent my last hour with Gerd. I talked about my recently finished diary entries of the memories that were creeping up on me and starting to be engrained in my mind. He talked about his parental

home, his worries about his loved ones, and his concerns for the future. He was so free and trusting in those minutes—he who had usually been quiet and proud, keeping his thoughts to himself. We promised each other that if one of us was to fall, the other one would pull his diary from the left pocket of his uniform jacket. I was not able to keep my promise.

The Russians did not come for us that day; it was as though they were to save us for another moment. We had the first death in the company that day. It was a pale boy who had leaped across the street in fright when a grenade hit, instead of seeking cover. There was also Karl Heinz; he stood with a sergeant major on an unprotected mound to watch the Russians. A burst of shellfire struck him down. Next to him, the always cheerful, slightly rotund sergeant major did not get up again.

It turned night again, and nobody came to relieve us. In the dark, I ate something provided by the Panje wagon [a horse-drawn cart] of the sappers unit. I observed two dark figures who carefully lifted a longish bundle onto a cart.

"Hey," said one to the other, "we cannot just put our dead major's head on the ground. Come on, take your coat off!"

The morning saw us hastily marching into great uncertainty. We walked endlessly in the woods and, as we found out later, we had been racing the Russians. During a break, we relieved a stingy hoarder of his hidden stash of condensed milk. He desperately searched for the tins but could not retrieve a single one. This is where I sat with Karl for the last time; I was tasting the sweetened milk with a little tin spoon. The uncertainty of our situation and our suspicions that this would not end well were the content of our short conversation. Karl was touchingly humble, and he let me talk and agreed with me. At the end he also said a few things. After this moment we never had a close conversation with each other again.

At a good distance from the
right and left side of the country
road we left the safety of the
forest to hurry with our heads
bowed parallel to the street, shot
at by the enemy, to the southeast
toward a stretched-out village.
When we finally rested after 10
kilometers, we found out that we
had been the last ones to escape
the Russian encirclement.

German people watching
us walking by from their farms

Sudeten German children, around
the summer of 1944 in Závada.

asked us if we were to stay. They handed us milk as we walked
by and told us they would stay on in their villages, regardless
of which army was going to come by. We admired those
Sudetendeutschen and the love they had for their homeland,
voluntarily exposing themselves to potentially arbitrary Russian
cruelty.

Just before Wretschin, a number of light German infantry
weapons were firing shots. They were the first and the last we
were to come across that month. We went by a big manor house
with a windmill and passed by friendly little farmhouses where we
would have loved to sleep for a night. We walked through woods
that were divided by a wire fence in the southwest direction of the
village where the Czech bunker line lay.

The Czech bunker line had fascinated me on my trip to Závada.
In 2013, over ten thousand of these structures were still littering
the landscape, standing randomly in the middle of fields or woods,
built by the Czechoslovakian government prior to the 1938 Munich
Treaty to defend themselves against Nazi Germany. In an irony of
fate, they were now utilized by the Germans. Few were actually

A bunker in the Czech bunker line.

used for defense, except in the area of Ostrava in Moravia where the *Wehrmacht* fought the Red Army. Initially they served as first aid shelters, as my father was to find out. In the last days prior to the annihilation of the German forces, they became the new main line of defense:

> Apathetically we dropped onto the forest floor and quickly, before the onset of darkness, made several small fires. We found a dead horse from which we cut the best pieces and tried very hard to boil them until tender with our rudimentary military cooking utensils. Soon we had to extinguish the fire, and we tried in vain to tear the meat off the bones with our teeth and to chew it soft. I walked with fat Kugler, who was the leader of company headquarters personnel. A little distance away from the others, he confided in me, telling me some of his concerns. He had invested some effort into not letting on to the others that it was worrying him how he could maintain his position of authority. When a little cart arrived bringing us sugar, bread, and even some sausages, everybody was wide awake again, until the forest floor became our resting place for the night. In the early morning, after the arrival of a company runner, we marched back to the street from which we had come the previous day, back to the woods where we had briefly rested the day before.

I correlated my father's account to the official daily report of the 18th SS Volunteer Tank Division Horst Wessel for April 18, 1945:

> At the northern rim of the Boor Forest, the Waffen-SS built a combat front in the area of the Ostrava defense belt assigned to them. This position was really unfavorable, as it ran across a wide forest opening with the road in the north running directly onto it. It did not take long until the fighting group received well-aimed grenade fire, which brought losses.[2]

Hans described the situation in more detail:

> It was an unfriendly, wet day, this 18th of April 1945.The clouds were hanging low, and the air was heavy. I became impatient as I pushed the little company supply cart up the long road, since nobody else was willing to take care of it. Everybody was already overloaded with carrying equipment. Bad humored, I pushed it into some shrubs in a pine forest when we were randomly allowed a rest. I leaned against a trunk and declared that I was fed up with senselessly marching around. This almost led to a serious clash with a dutiful sublieutenant. I told him that I had observed that there was fighting on both sides of the access road to Mährish-Ostrau.

Even a high-school student could figure out that the commands no longer made any sense from a military perspective. But there was a logic in them that foreshadowed the giant betrayal they would soon face. Hans speculated:

> Why was it so important to keep this road for two days longer against the approaching Russian wave, which was demanding such terrible sacrifices in lives? Was it so that, until the end, the paymaster official could show his shiny pistol to the hunger-stricken doughboy to deny him the access to the overflowing supply trucks and regular cars? Was it so that those precious

trucks would be able to get out of danger easily? Those
gentlemen supplied the battalion headquarters well, but the life
of a simple soldier counted for little in the computations made out
here. "Whoever takes one step back, will be shot." This was the
simple command with which the officers pushed along the men in
front of them, so as to protect their own bodies with theirs.

That was cruel but a whole lot less sinister than what was going
on at the home front. The regime, realizing its imminent demise
and military defeat, promoted a total annihilation strategy. As they
could no longer feed or care for their people, the Nazis could claim
one more horrific record: encouraging the largest mass suicide in
the history of Germany. The author Florian Huber recalled an incident where on April 12, 1945, after the last concert of the Berlin
Philharmonic, playing Wagner's *Götterdämmerung* ("Twilight of
the Gods"), uniformed Hitler boys stood at the hall's exits with
baskets, handing out cyanide ampules.[3] That was hard to believe,
but in line with the regime's scorched-earth policy. Meanwhile on
the front, the situation was deteriorating rapidly:

The high forest, which accompanied our muddy way while going
up and down the hills, became our last resting place. We were told
that here we could rest and eat our fill. We did not see much sense
in any of those commands. We had been marching and sleeping
for days. You found a chair left behind in the middle of the forest
and took off your ammunition belt, the little box with ammunition
and all your hand grenades. It was a welcome opportunity to
engage in combat with smaller prey, those little animals that had
started to live on one's hair and body and were constantly making
a nuisance of themselves.

Suddenly an order for deployment came for our third platoon.
We trotted in a row behind the messenger through the high
pine forest. It was a silent trek as the underground muffled our
footsteps, creating an eerie feeling as we passed by deserted and

half-finished dark dugouts. We passed ghostly white birch crosses, marking the fresh graves of soldiers. We stepped over brand-new machine-gun barrels, which nobody had bothered to pick up, because of the heavy weight of their own burdens.

We scattered and jumped a short distance, across an open field that was under enemy observation, to reach the first houses of the village of Zawada. There we could quench our thirst with the fresh, chilled water of a well. We went farther over ascending furrows of freshly ploughed fields into the center of the village, which was marked by the quadrangle of the manor house and a high granary.

In a whitewashed, low ceiling room of a farm you saw all the men of your group for the last time. At the entrance of the room was a box with brand-new stick hand grenades—without detonators. It was already 6:00 PM. You took off your coat and leather harness to sort out which ammunition and reserve barrels were essential to take along. You helped old Martenson, who was suddenly showing signs of insecurity, to put his harness back on. There was not much to say in this moment. One had the same distinct feeling one had already felt in the Flak as an antiaircraft artillery auxiliary, just before a great attack.

At exactly 6:30 PM, four German mine throwers, positioned in the garden, started with their clanking bangs. In rapid succession they had fired their carefully counted seventeen grenades. The Russians responded violently. This firing had been the preparation for a counterattack that at that moment was being prepared by a platoon of sappers who were stationed in front of us. For a few moments it became quiet. Then the brief clipped pounding of machine-gun shots could be heard. Short Porath jumped into our trenches commanding, "Move! Toward the manor house." We chased down the road, in competition with the repeated Russian grenade detonations. We caught our breath in a demolished restaurant and stormed on farther. In the cellar of the manor house we found the remaining frightened and exhausted sappers sitting on a bench. The attack that was intended to reconquer the northwest arm of the village leading toward the dense forest had failed. A group of their comrades was closed in at the front part of the village. The sappers were finished. They had been forced to dare an attack without sufficient preparation.

Just inside the barn door stood a lieutenant, unknown to us, with the other men. He handed you an automatic pistol that had been shot empty. We went running around the high barn to the fence of the house. In front of us was the straight line of the road that we were to conquer, with farmhouses flanking it on both sides. A dirty ditch ran along the right-hand side of the street; it was to drink much blood.

The entire left flank of this street was bordered at a distance of about 250 meters by a high forest occupied by the enemy. In a frontal attack, walking ahead on the right and left side of the street, we were to fight our way through.

"Third Group to attention!" shouted the lieutenant. He jumped to the left; you jumped to the right. He barely reached the fence of the first house. Then he spun around and fell down due to a shoulder shot. Georg felt pity for his groaning; he jumped ahead

Destroyed manor house in the village of Závada, 1945.

and brought the lieutenant back, supporting him in an upright position. You had thrown yourself in the dirt of the ditch; the hand grenade had been torn from your harness. Gerd was lying next to you. You indicated to him the right upper window of the red brick building. Our counterfire worked really well, until suddenly the gun jammed. You jumped across the street, crouched along the fence, toward the burning farm, where you looked around the corner. An abrupt movement to the left made you suddenly turn to face the muzzle of a Russian rifle at a distance of about 18 meters. He pulled the trigger and—startled by your sudden movement—he did not hit.

Passing a pile of wood and the well, you crawled toward the small hut where the Russian had been standing. Your gun had become unusable because of the mud, you had lost the hand grenade, and the ammunition bag had been torn open. You released the safety catch on the bazooka and were about to shoot into the burning building, as a short burst had just been fired from there. But you changed your mind and with only the gun you jumped into the field toward the dark pile. You noticed disappearing silhouettes at the fourth house. You were alone and were waiting for the others. In the meantime, they had circumnavigated the right flank of the village in a large circle, so as to reach the last houses of the village in large numbers and reconnect with my lonely post.

The village had been conquered again except for one last house from which an angry Russian commissary was shooting. The formerly entrapped sappers were enjoying their renewed lease on life. Rapidly it had become dark, and it was impossible to search the houses. In the cellars, even of the burning houses, the villagers had locked themselves in. A terrible night started. Porath reported excitedly of enemy shadows that he had seen as silhouettes contrasted against the dark sky against the right side of the ridge. You jumped up the slope, passing the dead Russian, who was lying on his back.

The dead Russian! Which dead Russian? Was I reading between the lines, as Franz had suggested to me, that my father, when he had jumped toward the dark pile, had clobbered a Russian soldier to death with the shaft of his broken gun? Mentioning that the body was lying on its back must have meant that Hans had to look at the dead face. The thought was horrific:

> The last part, you crawled upward with a new gun, its safety catches off. You heard, "Stop, who goes there?" There were four sappers who had dared to come this far out. They were occupying the right side of the dugout, while the left side was filled with the bodies of dead Russians. Even farther ahead was Albert, with his gun, shooting just over the heads of our comrades into the last house, where the Russian was holding out. Georg and Hans tried with hand grenades and bazookas to smoke out the tenacious enemy. In the morning his own comrades freed this brave Russian who had angrily defended himself. The village was illuminated in a ghostly way by the two burning farmhouses. Not a single leader stayed at the front; no food was brought and none of the promised relief reached us. The men were tired, exhausted, and cold. You stood with Gerd behind the pile of wood and constantly fired into the dark woods on the other side. The enemy did not fire one shot. Soon Gerd had to go back with a jammed gun.

Ossadnik's book includes the Russian account of what happened in Závada on April 19, 1945:

> The Russians attacked the area of Wretschin from the southeast and faced the Kampfgruppe Schumacher. At the same time, the Soviets strengthened their pressure on the forest of Zawada, reaching the village. From the air, they were supported by Czech flight squadrons. The street fights were very tough and lasted until April 20th. Every house had to be fought for separately. Those were bloody days.[4]

Destroyed farmhouse in the village of Závada, 1945.

What happened next was the result of a serious military blunder that is briefly recorded in the Tieke and Rebstock journal for April 19, 1945:

> The Kampfgruppe Schumacher was supposed to build a new front line between Buslawitz and Wretschin. Because of that it ended up in an exposed location in front of the old Czech bunker line. The position was precarious because it ran across a broad open space between the forest that could be accessed from the north by road. Soon the group received intensive fire from grenade throwers, which led to heavy losses.[5]

Jan Stacha had told me that the only entry for that day in the archives of the village had been restricted to the exact number of the loss of livestock. My father's account was the only one that recounted the battle in detail:

> Then came the insane order that you did not believe at first. The broad freshly dug holes on the open field, with no camouflage at all, at a distance of 15 to 20 meters away from the border of the village, facing the high forest, had to be occupied by us at dawn and would be the new HKL [front line]. There was no communication with the neighboring platoon on the right. The few sappers that were left

started to retreat inconspicuously. The situation was totally unclear. Together with Georg, you collected your men under the roof of a dark entrance to a cellar and waited. A second order came though; platoon leader Hoffmann appeared briefly. At least to go through the motions, the holes would be manned from dawn onward. At this moment, we occupied the entire front part of the village. If only the Russians had known that!

Dawn was appearing, and it was getting light. The guys slowly climbed into their holes. Our line went in a shortened form over the road to the right, where supposedly the sappers were to connect with us. When Gerd joined you at the front, you assigned him the outer corner across from the white house that was 150 meters away, from where he had a good overview over the shooting field. You dragged two MG cases into his hole and advised him to immediately run back the short distance to the fence of the house if he felt that he was without cover from the right. When you winked at him, he was busy adjusting his gun. It was the last time that you saw him.

That last sentence told me little. How had Gerd died, and was that too painful to record in detail?

Next to the half round of the MG positions, Karl looked out of his foxhole. In the next hole over was old Martenson, who was later to hang out of the ditch with only half of his torso left. You started to dig your own foxhole deeper and put a whole lot of hand grenades into easy reach. In the meantime, Georg struggled with four heavy firewood beams that he hauled to put over our holes to give them added protection. Then next to you was the young Wenzel, who was the only one who was to stay with you until you got wounded. Hoffmann and Gerlach made themselves comfortable in the wreckage of the former barn. Hoffmann was the first to try his new rapid-firing gun while standing in the roof truss. Subsequently the brunt of the heavy barrage was concentrated on this poor building. Very much in the center of the village next to the MG position of

the sappers lay Hans and the Tall One. We had been lucky this far
to keep the circle of our original six together. It was here that our
ring was going to be broken up.

At dawn we were almost ready with our preparations. The
gray silhouettes of our comrades were still scurrying about in the
approaching light. A German woman appeared from a cellar and
without any cover, drew water from the well. Coming close to our
holes she gave us the cooling liquid in a small porcelain cup. Then
she disappeared again; the enemy had not shot at her. It became
quiet again, very quiet as though nothing was going to move.

I wondered if the woman was the same one Jan Stacha had told me
about, who had bothered to retrieve the documents from a dead soldier to send them to his widow. Those small gestures of compassion
seemed to be the only glimmers of hope in this raging inferno. Jan
had confirmed that the remaining villagers had holed themselves
up in their cellars during the fighting, while their menfolk were on
the Western Front:

Without any warning, at exactly seven in the morning, an
unrelenting firing barrage was started by Paks and grenade
throwers. While Georg was trying to keep his mud-encrusted steel
helmet above the muzzle of his rifle, you were trying to refill the
magazine of your MP 42 with scavenged ammunition.

Georg did not hide the fact that he was really hungry, and
he wanted to devour the contents of a brown backpack that he
had taken from a dead enemy. There was bacon and bread. The
grenades started to hit worrisomely close by. Especially the enemy's
tree snipers who were shooting into our holes at an angle.

Then farther up from us started the howling, long-drawn-out
screams of a comrade. He must have been lying in the middle of
the village road. We could not help him in the tremendous fire of
rapidly hitting grenades. It was agonizing to have to listen to him in
each little firing break, when the force of the shelling subsided for a

moment. We must have been waiting for an hour and a half when suddenly to the right we could hear the hoarse "Urraeh" of the Russians.

In this moment, Karl jumped in. It was hard to huddle together close enough in the narrow hole. In his hand he held a ready-to-shoot MP. In those seconds, he was a hard, ready-to-fight soldier. Out of breath, he exclaimed, "I have been very lucky—I raced the bullets and won." At that moment, a shot hit his right shoulder. He sank back and for seconds he seemed paralyzed.

"You have to come with us! Where are you wounded?"

"I don't know, somewhere in my upper body." From the uniform a quiet trickle of blood flowed from the general vicinity of his collarbone. You stuck the bandage from the hastily torn-apart package under his jacket and carefully supported him while climbing out of the hole. Georg wanted to follow with the guns.

At this moment, when you got out of the small ditch, a grenade hit the ground between Hans and us. The small beam fell down and behind the smoke, Georg became visible again. You put your arm around Karl and walked with him upright the 15 meters to the sheltering fence. Shortly before reaching the wall, we walked into another short burst of fire. Hit mortally, he sank with a quiet, painful moan from your arms. You did not get hit yourself.

Georg and Wenzel luckily reached the fence behind you. You wanted to secure the street while Wenzel and Georg were to transport back the wounded, at least that was what you were hoping to do.

My father wrote to Karl's parents:

Shortly before the fence in relentless grenade shelling and MG fire, Karl was becoming limp in my arms, hit again by a shot in his heart area. He struggled and tried very hard to remain upright, but he could not keep up. Three of us tried to pull him along farther, but in vain, we could not take him with us.

The boys had been unable to take their heavily wounded, dying comrade with them. It was one of the many terrible things that Hans did not elaborate on in his diary. None of them had been there to comfort Karl in his dying moments. Could Karl have been saved?

I discovered in a letter to Karl's parents, written just after the war and stuck at the back of the diary, just how fond my father had been of his friend and how talented Karl must have been:

Dear Mrs. H., Very esteemed Mr. H.,

If I feel the need to get close to you at this time, even though up to now I have been a total stranger to you, I take this license because you and I are bound together by the precious memory of your dear son Karl—my good friend. He fell still by my side on April 19th, 1945, in the battle of Mährisch-Ostrau, Troppau. He fell for his German world and—to quote the writer Flex—he fell for his belief in the godliness in men. In this terrible hour, may it be of some consolation to you, dear Mrs. H., that he did not die in vain. He has joined that community of quiet spirits of great minds, among whom he had always felt at home.

In his young life he has been a great source of inspiration and support for the living. On one of our communal walks he mentioned that after this terrible fighting was over, German youth would draw the strength to start again from the sacrifices their mothers had made for them.

I met Karl for the first time on his beloved handball field. He was a famously good player throughout his school years. But only during our time at the Flak did I discover that Karl was not only a great athlete but also a talented painter. I found a friend and a fellow human being in him. This happened bit by bit. After I had greatly admired his watercolor of a forest clearing, he told me in his own way about his future drawing projects. Among our loud comrades who loved to discuss their thoughts in heated arguments, he was always quiet. He did not enjoy drawing attention to himself. Once we were reading Nietzsche's *Zarathustra* together and he envisioned the described world of icy mountaintops in winter storms.

In his small paintings, Karl loved the reddish-brown colors most. He succeeded in giving his subjects a personal note and a breath of warmth. If he wanted to draw people in action, he would always refer to Albrecht Dürer's drawn studies of the hands. He tried to capture the moments he had experienced down to the last detail in his carefully executed sketches. He was always observing and drawing, content to do so on his own. He had set himself the goal to turn reality into artistic truth.

It was destiny that we ended up in the same barrack as freshly recruited soldiers. For the first time, Karl talked of his desire of wanting to become an artist. Colors and landscapes, especially of old Nuremberg, images of the future and the past were conjured up by our conversations, and this is how we confirmed to each other that we were still alive. On Sundays we met at the radio, which were our favorite moments. We listened, doubly thankful that it made us forget the daily misery, to a symphony by Beethoven or Brahms. After such hours we usually went silently down the desolate barrack path until painfully ugly sounds would bring us back to reality.

I still see Karl in front of me. His shining eyes could not get enough of all the natural beauty around him. We talked about the miracle of the human eye, which is capable of absorbing enormous amounts of light from the universe, broken in the earth's atmosphere, and bringing it toward a point in the soul. Those were the happiest moments of our deployment!

I did not realize it at first, but I knew Karl's younger brother, because we had visited him and his family several times in Nuremberg when I was still a child. Neither Karl's family nor my father ever found out what happened to Karl or his body. My father's report had served the family to have him declared dead. The best my father could do was to spend time with Karl's younger brother.

14

—

SAVED BY A GRENADE

THE FATEFUL DAY OF April 19, 1945, was not over, and once again my father's account of the Battle of Zawada was the only one that survived:

It was in the nick of time that we stormed down the streets and were among the last ones to reach the manor house again. Hoffmann wanted to take us on a safe detour, but then a brave major came out and with his drawn pistol held against us, drove us back for a frontal attack on the open road under the leadership of a lieutenant. You jumped across the street from the corner of the wall to the transformer installation hut to wade forward in the ankle-deep mud with your comrades. Then Russian grenade fire hit the road, the wall of the manor house, and us directly. In this moment the corner of the manor house received a direct hit, where Albert, Georg, and Hans stood. Through the gun smoke one could see them hastily making their way to the company command post.

In this moment the lieutenant in front also received a shot through his neck. The lieutenants were wearing out really fast! Since the Russians were already firmly entrenched and shot at us frontally with MGs above our heads into the splintering road, we gave up our crazy attempt and withdrew into the transformer installation hut. Poor Gerlach was leaning against the yellow wall with his head smashed in.

Suddenly Hoffmann was back again. In the impending danger of being encircled by the enemy, those of us left over followed him blind. He raced to the left southwest corner of the village and was trying to win some height toward the forest. But it was in vain. As we crossed the farm garden, Russian Pak grenades exploded among us. Four comrades, among them the Tall One, were no longer able to crawl forward. You were lucky to reach a projection of a wall in the moment of the explosion. The situation was completely unclear. Except for the few remaining members of our platoon and a handful of sapper combat engineers, there was nobody in sight.

You dragged the Tall One and another guy who could not walk some distance back, passing a harnessed team of horses. Directly hit, the animals had been completely torn apart and lay there in the middle of a sea of blood. The village main street had been raked up by the barrage of firing. The Tall One assured me several times with a beaming face that unless one got hit, one would never make it out of this hell alive. Did those two ever make it home?

Suddenly, a cursing first lieutenant stood in front of the manor house's main barn. A few men were ordered into the barn, some

Bunker in the forests of Závada where Hans was treated at a first aid station.

into the stables, and a number of men were sent into the three-story-high granary. The gate was barricaded behind us. Through the wire mesh of the windows, we picked off those Russians who tried to get around us.

"For every fallen comrade, twenty Russians! After that you are allowed to get yourself killed," were the encouraging words of the first lieutenant. Under the stairs on a little bit of straw lay a poor, dying infantryman. Nobody had time for him.

Unexpectedly, a young Russian commissar jumped into the barn. He shouted, "Ah . . . *Germanskis*," fell down, and kicked the bucket. You stood on the top floor of the granary and fired and fired and didn't see anything anymore. During those days you were deaf. Again, and again, the same song was thundering in your head: "Once I had a comrade . . . a bullet it came flying, was it meant for him or me?"

It was lunchtime but not even a tiny bit of provisions made it through to us. You were astonished at what your body could endure. Suddenly half the barrel of your rifle was split, and you didn't know how it happened. Somebody wanted to give you a new one, totally covered in blood, but you took another old one instead. Of the comforting, familiar faces you had grown so fond of, nobody was around anymore. You seemed to be the only one who was still left of our old group of six. You did not want to go on living anymore; you just wanted to lie down and sleep, just sleep. From the chalk wall behind our heads, the mortar was spraying out. The Russians were shooting into the windows. It would be so easy to just stick out one's head in front of the window frame.

My mother had mentioned that my father had been suicidal during those last battle days. He had told her that it had been his older comrade who had protected him from himself when he had tried to stand in front of the window. I was interested if suicide by enemy fire was a common occurrence and naively tried to research the subject. Soon I realized the futility of it. It was hard enough keeping track of who was still alive. Whether a soldier had stuck out his head on purpose or had just been hit accidentally was of no interest to any recordkeeping.

> You glanced outside. There was bright sunshine; here and there lay the motionless, bold bodies of Russians. Over there—you strained your eyes—by the charred house, in front of the familiar red brick building—he must be lying there. Maybe he had lived a little bit longer? It was horrible.

This reference to Karl was heartbreaking. I could not even start to imagine what my father had felt leaving his best friend behind in desperate need of help and comfort in what were probably his last hours.

> There was the sound of a dull bang and thick, acrid smoke. A jagged hole was torn into the front wall by a Russian Pak. You picked up a hot splinter the size of your palm. It had not hit any of us. Now we were no longer in the mood to wait for the next direct hit. Three of us climbed down the stairs. But the officer gentlemen who sat in secured positions downstairs chased us up the stairs again. What was the life of an infantryman worth?
>
> We watched two more detonations, and afterward we stayed downstairs. We had another mortar with thirty-five shots at our disposal. By using a field telephone, we coordinated with the mortar operator to fire close to the wall of the granary into the blind spot, which we could not reach with our rifles. The man knew what he was doing. Then the fire eased up a little bit, and soon we had heavy, white smoke in our faces. The last five remaining houses on the outskirts of the village were burning down.
>
> You could rest a little bit on the pile of soybeans, from which it was hard to get up again. You couldn't hear anything anymore. In the approaching darkness, we left the fighting line to the arriving

relief infantry platoon. There were only nine men left out of the thirty-one who had been ordered to fight in this location. In the living room of the small farm you found the nine coats of your closest comrades untouched. You had secretly hoped that maybe some of them might have returned wounded and taken their coats and equipment with them. By the light of a small candle stump, you gathered up your things. You could not bring yourself to search the coats of your comrades for documents.

Again, heavy Russian fire chased us from the burning village into the dark fields and into the woods through which we had walked the day before. This had been Zawada! You dragged yourself with the only saved MG down the street to the village of Wretschin to quell your burning thirst at the village well. Late in the night, some members of your unit arrived in the already familiar forest behind the Czech bunker line. The other ones were ordered to dig more trenches during the night. You slept the sleep of the dead in the earth hole of a comrade.

The next day on April 20, Hitler was celebrating his birthday in the safety of his Berlin bunker where he had been hiding since January 16, 1945. While the Führer was throwing a tantrum, firing Goering and demanding that Himmler be arrested, the 371st Infantry Division, in which the Feldafing boys had been fighting, was finally allowed to vacate the strip of deadly foxholes in front of the village and retreat to the bunker line. But as Hans observed, that was too late for Karl and the others:

Early the next morning, you experienced how inventory was taken. They were just crossed off the list, just the same way that they had died. It was incomprehensible. Afterward, the Hungarian Schmidt, Georg, and I were promoted to the position of senior privates. Then we moved deeper into the woods, nearer to the main battle line. You told the skinny, freckle-faced Michael about your last minutes with Karl. He did not say a thing. A day later he

205

was single-handedly to defend a gorge from three Russian attacks solely with his MG. The same night, he received the Iron Cross for his bravery and shortly afterward was killed by a direct hit.

We had peace for a day. On the company bicycle you drove to the manor house in Wretschin hoping to tell Georg about his promotion. But even in this neighboring village, just 3 kilometers away, all the wounded had already been evacuated. So, without having accomplished anything, you returned to the woods. You waited with the others for the next deployment, now with the rank of an MG shooter, First Class. You enjoyed Hoffmann's apricot marmalade, which he had carried off from the cellar of a small store in Zawada. It was not a comfortable rest. Hostile artillery was shelling the woods during the entire day. On the German side there was no more heavy artillery, human bodies were fighting against steel!

With the approaching sunset, we received a new deployment. We had to go along the paths that were radiating out of the gray, round bunker as shooting positions. Our platoon, reinforced with new men, occupied 2 kilometers of the forest's edge. You stayed with Wenzel in a small, muddy, knee-high MG hole; it had been built as a small dugout by the previous occupants. You put your gun in position, camouflaged yourself, and anxiously observed the field in front of you. Suddenly flares illuminated the surroundings and dark figures came by whispering, "Don't shoot in the next two hours—we are laying down landmines." Could that figure have been a Russian? The sky opened up a little bit. It seemed as though you could observe dark shapes in front of you. Did they not seem to be slowly approaching? You looked more carefully; were they only apparitions? There was nobody to consult. The relief was sleeping soundly. You fired a few shots toward the dark silhouettes. Nothing moved.

Suddenly, star shells were fired above your head, splintering the tree branches. You tried to locate where the fire came from but could not discern from where in the trenches they had been fired. This is how the first strange night passed. Three days of fighting to hold our strategic position ensued. There were two hours of sleep and two hours of watch. In the morning and in the afternoon, the Russians subjected us to hostile firing with anti-tank guns and mortars. Then the brown swarms of Russians came toward us, attack and defense. In front of us, the field ended in a hollow in which lay the village occupied by the enemy. On the other side of the village, the fields were ascending again.

As the crow flies, 2 kilometers were separating us from the forest edge on the other side and the enemy lines. From there came flashes. When we heard a weak, short knock from the other side, we would put our heads down, and shortly afterward a grenade would detonate next to us or in a tree. On the other side of the forest edge, we observed the endless procession of arriving supplies and fresh ammunition. From the distance we were powerless: there had not been any German artillery for a while. Clearly the Russians did not know what to do with all their excess ammunition. It was here that we finally lost our belief that in the end Germany was to win the war.

The Russians kept playing gramophones. In the quiet of the night, there was also somebody talking through a loudspeaker, but one could not understand him. Soon the forest was white from flyers that had been shot across. They said, "To the Soldiers of the 96th Tank Division . . . This flyer is a pass . . . Every second German has an Iron Cross; every second Russian has a mortar on his back.

The loudspeaker operators encouraging German soldiers to desert were known as Seydlitz's people. General Seydlitz, a well-regarded career officer, had given his men permission to voluntarily surrender at the Battle of Stalingrad against Hitler's orders. He was immediately relieved of his duties and became a Russian collaborator. There were rumors that besides organizing the propaganda campaigns, he was also the head of an army that consisted of German prisoners of war who were trained to wreak havoc among German troops. Hans had expressed his doubts about the identity of the person who had told them to hold their fire while mines were laid. He and his comrades had heard about acts of sabotage that were attributed to Seydlitz's people on behalf of the Red Army. In the end, General Seydlitz himself had little to show for his efforts on behalf of either power. The Reich sentenced him to death as a traitor in absentia and the Soviet Union gave him a twenty-five-year prison sentence.

During the night, the intimidated platoon leader of the neighboring company came to us:

"Don't tell this to anybody, but in the night two of my men ran over to the other side."

On the second night they forgot my relief. I stood for six hours in the constantly blowing wind; my coat felt like lead from the rain it had soaked up. I had to keep my eyes open with my fingers. The muddy water rose up to my ankles, but there was no way to scoop it out.

In the morning of the third day, the commander gave us some recognition for sticking it out in this windy corner, and the announcement came that the general attack of the Russians was imminent. The remaining parts of our platoons had been significantly decimated and the defense became weaker. With my left hand, I held the carefully folded ammunition belt against the mud wall and my right hand was on the trigger. You waited and crouched down to avoid the firing. After one hour under heavy drumfire, you had the weird burning, partly numb feeling and urge to stand up. At great pains, the faithful Wenzel managed to keep you down. You crawled slowly over an overturned tree trunk to say farewell to Hoffmann. The gaunt König carried you back. You had been hit.

König bragged how he had shot and hit just as though he was at a shooting gallery. He tried very hard to help you with your crawling and limping. The last part, toward the first aid bunker, he managed to transport you in an abandoned wheelbarrow. At the entrance, somebody was looking with glazed-over eyes at his arm torn apart by exploding ammunition. There was a disgusting smell in the dark, sparsely lit bunker. Outside, König had taken off your helmet and ammunition belt. He watched as they carried you in. Did he ever make it home?

At that moment did my father wonder if he would make it home himself? Did he dare to look at his injury? It must have been substantial. I remember that as a little girl at the beach with my father, I ran my fingers with childish curiosity over the large area of odd, shiny scar tissue on his leg. When I asked him about it, he said dismissively, "Oh, that's from the war," unwilling to recall further details. In the spring of 1945, it must have been frightening to be unable to walk, at a time when the rapid disintegration of Germany sent his compatriots running to safety, and with the Nazi functionaries leaving the sinking ship first. Did he wonder if people would take pity on a broken boy when there had been so little concern for a healthy one?

15

GERMANSKIS ON THE RUN

I LOOKED AT MY COMPUTER in dread. Working on the manuscript meant descending once more into the misery of millions of fleeing Germans who, while coping with the destruction of their world, understood that overnight they had become the pariahs of Europe. The ethnic cleansing of Germans had mainly happened in the east, but in 1946, even countries like Holland drove out its twenty-five thousand German residents, coming in the middle of the night, seizing all their assets, and sending them on their way with only their suitcases. The operation was called Black Tulip and was virtually forgotten in the coming decades.

I visualized the numbers involved and realized that 12.5 million people fleeing into the West German area of roughly 95,000 square miles was the equivalent of the entire populations of Alabama, Louisiana, and Arkansas crowding into the states of New York, Massachusetts, and Maine all at once, with those states already on the brink of famine and a dire housing shortage. Not to mention that even though those immigrants spoke the same language, their accents and religious and cultural traditions were different from their involuntary new hosts. But not all refugees made it. Again, the numbers I found of those who died or were killed on the way varied widely. Some historians spoke of only five hundred thousand, while others quoted three million. Those who survived their arduous journey were marked for life. While I was growing up in Rheinbach in the 1960s and '70s, even we children knew who in our class had refugee parents.

Where were their unrelenting Nazi leaders now that true leadership was required to solve this monumental logistical problem of defeat? Where was Baldur von Schirach who had made his boys sing, "The flag is more than death"?

He abandoned his unit of juveniles as they were fighting to defend Vienna. Schirach, afraid of bombs, had built himself an impressive bunker underneath the city and escaped totally unharmed. Growing a beard, putting on glasses, and securing papers as "Dr. Falk," he offered himself to the Americans as an interpreter before being taken into custody. In Nuremberg, he was sentenced to twenty years in prison for having facilitated the deportation of the Viennese Jews to the concentration camps. For his role in grooming the German youth into becoming child soldiers, he went unpunished. An opportunist by nature, he was one of the few who denounced Hitler at his trial.

His Hitler Youth successor, Artur Axmann, defended the Nazi system up to his unspectacular death in 1996. In his only interview, Axmann confirmed that he had been wounded in 1941 and recuperated at the Capri villa of his friend Dino Alfieri, a member of Mussolini's Great Fascist Council, acknowledging that his boy soldiers did not enjoy such privileges.[1]

In the last days of the war, Axmann had been commanding an HJ battalion in Berlin. Weekly newsreels of the Führer handing out tin Iron Crosses and talking to boys showed that some of them had been as young as twelve. In his interview, Axmann confirmed that he himself had spent the most brutal days of the battle for Berlin inside the Führer's bunker, not with the children. On May 1, 1945, the day after Hitler's suicide and shortly before Germany's official capitulation, he fled. After the war, he was only given a nominal prison sentence. Meanwhile, his boy soldiers were fending for survival on their own:

Together with Schmidt, I was loaded onto a small, gray amphibious vehicle that recklessly drove down the muddy forest tracks to a village where there was an ambulance waiting. Later I found myself in the classroom of a school in the town of Schönbrunn in the care of a very kind medical NCO [non-commissioned officer]. After an injection and an operation, I got to meet the Catholic army chaplain. Despite the approaching fighting, he walked through the rooms of misery and dispensed solace to the convalescents and the dying. He read a story from the Old Testament and from Walter Flex.

On the second day, I was loaded onto a cattle train with a card around my neck attesting to my status as wounded. The closed wooden compartments had been fitted with thin plywood beds. The train was not marked with a red cross.

The little train started its trip with the destination of Olmütz. At every station, wagons were added and the train became slower and longer. Finally, we were about a thousand wounded, whom no city or military hospital wanted to accommodate. We had no doctors, no provisions, and only a few nurses. The bandages turned into unshapely, purulent masses. The two paramedics assigned to each compartment were powerless against the unfolding misery. Urgent lifesaving operations could not be performed. Everything was incredibly dirty. The trip had already taken four days when it stopped at around lunchtime on an open track about 100 kilometers west of Prague. In the stiflingly hot midday atmosphere, the droning of a faraway airplane could be heard.

Out of nowhere, there was crashing and splintering. The two paramedics and anything that had the use of their legs clamored outside the train wagons and ran onto the open field. In sudden terror and mortal fear, I pressed myself against the wagon walls as my neighbor collapsed, dead. Metal pieces had splintered from the open wagon door. The bluish-looking, acrid-smelling smoke of nitrocellulose filled the groaning wagon. Suddenly I felt a burning pain in my injured leg. Two times the roaring din reoccurred, but suddenly it became still. Eleven Mustang planes had attacked our wagons, under the impression that it was an ammunition train.

Only when they had spotted the white bandages in the field had they turned away. In the wall of your bed stuck a not totally detonated explosive missile that had only partially burst open. It had found its way from the torn open wagon floor through your bed from bouncing off the rails outside. It had injured your foot. This attack led to 70 dead and about an additional 190 heavily wounded casualties on the train. The Czech population in the nearby village stood by the railway line and watched the sad spectacle without offering help. Only one Czech doctor and four Sudeten German women helped as much as they could. In Saatz, those with head or abdominal injuries were unloaded. The train was suddenly directed to the north in the direction of the city of Dresden, already conquered by the Russians.

Franz, my father's classmate, had told me that it was known to the German soldiers that on the Eastern Front, the SS units had committed atrocities against the Geneva Convention when dealing with prisoners. Everybody expected the Russians to take revenge. In addition, Goebbels's propaganda machine had made them out to be brutal and primitive. Being taken to Dresden meant being taken to a place where the Russians hunted down *Germanskis* at will. Any German soldier in the eastern territories with the ability to walk tried to make it through to the American or British lines. But Hans's luck had not run out yet:

Finally, we were to be released from our odyssey by the friendly town of Bilin, which was in the hands of Sudetendeutschen. As we were taken off the train, a paramedic told us that we were supposed to have been handed over to the Russians.

A welcoming and attractive town awaited us. Two little boys visited me at the loading ramp of the cattle train. All the suffering of the last days finally seemed over. I talked with them about Karl May, Tom Sawyer, and Buffalo Bill. They promised to visit again soon. The boys' school had become our makeshift hospital. Relieved, I sank back in the simple bed covered with white sheets. Finally, a bed, peace, and sleep! I slept for three nights and three days and when I woke up, I saw everything through a pink veil and felt the soft hands of the nurses who cared for me and fed me. Flowers stood on the table, real flowers! The Sudetendeutsche came with newspapers and books, bringing us their precious jars of preserves and a little bit of cake. They themselves were already going hungry.

Hans's concern for the Sudetendeutsche who had given milk to the boys when they had marched by their farms, and who were now sharing their last food reserves with them, was well founded. But it was not the Russians who were eventually to kill them. In several massacres right after the war, the ethnic Czech population killed several thousand in retaliation for what the Nazis had done. It was Karin, the wife of Franz, my father's classmate from Feldafing, and a Sudetendeutsche herself, who told me her story.

She was a teenager when her family got driven out of what had always been their home country. Almost all Sudetendeutsche who survived ended up as refugees, fleeing to Germany in 1946–47. Karin ended up in Munich with her mother and her sister. There were 3.5 million ethnic Germans who had lived in Czech regions since the Middle Ages and ended up as displaced persons. Karin talked about her family's property that had been taken by the

Czechoslovakian state without compensation. To this day there are German aristocratic families who are fighting for the return of their estates, as they can prove to the courts that during the Nazi occupation they sided with the Czech government. Sudetendeutsche survivors and victims of Czech persecution have formed organizations that continue to lobby, with very limited success, to have the sustained injustices recognized by the Czech or German governments. Not all Czechs felt that the treatment of their German neighbors had been justified, although during the communist regime in Czechoslovakia, much of that history was suppressed.

But in 1945, right after the war, the Sudetendeutsche did not yet realize what a catastrophe was to befall them, and they helped the German soldiers as well as they could. They must have been hoping that somebody was helping their own injured boys who had been sent to the Western Front:

> The nurses were patient and again and again fetched fresh water to take off the layers of dirt from hands and bodies. The bled-through uniform pieces were removed and new ones were substituted. Oh, I felt so incredibly good in my weakness that had been induced by the sustained blood loss. To think of nothing, to keep the memories of all that had happened in a small secret compartment, always lying there, all calm and relaxed. But then the nights became long, and the night nurses did not have enough painkillers. Two doctors with rolled-up sleeves were losing control of the situation. They were cutting and cutting; more and more limbs required their services. Four hundred patients were put up in the small school. Later the bandages were only changed twice a week. It must have been revolting to the poor nurses to deal with the stench of the yellow-encrusted, soiled sheets they had to air out.
>
> Soon the blanket was crawling away, as so many little white and black animals lived in it. Twice your temperature went really high

and you saw fire in front of your eyes. Only after many days did you start to pay attention to the conversations of the new arrivals. The army on the Western Front was being dissolved. Goebbels held a speech . . . the Führer was dead! You looked with disbelief into the indifferently smiling faces of your older compatriots. They commented, "Finally!"

But was not the whole world collapsing? There should have been a scream from the voices of thousands. Unceremoniously, the German world had collapsed. But your spirit, your will to live, was awakening again.

You heard that the Russians had broken through south of Dresden in the direction of the towns of Brüx and Aussig. Whoever could walk was advised to pick up some field rations for the journey and start their trip on foot. The other ones were simply left behind. The military hospital was dissolved. More frequently the cars of the Wehrmacht, heavily loaded with provisions, were driving by the front of the building. Where did all those cars come from?

Willingly I accepted help from the two pale seamstress girls who were crying. They could not understand how we were to be simply left behind. They promised in with absolute urgency to arrange a vehicle. Carefully they dressed me by tearing open one of the pants legs. Amid the general disbanding, they carried me down to the street. A decent captain of the medical corps stood there and forced the fat, timid faces of the paymasters and majors behind the windscreens to stop, and each to take at least one wounded with them. This is how I got to travel together with Schmidt in an uncomfortable resting place between canisters of wine, cigarette boxes, tins, and bread in such a bigwig car. They were still so stingy on this terrible day of retreat. The car radio booming in our ears was transmitting the victory celebrations and speeches from all over the world. It was May 9th. Germany had unconditionally capitulated. Schmidt's femur had been shot right through and it had hit the sciatic nerve. Lying on the pillow that he had salvaged, he was rolling from one side to the other, moaning heavily. This was due to the car speeding to ensure that it would escape the rapidly approaching Russians. Schmidt told me how he had gone from his position in the woods to the company command post to fetch some food for his group in the early morning hours. When he came back, all his men had vanished.

Thousands of the most diverse trucks were driving in three lanes in a never-ending queue down the great retreat route in a southwesterly direction toward Karlsbad, to the American lines. When the little car door was opened for the first time, I saw the size of the convoy. I did not believe my eyes. Where did they all come from? At the front there had only been a Panje wagon that had brought us food. But here there was an abundance of tires and gasoline. Everything rushing back in a mad disorder, officers and soldiers, general staff, and privates. Nobody took any notice of anybody else. Nobody wanted to lose his precious hide at the last moment.

In the evening, I finally lay in a big, beautiful bed in the large city in a real army hospital. I should have been happy: freshly deloused, bathed, with fresh bandages, and more or less fed. But I could not lose that oppressive feeling of the muggy stillness of the surroundings. Whoever had legs was also leaving this nest to walk toward the west. The rats were leaving the sinking ship.

Trucks and buses left. It became quieter and quieter. For half a day we did not see a nurse. I could not stand it any longer and wanted to drink some water in the middle of the night. Everything seemed to burn. That is how the night nurse found you collapsed at the sink.

Was not everything in order? Did the Americans not stand ready at the entrance of the city to occupy it? On May 13th our destiny had been sealed. Overnight we had become Russian prisoners. The American patrol cars with their big white stars on the car bonnets, after which I looked with almost longing eyes, became more and more rare and finally disappeared altogether. Instead my ears listened to the bellowed, strange marching songs of the little brown and totally shaven figures as they continuously marched by, clad in cheap cloth. For the first time in my life I saw them this close. When I sat up and looked through the balcony door, I could see a real, red flag attached to the house opposite.

In the night, a barely interrupted shootout started: Germans, Czechs, Russians, and Americans—nobody was entirely sure to whom the town belonged. What was going to happen to us? Which of the hair-raising rumors we had heard were true? The Russians lay raucously shouting on the steps of the hospital and were celebrating their victory. At night they broke in, so that the nurses had to hide in the beds with wounded patients. Senselessly they destroyed all the food stored in the cellar. From then on there was nothing to eat anymore. Russian doctors and Czech military personnel searched the wardrobes, beds, and walls for weapons. Then they started to carry out more and more beds. The heavily wounded ones could no longer be cared for; most of them died. The few brave nurses who had not fled were totally overworked. Whoever could walk reasonably well disappeared at night toward Eger. Czech police moved into the neighboring house, armed to the teeth with brand-new German MGs, steel helmets, binoculars, pistols, and ammunition belts. Soon they openly plundered any refugee who came by in the street down to their shirt. Frightened, the refugees would move on. We saw it and we kept quiet.

Over it all smiled a balmy spring sky, which felt totally out of context.

One could feel how the forests of Karlsbad were starting to green. The blossoms on the apple and cherry trees that had lined the roads of our retreat were brightly blooming. The pointy, gilded onion tower of the Orthodox church, once upon a time donated to the venerable Karlsbad by a Czar, was shining over us.

We were not allowed to leave our building, with the threat of being punished with liquidation. We would not have been able to anyway. In the morning, they fed us a cup of water with some bits of dried vegetables. At lunchtime there was a precious plate of bean soup. In the evening there was another plate of the tasteless, whitish broth. One's own will was no longer relevant. One had to wait out what was about to happen. Tenaciously and agonizingly, the thoughts started to come, and they always turned in circles. Slowly the hours ran by. A thousand times I had counted the design pattern of the tiles on the wall, from front to back and in reverse.

From confused thoughts, one theme started to emerge. For me there was not going to be a passive, gradual decline in an eastern prison camp. At the first opportunity there would be flight, which would be either successful or bring a rapid end to a life that had already become senseless in so many ways. It had felt like a joke that one had been spared by destiny so far, and now it seemed entirely possible that one was to lose one's life in some totally meaningless way. First, we were to be transferred to Germany but then to the east. Apparently in the Komotau prison camp, typhus was raging.

I was lucky—because of my inability to walk, I was assigned to the last of the three transports of wounded out of Karlsbad.

Other eyewitness records confirmed what my father had said about the sacking of Karlsbad by the Russians. Liesel Lentz recalled how they had occupied her house, vandalizing it and using up all food supplies.[2] Like the nurses, she and the other women had to hide once the Russians started drinking. But she also remembered a kind Russian cook who had diverted food from the Red Army canteens to feed her family and other Germans. Neither kindness nor cruelty runs along lines of national identity. But her most traumatic experience was after the Russians left. Her family was turned out of their home by Czech militia with guns, who confiscated everything and sent them on a foot march to West Germany with a suitcase and a baby carriage.

Back in the late spring of 1945, Hans was in no shape to walk anywhere yet:

From a truck I was carried onto a long Italian field hospital train car, which had bunk beds three levels high, covered with thin mattresses. Czechs were wandering along the tracks with hostile faces. Fat Russian officers shrugged their shoulders; they did not know where the journey was going. One pound of bread, 85 grams of canned meat, and three packages of dry flat bread were given to each person. It was wonderful to sink one's teeth into the bread and calm one's hunger. Soon the rations were eaten. It turned out to be the food allocation for a full ten days.

The morning sun was shining on our train car that rolled along with occasional jerks. Czech militia were bumming about on railroad stations decorated with garlands and emblems. Suddenly, between the forest-covered hills there was an indentation, and a broad, green band became visible: the River Elbe. The forests appeared to be climbing higher and higher as naked yellow rock walls were revealed. It was the *Elbsandsteingebirge* [Elbe Sandstone Mountains] and the border. German land again! People were waving to us the same way as when we were traveling in the opposite direction. Now I am the only one left of all those I cared about. Alone among strange faces, lying miserably on my cot, I am looking with wet eyes on the unchanged majestic beauty of the surroundings. There in a reversed order, the imposing grayish-blue and white rock formations are passing by that I had enjoyed seeing in "the circle of the six" [the group of boys who had gone into war together].

We reached Pirna. Brown, stockily built figures were yelling on the riverbanks while they were watering some shaggy horses. They gestured to us, threatening us with their fists. The train stopped. Like a wildfire, it spreads through the city: a German transport of wounded soldiers. Despite the Russian guards, the inhabitants of the city came to us with their little handcarts, cooking pots, bowls, and buckets. Nobody had called them. They had regarded taking care of us as a matter of course.

Then the train started to move; it went for about 2 kilometers and stopped in a railroad terrain that was burrowed through by bombs. Bent-out-of-shape rails and derailed train cars completed the usual picture of war destruction. Ten thirsty days we were to spend here, hungry and filthy. We would have felt threatened if it had not been for the faithful inhabitants of Pirna and the nurses who stuck it out with us.

Skyline of the historic town of Pirna in 2013.

When I had visited Pirna, I found records that showed how the townspeople had gone out of their way to help the thousands of wounded and dispossessed who flooded through their city in the aftermath of the war. It saddened me that the association with the horrific Sonnenstein facilities overshadowed all this kindness. But in 2020, I was happy to discover that some of that humanity and the fate of those on the receiving end were shown in a special exhibition in the city's museum named *Children of War.*

Ordinary everyday items, like a baby carriage or a torn-out calendar page, were used to tell the stories of those who had turned to the city seeking help. But what impressed me most was that the curators had invited children of war from the current refugee crisis, which in 2015 had brought 1.5 million people to Germany, to tell their stories. For Hans, Pirna was only one of many stops on the way back, but he remembered it with gratitude and toward the end of his life went back to visit the town once more.

Day and night, the trains taking Russian soldiers back home were passing by. The wagons were decorated with green, wilted twigs, and chalk marks of the hammer and sickle. The wagons were also loaded with threshing machines, cars, and even buckets. Everything that could be mechanically produced was hauled away.

The heat and the foggy dryness became unbearable in the wagon. Once in a while one could put one's hot hands into a bowl of tepid water that the nurses brought. It felt so good! During the night of the eleventh day, the train slowly started to move. The commander in Dresden had blocked the passage of the single-track railroad line. Now we were distributed to the surrounding military hospitals, which were mostly overcrowded already. But it was good luck. We stayed in Germany.

The statistics of the time supported my father's sense of a lucky escape. Out of prisoners in the east, one in three men died, compared to one in one hundred of men taken into captivity by the Allied forces in the west. Staying on German soil also meant the support of the civilian population:

> The recuperation station of Bad Gottleuba lay in a beautiful, rising park, a former spa. Here I found peace for a month and a little bit of mental stimulation. Only the hunger was hard to bear. But I traded pages from the little linen covered edition of *Faust* for cigarette paper. With 10 peeled potatoes and 200 grams of bread, things started to look up. When it got really bad, I gathered my courage and climbed over the fence to limp to the neighboring village to search for a few potatoes that I would bake on a small fire, hiding behind shrubs under a bridge. Soon I was well enough to help distribute the food, which earned me another portion. There was the little, gray chief-of-staff physician who held a presentation about different German art styles. When he left, he gave me brown pants as a present in which I was soon to try to cross the Russian occupied zone. Without really noticing it, I started to become a human being again. I had a haircut, enjoyed bathing in a real bathtub in the spa's guest facilities, and did not even forget to shave daily. I enjoyed reading Scheffel's medieval novel *Eckhardt* and felt like one of its characters, "Brother Cheerful," who had won the bet with the devil.

A German proverb says, "A great war leaves the country with three armies—an army of the crippled, an army of mourners, and an army of thieves."

At eighteen years old, my father had become part of the army of the crippled. Now with a physical impairment, he would be recognized by the German government as 40 percent disabled for the rest of his life. His supreme commander, General Field Marshal "Bloody Ferdinand" Schörner, commander of the *Heeresgruppe Mitte* on the Eastern Front, had joined the army of thieves. On May 9, two days after personally shooting twenty-two young German soldiers as deserters in Lednice, about 150 miles away from

Zawada, he disguised himself in civilian clothes and stole the money from his units' army coffers. He flew in a private plane to the Alps dressed in a pair of lederhosen.

How did Schörner fare after the war? The Americans captured him and handed him over to the Russians. He served ten years in a Russian jail and, later, four years in a German jail. After that there was some public debate about awarding him his *Wehrmacht* pension.³ In the end, he was paid and lived a comfortable, quiet life in Munich, living to the ripe old age of eighty-one. The story reminded me of another German proverb, "The unimportant ones are hanged; the big ones are allowed to run."

I checked if abandoning the Germans who had so faithfully followed them was a general trait among high-ranking Nazis. It appeared that the party members usually ran away first without giving orders for their soldiers or the German population to save themselves. That was certainly in line with what my father had observed while the *Wehrmacht* was in retreat.

I looked into the biography of another Nazi in charge of children. General August Heissmeyer was an SS officer who had been the Napola inspector of all military child training. In the last days of the war, he was fighting with a group of Napola pupils to defend the airfield in Spandau in Berlin. When the cause looked lost, he got out of his uniform and fled, abandoning not just the Napola boys but also his own two sons. He surfaced three years later with his wife, Gertrud Scholtz-Klink, leader of the National Socialist Women's League, as a farmhand in West Germany. What happened to their children is unclear, but it is presumed that they survived, which is more than can be said for the children of Scholtz-Klink's old adversary, Magda Goebbels. Goebbels poisoned her six youngest children before committing suicide with her husband in May 1945.

I contemplated the horror of those stories. Being a mother myself, I could not imagine an ideology, a religious cult, or even my

225

own safety more important than the welfare of my child. But I had been educated by a generation of Germany's war children who had instilled different values in their own children.

Another story that I came across had a better end. When I turned the diary upside down, a 1950s newspaper clipping fell out. The article's title read, "Martin Bormann ordained as priest."

It referred to one of Hans's schoolmates at Feldafing and Hitler's godson, Martin Adolf Bormann Jr. His father Martin Bormann Sr. was Hitler's former deputy and had disappeared from Berlin on May 1, 1945, as the Russians took over the city. For decades, sightings of him were reported all over South America. His fifteen-year-old son was traveling alone across Germany, unsuccessfully trying to locate any family members. A year later, he learned of his mother's death in an Italian prison from the newspapers. Having been raised in a Nazi household herself, Gerda Bormann married Martin Sr. at age nineteen, and by the time of her death, aged thirty-seven, had given birth to ten children. Martin Adolf had been her oldest son, nicknamed *Krönzi* for "crown prince." His father never reappeared. A DNA test in 1998 finally confirmed that a skeleton found in a ditch close to Berlin's Lehrter train station, with a broken glass vial between its teeth, was that of his father. The son was adopted by a Catholic farmer in the Alps. Under the influence of this pious man, he became a theologian. I could not help but think how lucky Martin Adolf had been. He had been given another chance and a second father.

Thousands of children like him, who had been orphaned or separated from their parents and left to their own devices in the chaos of the war's aftermath, had ended up in dire circumstances. For years, the Red Cross aired programs featuring children who were looking for surviving relatives. Those too young to know their names were particularly disadvantaged. Prior to DNA testing, children were often irrevocably lost to their families. About forty-five thousand youngsters, labeled *Wolfskinder* (wolf children), were roaming the

Baltic forests, the older ones taking care of their younger siblings. Several films based on survivors' accounts have been made over the years.[4] Many of them had seen their parents killed in front of them. Some managed to survive in the woods for years, turning feral, scrounging for food or stealing from farms. If caught, they were put in Russian orphanages, and some were adopted by local farmers who had to change their German identities. Children who made it farther west arrived in the German region of Mecklenburg-Western Pomerania, which registered thirty thousand unaccompanied minors. In a hurry, the region created 120 provisional orphanages, but the local communities were totally overwhelmed by the mass of victims and their physical, psychological, and medical needs. However, once again, the wolf children and the Meck-Pom orphans were among the lucky ones: They were alive.

My father, prior to his death, had once told me about the *Wilhelm Gustloff*, almost in embarrassment rather than in outrage over an atrocity committed against civilians. It had clearly anguished him to talk about it. He saw the Guido Knopp documentary, *The Last Voyage of the* Wilhelm Gustloff, which had brought back lots of unhappy memories for him. The biggest catastrophe at sea ever was not the *Titanic*, with the death of about 1,500 passengers, but the attack on the MV *Wilhelm Gustloff* with over 9,000 casualties— German women and children fleeing the Baltic region. Several hundred BDM (Hitler Youth girls) were crowded into the ship's former swimming pool. There were pregnant women who went into premature labor, and infants drowned. With only three hundred survivors, the eyewitness reports were heartbreaking.

A Soviet U-13 boat, under the command of Alexander Ivanovich Marinesko, had sunk the former Nazi cruise ship that had been part of the "Strength through Happiness" program. The Russian commander was later awarded the Order of the Red Banner medal, although it had been recorded that he knew that the ship carried civilians. A few days later, he went on to sink the German ship

Steuben carrying wounded military personnel and over 800 civilians, with an estimated 4,267 casualties.

All these numbers are staggering but make sense when looking at the overall statistics. After the Second World War, Germany lost 25 percent of its territories in the east, turning twelve to fourteen million Germans into homeless refugees overnight, of whom hundreds of thousands perished on their journey to the west. But children did not die only in those refugee treks. All over the Reich, children had suffocated in cellars while their cities were bombed, were blown up while manning antiaircraft guns, or succumbed to disease and hunger.

In an ultimate betrayal, the Nazi regime caused the death of at least one million and most likely a whole lot more of their own children, either by using them in the war, or as collateral damage in the destruction of Germany and the expulsion of Germans from the east. As there was no interest in collecting such statistics, exact numbers will never be known. Nobody wanted to count how many infants froze to death on the refugee voyages across the Baltic Sea, or how many children were among the ten thousand dead civilians in the Soviet-encircled forests around Halbe near Berlin, shot in mortal fear by their own mothers.[5]

In 1993, the theologian Martin Bormann, who had dropped the "Adolf" from his name, accepted an invitation to Israel by the psychologist and author Dan Bar-On. The well-known Israeli researcher had traveled to Germany to interview the adult children of Nazi criminals. He wrote *Legacy of Silence: Encounters with Children of the Third Reich*, published in 1989. Having studied transgenerational trauma in the families of Holocaust survivors, Bar-On became interested in what the legacy of the perpetrators had done to their own surviving children. His research yielded the complexities of father–child relationships under such extreme circumstances. In his attempt to categorize his findings, he struggled with drawing general, applicable conclusions, as many of the stories of his fifty interviewees were unique.[6] Questioning his own ambivalence toward his research, he wondered, "Am I afraid that if I look too closely I will see ordinary human beings?"[7]

I contemplated how my young father must have felt about the guilt, the shame, and the utter humiliation. Hans had been a good boy, worked hard in school, made Auntie and his grandparents proud, worn the required uniforms, and volunteered when he was told that the fatherland needed to be saved. But on his long way home he discovered that it had all been futile and monstrously wrong.

16

—

A LONG WAY HOME

I**T WAS AN ABSOLUTE** miracle that this piece of paper survived. By accident, I found it among old family letters. It was actually two incredibly brittle pieces of paper taped together. The top one was a confirmation of discharge for Private Hans. The second was a pass that allowed him to travel back home to Bremen. The most interesting part of the document was the signatures and stamps that confirmed what my father had written in his diary:

> The last examination by the doctor came. I had washed my bowl and was sitting ready, dressed, on the side of the bed. The doctor asked, "You want to be discharged? Fine, but it is on your own responsibility."
>
> An hour later the decisive moment had come. You drew back the woolen blanket that had been used as a curtain and stepped forward, heavily leaning on your stick, passing the watch post, into the office of the commander. Disapproving eyes looked at you. I was asked, "You SS, you SA? Take off clothes! Where wound? Turn! You go home."

Hans was discharged from the Lazarett—the military hospital in Bad Gottleuba, a former spa town as indicated by the prefix, which means "bath." The discharge I held in my hand was signed by the doctor; the pass was endorsed by the town mayor's office. There was a space for comments in Russian, as Bad Gottleuba was in the region of Saxony, under Russian administration.

> A happy, thankful feeling ran through all of your body. The first step toward freedom had been made. Carefully you stowed away your discharge papers and passed a heavily armed Russian. As in a dream, you walked through the streets able to go wherever you wanted. You are free! They can do nothing to you now. You eat for the last time with the friendly peasant woman whom you have been secretly visiting several times. Even your hospital comrades and orderlies could not be told about her, because some of them might have enjoyed reporting you. The poor guilty one would have been sent to the Pirna detention camp.

To me, the most interesting parts of the discharge document were the dates and the additional stamps and signatures that were in the margins and on the back. The discharge was dated July 12, 1945. A stamp on the back from July 13 certified that Hans had been given some provisions. Food was severely rationed, and draconian measures were taken against those breaking the rules of strict distribution. Hans had been wounded in April, and now in July he was finally well enough to be sent home:

> In the afternoon, the small local train drove you through the blooming and ripening countryside. But in Pirna you were seized by doubts and the oppressing uncertainty that you were fair game to any Russian who put it in his mind to take you with him.

His fears were not unfounded. After the war, every German was an attackable target to Russian soldiers, especially women. But rapes occurred all over Germany. Even in the western zones, not every soldier was a gentleman who showed his appreciation for favors rendered by impoverished *Fräuleins* with generous presents of chocolate and silk stockings. After the 2008 film *Anonyma* was released, a number of German women in their seventies and eighties came forward to publicly talk about their experiences of being raped as children and teenagers.

> Women were heavily panting as they repaired the railroad installations. The wretchedness of the refugees left me with many unhappy impressions. Their numbers in the dirty railroad station seemed limitless. There were Germans who had been deported and robbed of everything.

The women my father referred to were a common sight all over postwar Germany. Known as *Trümmerfrauen* (rubble women), they formed work chains and removed the debris from their bombed-out cities and repaired what they could, while waiting for news to find out if their menfolk had been killed, wounded, or taken into captivity. Some of them would wait for eleven years. It was in 1956 that West Germany's Chancellor Konrad Adenauer went himself to the Soviet Union for the last living prisoners to be freed. The numbers I found suggest that over 11 million men fighting for the *Wehrmacht* or the SS were taken into captivity. According to Red Cross records, another 1.3 million men were unaccounted for, in addition to the confirmed deaths.

> You went into the city and asked to have a pass issued, which later on was to help you a lot. If you would have known how close your friend was at this moment, you would have not been in such a rush to leave.

I will never know who this friend was. Maybe Georg? Who of the Feldafing boys, "the circle of the six," had survived? It was one of the many secrets the diary left me with. But I did find the additional pass he had been issued in Pirna. It had a gray and burgundy stamp in its left corner, attesting to the fact that my father had paid one German mark for the service. It was called a certificate and looked more official than the pass issued at the hospital. An

English translation was included. Both the original pass and the transit certificate had one of Hans's thumbprints in lieu of a photograph:

> On the way back to the railroad station, a sinister looking figure stops you and tells you that you will be shot, unless you pass the border at a certain spot. Shy, you circumvent a Russian patrol, and after a long wait you see the train approaching. You borrow an old newspaper and look at it without much comprehension. It seemed to be like a piece of paper from the Middle Ages. Your route went over Dresden, Riese, Falkenberg, Wittenberg, and Rosslau until Biederitz, 2 kilometers from Magdeburg.

In Biederitz, my father's pass was stamped on July 16. Another fascinating stamp that decorated Hans's transit document was from the city of Salzwedel, which was to be his next destination. In its center there was still the *Reichsadler* (Imperial Eagle), the traditional symbol of German statehood, but the swastika on which the eagle had been perched had been carefully scraped off the stamp, leaving the bird floating aimlessly in midair.

> Every night, you were welcomed in a friendly manner by some strangers. You were told the fates of many people. The suffering they experienced was shared by all and had created a firm bond between them. There was no need for many words; everybody knew what it was all about. There was a poor young woman in Rosslau who had lost her small child and her husband. Daily she had to do heavy, shaming, and degrading work in the Russian barracks.

I assumed that it was my father's delicate way of describing that the hapless woman had to work at best as a washerwoman and cleaner or at worst as a prostitute, or both, presumably paid in food. But maybe she was fortunate, as most women were neither asked nor paid. In East Prussia, Pomerania, and Silesia alone at least 1.4

million women were raped. The historian Anthony Beever called it "The greatest phenomenon of mass rape in history."[1] Hans wrote:

> There were the families who got threatened and robbed on a regular basis at night by armed Polish gangs. And finally, there were the overripe grain fields, which no peasant wanted to cut. The traces of the fury of war accompanied the streams of miserable refugees of which you were one and where you saw incredible suffering.

Watching powerlessly as German civilians were mistreated without being able to do anything about it left an impression on my father that was to stay with him for the rest of his life. The disruption of the harvest was going to haunt the German population for the next two years. They were dependent on the mercy of the Allies for food deliveries.

At the Potsdam Conference in the summer of 1945, the Allies decided to keep the German standard of living as low as possible. The calories that were provided on the rationing cards were so low that those documents were colloquially called *Sterbekarte* ("the card to die on"). The winter of 1945–46 was hard for Germans in their destroyed cities, but the following hungry winter of 1946–47 was disastrous. The brutally cold temperatures claimed many more lives in an already weakened population, helped by an outbreak of typhoid.

It was an experience that would haunt my fourteen-year-old mother for the rest of her life. Her mother had sent her to the countryside to trade the last of

Photo of an anonymous peasant woman during the war years.

235

the family silver, which she had dug up from the garden, for potatoes. But the police were waiting at the train station to take the potatoes off her and accused her of criminal black-market activities. She recalled, "A girl who had accompanied me was so distressed that when they tried to take her precious pound of butter off her, she gulped it down. After that she could not stop throwing up in between sobs."

But in the summer of 1945, Hans was helped by the fact that he had been recuperating in hospitals long enough for it to have become warm and that he was traveling mainly through rural, agricultural areas where there was still more food than in the densely populated cities:

> Then, one morning, you climbed down the stairs of the small railroad station in Biederitz. In the middle of a dusty street through which some trickles of blackish waters ran, refugees were squatting. In a circle of 400 meters, everything was blocked by a half-moon made of a chain of Russian guards. Here nobody was allowed to cross the border over the River Elbe. You were standing there at a loss and looked around. Then a man with an ugly vulture's head waved you to his window and described to you a dangerous small path around the chain of guards where in a big circle you would reach the stream of the Elbe. That is, if you felt up to it . . .
>
> You sneaked out of the village from the back and hiked many kilometers to the south. Every time you tried to break through to the riverbanks, you were warned at the last moment of a Russian guard post. The Russians were not to be trifled with . . . Again, at a loss, you rested at the entrance of a village. There a playing boy came to you and brought you to his grandfather, who was very friendly and gave you some food. Upon inspecting your pass issued in the Russian zone, he claimed that you could safely attempt to cross at a checkpoint.

He dressed in his best suit and walked with you through the kilometer-wide river meadows from which one could see the silhouette of the city of Magdeburg, the desired destination. With his walking stick he gave a long-winded explanation of the topography of the landscape. Suddenly you reached the towering Russian guard hut from where you were already observed with suspicion.

The gentlemen were just having their meal. One of them could read a little and with some humphing read out the letters to his comrades, who approvingly nodded their heads and let you pass. Beaming with joy, the friendly grandfather said goodbye and wished you the best for your trip. Soon you found yourself alone in endless flat meadows only interrupted by a few patches of high reeds and bushes. Suddenly a bullet shot by your side. In the next minutes, a few more were to come. It was a "friendly" souvenir from the Russian guards sitting in the bushes, incredibly bored. Some of them you asked for the way; some of them asked you for your papers.

It was getting unbearably hot, and you continued to hobble along bare-chested. Suddenly, you felt like Little Red Riding Hood as you came to a big meadow where lots of Russians were making hay. When they saw you, they pretended to be Germans and asked you where you came from and where you were going. You treated them as though they were Germans and asked them to pass over their coffee pot from which you drank a considerable quantity of the precious liquid. You knew in advance that they would point you in the wrong direction and in high spirits you followed your own route. Then at a distance of 300 meters you saw the stream of the River Elbe. All you had to do was to walk along its shore to reach the city bridge and be safe. Suddenly another brown guard came from behind a tree, who startled but did not stop you.

Totally exhausted, you found yourself in the midst of the bleak ruins of Magdeburg, a provisional resting place for the night in the company of a very miserable refugee woman. But secretly you were elated: the first step toward freedom had been taken. The following days saw you traveling on car bumpers and car roofs in a northwestern direction. You already felt close to the yearned-for destination, when shortly before the city of Salzwedel, you stopped in this small village from which it was only another three hours to reach home. The challenge now was to cross the desolate meadows and wetlands to get over the border of this province.

Absorbed in thoughts, imagining the potential reunions at home, you walked along the long road toward the first border village, when an astonished railroad worker asked you if you intended to continue on this road. "If you go to the village in front of you, you will be arrested immediately. The Russians allow nobody near the English–Russian border." You were stunned when you heard those words. The fantasy world of the family reunion sank into a bottomless abyss. Only 8 kilometers away from the border, yet it seemed to be an unbridgeable distance. Would it all have been for nothing, all the struggle, all the sticking it out during the flight, only to end here at the border?

Slowly you returned to the railroad station and asked a peasant for work.

The days of harvesting were strenuous, and your still festering wound affected you a lot. But you went out to the field and thought day and night about how to cross the border. Carefully you kept away from the Russian border guards, knowing that the success of your venture was dependent on split-second timing. Finally, you convinced the milkman in a border village to take you with him on his rounds.

Right in front of the village commander, dressed in a workman's jacket, you climbed onto the wagon and made it through the barrier at the border village, which was opened by a sleepy guard. You made an effort to guide the horses as closely as possible next to the little milk sheds, so that the old cart driver could unload the milk cans. With curiosity, the soldiers of the border guard, who had installed themselves in the community house of the circular village, watched you. You enjoyed wonderful milk porridge with the family of the farmer, so you could return right away to harvesting the field. Then it happened that three-armed sons of the east invited you to come with them. Now everything was over.

At the Russian Army command headquarters you had the honor to stand in front of a commissioner who interrogated you as an alleged English spy. It did not take long, and you saw your well-filled wallet disappear into the brown uniform of a Russian after he had not neglected to write your name and the date in a big book. You had to wait in a corner, and a rusty knife was made available to you with few leaves of Machorka tobacco, which you chopped up for your personal use.

Together with one other man who had been picked up, another episode of suffering started, accompanied by an honorary guard. I was without my walking stick. My bandage was torn open. From village to village, more prisoners joined us, although they had come from the other side, making themselves suspicious by crossing from the English zone into the Russian zone.

Hans's pass had a Russian signature at the top right-hand side of his discharge document. It was dated July 19, 1945. It must have been the date he went into Russian captivity. His fellow prisoners, in their naivety, had not understood that the Cold War had started and that voluntarily returning to what was now the Russian zone had made them instantly suspicious to its new occupation force:

The travelers from the British zone all had astonished faces. This is not how they had envisioned their homecoming reception. How many times during the long nights in the field hospital had you imagined how you would walk through this little town, just the same way as when you had said goodbye, proudly in uniform. Now you had to walk through the streets in the middle of Germany in a group of preposterously miserable, suspicious characters, who were anxiously watched by German faces full of pity behind windows and doors. So, this was the return from war!

Nobody took special notice of you when you stood in front of the Russian commander of Salzwedel underneath the gold and glass framed picture of Stalin. The memory of sleeping on the cement floor of the cellar of the former air-raid shelter became one of your most vivid memories of the entire ordeal. On the stairs to the upper world, a guard had made himself comfortable. The night in the tight space was insufferable. You were lying on some large sheets of wrapping paper and had your head on your little bag.

It was morning. The rushed and busy legs of women, children, and men clattered by on the pavement in front of the small barred window. Did the German people know that among them Germans were incarcerated and had to suffer? Did they know that worms and maggots can chew up one's body? A Russian with a bald, shaved head drove us out into the street, where a reinforced guard unit waited for us. We were given one can of Wehrmacht beans for two men: our food allocation. Despite the guards, the inhabitants of the house handed water, coffee, and bread down to us. Now our pitiful bunch was dragged through the town. Apples and cookies were thrown out of the windows toward us from both sides of the street. We felt pathetic.

The march in the heat lasted for hours. You moved almost at a crawl behind the group with the white flag of your opened bandage flattering behind you. The young, busily gesticulating Russian behind you who talked so loudly of "Stalin" and "America kaput" did not let you stop to bend down and fix it.

Finally, in the late afternoon, after great detours and indecision, the relieved guards stuffed us behind a great barn door where many others with the same destiny were already waiting. The villagers had to drag buckets of over-boiled potatoes to us, which was our food. An inconsolable woman with her child had accompanied our procession. Soon one heard her screaming and crying in front of the main building of the farm. On the other side Poles and Yugoslavs were enjoying the sun. They were allowed to move freely, drink jugs of milk, and play cards in their separate quarters. There was one outhouse for two hundred Germans. Soon one had pains; if one wanted to use it at midday, one had to get in line in the morning.

You spent four days there in the expectation of a dubious fate. But suddenly the doors opened. All who wanted to stay and live in Saxony, now a province under Russian administration, were allowed to leave and go wherever they wanted to. But this was without any papers, so one stood the risk of being captured again by any Russian who felt like corralling a few *Germanskis.*

This anecdote of how my father had been able to get away from his Russian captors had been one of the few stories we were told as children. He had explained that only a few men had declared that they would settle in East Germany. He was among them, calculating the risks of either decision. He had been right. The risk of being shipped off as a prisoner to Siberia as a West German was a potential death sentence. But Hans was determined to stay alive:

But you had become more careful. On the old farm they did not want you anymore, so you looked for other work and carefully hid from the Russian soldiers. The hot time of binding the grain bushels, carrying them into the barn, and preparing them for threshing took its toll on you. You were admitted to the Salzwedel hospital. After being discharged at the earliest possible moment, you heard some whispering at the train station. "Take the short train to Duderstadt, then go by foot to the village that is 500 meters from the border. There Mr. X has already been informed." You decided to bet everything on one card. You were tired of the eternal insecurity: either succeed or fail.

From all your luggage, only the *Faust* remained. A spoon, a fork, a knife, and a bread crust went into your pants pockets. That is how you climbed aboard the train dressed in a sweater and brown trousers, hands mostly in your trouser pockets. What would the next hours bring?

From the beginning, Hans taking along a copy of Goethe's play *Faust* had captured my imagination. I recalled the medieval story that predated Goethe of man's quest for superiority. For the ultimate human experience, the highly learned Dr. Faust is willing to sell his soul to Mephisto, the devil in disguise, who promises to fulfill all of Faust's grand fantasies. It is a bargain that ends in deep disillusionment.

In Goethe's version, the innocent girl Gretchen, who is only a pawn in Faust's ultimate quest, features prominently. She is seduced into believing that she will find happiness if she succumbs to him. She pays the price for being so gullible by going insane and being hanged for having killed her own child.

At first it had seemed like an odd item to take on a journey where, in another time, Hans might have taken a Bible along. Of all the books available to him, why *Faust*? Had it become his Bible? Had he hoped to find answers in the ancient tale of how man could overcome his entanglement with evil? Was it the last sentence of the play that had given him hope? "He who strives on and lives to strive, can earn redemption still."

I had not realized that the little book had survived until I cleared out my mother's nightstand after her death in January 2020. While my father had saved all his papers, my mother's style of housekeeping was to throw everything away. So, I was astonished that she had kept it. It must have reminded her of their happier, early marriage years, when they had shared their childhood war stories and found warmth and compassion in each other's company.

Touching it was emotional. Measuring only inches, it was printed in tiny letters on very thin paper. The 1868 edition had belonged to Hans's grandmother, the Consul's wife, when she had been young. In faded ink letters, her name was written on the first page. It was held together with dirty pink medical tape, as my father had torn out some of the less important pages and traded them for cigarette paper.

At the destination's train station there were Russians, but they left you alone. Hurriedly you walked in the late afternoon sun toward the border, asking for information on the way, prepared for new, unpleasant surprises. Finally, at the village entrance you ducked straight into the first farmhouse. Only a Russian on a horse at the watering hole had seen you. The dog yapped, the farmer threw up his hands in horror and said, "You'll be lucky if you are not picked up in the next ten minutes. Yesterday the secret path was discovered and as of now two hundred border crossers have been arrested. There, you can still see the last group in the distance. They catch everybody in the border area. Out of the question! You cannot pass here. Who has already seen you?" You told your story and waited. Nobody came; it appeared that the Russian had said nothing. Discouraged, you stood there and were ready to give up everything. Back to the hospital?

That night you hid in the straw and the next morning, with a bar over one shoulder to look like a workman, you left the village from the back. You sneaked through the forests and shrubs; you crawled through the farmed fields and listened and observed. You asked the peasants in the fields some questions and you circumvented the neighboring village by some distance, where the regional Russian commissary was wreaking havoc. You got close from the other side, saw a nearing hay cart, took the reins from the farmer, put on his straw hat, and asked him for assistance.

He took you into the village and wanted to help you. Passing the Russian guard, you made it to the farm where you would be safe and went into hiding. The farmer tied a rope twice around the mouth of a cow and gave you the other end to hold. Then the two of you went onto the meadow and looked at the bushy, marshy borderline at a distance of 2 kilometers.

It must have been 11:00 PM when the patrol was over. The loyal farmer put out the lights; his wife gave you a substantial sandwich, a big hug, and wished you all the best. You were alone with the softly blowing wind, with the twinkling stars and the brown field. So very alone, walking toward what appeared to be a threatening black belt, in which hidden guard posts were on the lookout. It was a strange feeling when you crawled around the corner guardhouse out onto the open field.

There were the upright stacked oat sheaves, where two comrades, sharing your fate, were supposed to be hiding. You called in a low voice and touched the stacks: nothing was stirring. So, you continued walking and constantly looked around to see how your silhouette would contrast against the horizon. A flashing glimmer of light flitted over to you; over there was the English zone, with the promise of freedom and home. The closer you got to the rustling willows, reeds, hogweeds, and abandoned meadows, the more you crouched down. On your right, shots rang out. Then it was quiet. A hoarse, howling bark sounded in the bushes in front of you. In your mind you saw a Russian with a tracker dog lying in the grass. You imagined images of you getting lost and, in the morning, turning up in Russian territory again. Slowly it was becoming eerie. You reached the borderline of the shrubs and tried to continue straight, when you fell with a loud crash like a boar breaking through the underbrush, into a gurgling bog hole.

Startled, you stayed stuck in it and listened. Nothing stirred except that there was another howling. It later became clear that it had been a fox. Other people who, like you, had crawled over the border on their stomachs had been startled by him as well. In desperation you simply walked along the edge of the shrub line and looked for a spot to go through. Those were the most dangerous moments. You climbed over a fence and found yourself in the almost impassable wilderness of an overgrown marsh. There was a little black-looking stream. You took off your shoes and very quietly waded through it. Air bubbles came up from under your heels. Deeper and deeper the path went into this tangled wilderness. Then finally a fence again, a marshy meadow, and a road with a sign that said in English, "Road and Shoulders Clear of Mines."

You had been saved. On English territory, free and unharmed. A deep feeling of happiness and thankfulness streamed through you. You walked a little farther along, staggering in happiness, and lay down between the potato plants and stared at the bright blue, shining sky, where thousands of gleaming stars were still visible. You ate your well-deserved sandwich and knew tomorrow or the day after you would be back with your loved ones.

My father's long way back home from the war had almost ended, but his even more difficult path of what Germans call *Vergangenheitsbewältigung* (coming to terms with one's past) had just begun.

THE BACK-TO-FRONT FILE

What happened after the diary ended? A faded cardboard folder held some of the answers. In my father's distinct handwriting, large letters across the front instructed the reader, "Read from back to front." Inside were letters written on thin airline parchment paper and telegrams with cut-out sentences. All were neatly hole punched and filed on top of the other.

After making it home to Bremen in the summer of 1945, Hans spent time with Auntie Tali while his leg was still healing. He was now eighteen and eager to finish high school. But most importantly he longed to see his family in South America, whom he had last seen in 1937. Correspondence was difficult, as the city of Bremen was in the British Sector and international mail was strictly censored, routed via London, and took forever to arrive. Somehow, the family knew a lady in the Swiss town of Prangins on Lake Geneva by the name of E. Forel Steinheil. Many of the letters in the folder were addressed to her, and she responded.

Who was she? I will never know. Judging by the correspondence that went back and forth, the woman was a saint. She did her utmost to help Heinz and Hilde in Brazil to establish whether their son Hans and the rest of the family had survived the war in Germany. Hilde and Heinz found out late in 1945 that their boy was still alive.

When Hans received the first letter written to him by his father in years, in early 1946, he immediately surrendered himself to a camp for displaced persons. It was called Kevelaer in the British Zone, close to the Dutch border in West Germany. Two million people from fifty-eight countries passed through this camp. The camp was disbanded in November 1946.

The care for displaced persons (DPs) in Germany fell under the responsibility of the United Nations Relief and Rehabilitation Administration (UNRRA). The agency struggled to perform the urgent job adequately. Transit camps were necessary to establish barriers so that every western-bound DP passed through a system of medical and security checks before being repatriated. The military framework was there—as were the transport, food stocks, and anti-louse powder—but the UNRRA teams were not in place, and staffing for setting up and controlling those camps was inadequate.

I have no account from my father's time in the DP camp. Through reading a number of other published reports, I gather it must have been another unpleasant experience, but nothing that could shock him after what he had already been through.

On the surface, the work of registration, delousing, and feeding the DPs was the same as those for refugees. Old photographs show that the DPs of Kevelear seemed to have been housed in tents. But while the refugees were mainly frightened and dispirited families that were typically easy to handle, the DPs consisted of newly liberated, often young, men who wanted to secure whatever spoils they could and avenge themselves on the German population. There were many nationalities. The work was complicated by the necessity of keeping nationalities who had fought each other apart and segregating eastbound from westbound people.

The military agencies did their best to keep those people from looting and roaming the German countryside, but it was hard to get a grip on the prevailing lawlessness. It did not help that some camps were located on former prisoner-of-war compounds or concentration camps, such as Dachau. Most were overcrowded, with only the bare essentials of life, and the DPs resented having to live in camps similar to those they had been placed in by the Germans.

My father had gone to the DP camp to start the process of repatriation. He was a Chilean citizen and, therefore, entitled to return to Chile, as long as relatives there would vouch for him and he could secure passage. But whatever he had been paid by the German army, he had lost during his short Russian captivity; the half marks per day he was owed for working the Flak never materialized, and Auntie Tali and the grandparents had nothing left, with their house bombed to the ground. The old Consul, prior to his death from being unable to secure insulin for his diabetes, had invested the fortune he had made in colonial Burma in stocks and bonds that had become worthless.

It fell on Hans's father, Heinz, to come up with the money, but he had problems of his own. The regulations said that Hans could be repatriated to his native Chile, but his parents were, by now, living in Brazil. Once he was in Chile, the plan was that he would have to make his own way to Brazil. But even getting to Chile proved impossible.

Today, it is almost forgotten that the Brazilian government had followed the example of the United States during the war by interning many of its citizens of Japanese and German descent. My grandfather, Heinz, had been kept a prisoner on the Ilha das Flores (Flores Island) in the Bay of Guanabara just outside Rio de Janeiro, where he contracted tuberculosis. After his release, he was ill, broke, and his marriage to Hilde was failing under the strain. Nevertheless, she stood by him and nursed him back to health.

Besides the letters to and from Switzerland, the back-to-front file contained a whole correspondence between Brazil and Chile. Heinz beseeched his brother-in-law, Uncle Fritz Marquardt, in Chile, to help him get his son back to South America. Heinz scraped money together, sending it in installments for Uncle Fritz to buy a ticket. After five unanswered letters and two desperate telegrams from Heinz, Uncle Fritz finally answered that he could no longer help, as the program for the repatriation of displaced persons had been changed in the meantime.

Hans had waited and waited and waited in Kevelear for his ticket to come. With his father not able to come through for him, Hans gave up and decided to complete his education in Germany on his own. At the end of the war, Feldafing School was closed. The Allies had realized that it was no ordinary school and barred the former students from higher education until 1949. Had they stayed in school, they would have had their *Abitur* already. Some schools had handed out emergency diplomas, recognizing the boys' military service as school time. But these were usually not recognized after the war.

The Feldafing boys had a different problem. They needed to graduate from a regular school to circumvent the schooling ban, imposed on them by the Allies, to get what was called a clean *Abitur*. Now their strong camaraderie and solid survival skills came in handy. An informal network sprung up. "Tiddy" Schrimpf, a former classmate of Hans's, told him that his local high school in the town of Mülheim in the industrial Ruhr area was willing to take pupils, no questions asked. The school director was sympathetic to the boy soldiers who had returned from the war and willing to help them to find their way back into civilian life.

It was the first time that Hans had come to the Ruhr area, living in the household of his friend Tiddy. He made lifelong friends with a classmate, Ludwig, a local boy also born in 1927. Ludwig, the son of the schoolteacher, Fritz, and his wife, Hildegard, gave Hans a first experience of how an average German family lived: two parents, four children, and an assortment of pets.

At a high-school dance at Ludwig's house, Hans finally got to do some of the things associated with teenage life. He had a crush on Marlene, Ludwig's eighteen-year-old sister. Their younger sister, Erika, was only fourteen years old and not allowed to join in, but she had certainly noticed Hans.

During his school days in Mülheim, Hans asked to be confirmed in the Protestant Lutheran Church, something that had been impossible under the Nazis. For the rest of his life, church was important for him, and he served for years as a Presbyterian alderman in Rheinbach, the town where I grew up. It struck me how important religion had been for those who returned. I remembered the newspaper clipping from the 1950s that reported Martin Bormann's son had been ordained as a Catholic priest.

Hans felt close to Ludwig's family. Political subjects and the war were taboo topics for Ludwig's father Fritz, the biology teacher, whose main interest in life was to maintain his flowering garden and hives of honeybees. Sticking to safe subjects had kept them out of trouble in turbulent times. The defense mechanism against wallowing in painful memories also had a practical reason: to keep difficult secrets buried. In 1941, Fritz's father, Hermann, who had always been an outspoken, self-declared pacifist, had not returned from his usual evening walk by the River Ruhr. His body was found weeks later floating in the river. Deemed an accident, the family had always stated that he had slipped on the path and fallen into the river. They were even willing to contemplate suicide. But the sinister explanation that as a pacifist the Gestapo might have targeted him was never contemplated.

In addition, when Fritz had heard of the end of the war, he had spontaneously given the order to sink the ammunition supply of the whole convoy he had been in charge of into a lake in the Black Forest. Technically, he could have been court-martialed even after the war.

Hans finished his *Abitur* in a year and said goodbye to his new Mülheim friends. He wrote to his father again and asked he if could come stay with the family in Brazil. Again, he was disappointed. Instead, in 1947, he enrolled at the University of Göttingen. It required some perseverance on his side to get registered.

The lady I had known as a child as Aunt Ellie, who occasionally came to visit us, was in fact not a blood relative but had been Hans's landlady in Göttingen. To be admitted to the university, he had to prove that he had found accommodation, which was not easy in a bombed-out city. He walked the streets and asked every passerby, "Excuse me, would you by any chance know anybody willing to rent a room to a student?"

People declined warily; they had heard countless such pleas. Twelve-and-a-half million East German refugees were looking for places to stay in West Germany, competing for scarce, still-intact housing.

By the time he asked a small, dark-haired woman with a tidy chignon and a kindly, intelligent gaze, he was ready to give up. She took a long look at him. He must have reminded her of her own son who had been about the same age as Hans before he went missing in the Battle of Stalingrad. She explained, "I only have my son's bedroom, which I am not renting out since I am saving it for him. But I will let you stay in it, because if my boy is still alive, I pray that somebody will help him as well."

Her kindness and her unwavering belief that her son was alive were rewarded. Her only child, Tillman, came home in 1956 in the last batch of German prisoners. Their release from the Soviet Union was negotiated by the Federal Republic of Germany. In 1942, Ellie had sent a boy into war and in 1956, she got back a man, who, after years of Siberian hardships, felt like a stranger in the new Germany. But he was alive and that was all that mattered to his grateful mother.

In the postwar years when my father had been her substitute son, Aunt Ellie and Hans became lifelong friends. Being a war widow with limited means, she had taken a job as an assistant for a renowned history professor at the same university where my father was studying. She transcribed his handwritten manuscripts and typed up his PhD. When she came to visit us, she looked over my history schoolwork with a grandmotherly kindness and lauded my efforts. I think that was when I decided that I would go to university and study history myself.

In 1949, after two years of studying, Hans, now twenty-one years old, had finally earned enough money in his student jobs to secure a passage to Rio de Janeiro to be reunited with his family after more than twelve years. In his letters, his father had convinced him that the old world was dead and that the new one was waiting for anybody who was willing to try his luck. Hans was ecstatic. Finally, he met his brother, Helmut, whom he had only known as a toddler.

But things did not go well. Hans found no answers as to why the family had abandoned him in Germany. Their assurances that they had no choice, with the war, did not convince him. Father and son were living in different worlds. Heinz was eternally looking for the next business opportunity and told his son to go into commerce. Having studied literature, philosophy, and history in school and university, that was of no interest to Hans. But he needed to earn a living. Since he had experience with 8mm films, having filmed shot-down planes as a Flak helper, he took a job with a newsreel company that produced weekly films to be shown in Brazilian movie theaters. Before long, he was going to the Amazon to film documentaries of indigenous peoples. But what he really longed to do was continue his university education.

Before coming to Rio, Hans had become engaged to a German girl by the name of Ingeborg, enamored by her intelligence and blond beauty. She was from a family of Latvian country gentry who had come to Germany as refugees. As soon as he had saved enough, he sent her the money for a ship's passage. Upon her arrival, she confessed to having had a fling with his friend Tiddy. It broke his heart, and that was the last straw. He gave her the money to return to Germany. Panicked and on the rebound, he decided to leave

Brazil himself.

Together with a friend he had met in Brazil, Dierk van Eyken, who later was to become my godfather, Hans followed an appeal by the Canadian government for qualified immigrants. By now he was twenty-four years old. With the rest of his savings, he arrived in Montreal and registered at McGill University. In order to earn money, he started working in a factory assembling refrigerators. Lacking warm clothing, the cold winter found him ill prepared. He lost his strength and contracted tuberculosis. From an entry in the front of my father's small *Faust* book that he still carried around with him, I had learned that in 1952 he was quarantined in the Laurentian Sanatorium in Sainte-Agathe-des-Monts in the province of Quebec. But as he was not a naturalized citizen, the Canadian government ordered his deportation and gave him the choice to return to Brazil or to Germany. He asked his father if he could come back to the family. In a letter that Hans saved for the rest of his life, Heinz informed him matter-of-factly, "My dear son! Your mother and I are getting a divorce; she is now living with your brother Helmut. The house has been sold, and I am planning to remarry. If you choose to come to Brazil, I can make a reservation at a bed and breakfast for you."

Bitterly disappointed, Hans returned to Bremen, where Auntie Tali once more received him with open arms. But her affection could not heal him from a state of bottomless depression. Tuberculosis, still known then as consumption, was treated by giving the patient lots of food so they would put on weight and not be "consumed" by the disease. No longer the muscular, blond, blue-eyed, handsome youth, Hans had become fat. A photo taken at the time shows him clutching a kitten, prematurely balding, and looking overweight and bloated.

In the meantime, in Mülheim, Erika (Ludwig's younger sister) was now grown-up and struggling to put the war—and the two severe and hungry winters that followed—behind her. Her elementary school years were marked by constantly hiding when the air-raid alarms were sounded. Mülheim, as part of the heavily industrialized Ruhr area, endured 153 bomber attacks. In the end, her mother, Hildegard, grew so tired of herding her children into the basement that she put their beds into the coal cellar. At age nine, Erika had been evacuated to Pardubice in Czechoslovakia as part of the dreaded Nazi program *Kinderlandverschickung* (KLV)—officially to protect them from bombings, but more importantly, to separate

Hans, around 1953, prematurely balding and overweight, holds Erika's kitten. After falling out with his father in Brazil and battling tuberculosis in a Canadian sanatorium, he suffered a nervous breakdown.

children from parents who were losing their confidence in the almighty regime. With their children kept like hostages in the care of the Hitler Youth, parents' compliance was all but ensured.

Erika had been so distressed in Pardubice, where she had been kept in a former sanatorium, that her father had negotiated a farm stay in the village of Zechin that belonged to distant relatives as an acceptable alternative. Unfortunately, it was located only 8 miles from Seelow Heights near Berlin where the last bloody battle took place, claiming about thirty thousand lives in April 1945. Her seventeen-year-old brother, Ludwig, almost lost his own life for leaving his unit to rescue twelve-year-old Erika just in time before the fighting started. In civilian clothes, claiming that he and his sister were refugees, they were allowed to travel in an empty ammunition train under a tarp in freezing temperatures. Passing through the town of Küstrin, they witnessed its destruction by relentless bombing. Not a single house survived. The town was never rebuilt, as the last German inhabitants were expelled after the war when it became a Polish town.

Erika never acquired a high school diploma. This was going to cause her problems later in life, as all three of her siblings had gone to university and her husband earned a PhD. An infamous aunt, the resolute midwife Hannah, had lured her to the town of Münster where a position as a housekeeper awaited her. Erika ran away. Her father was furious and sided with his sister Hannah.

After that she was sent to a farm in the lower Rhine area to learn home economics. She was now eighteen years old. She recalled later in life how she had worked like a maid, making twenty lard pancakes every morning for the breakfast of the famished farm hands. One of them sexually assaulted her and she ran away again.

Her parents, unwilling to acknowledge what had happened to her and embarrassed for having such a troubled young woman on their hands, enrolled her in a program to train as a nursery teacher close to home. The following year, Hans reconnected with Ludwig and came to visit Mülheim again. His former crush, Marlene,

Erika (11), Dierk (5), and Ludwig (16) in the summer of 1944. The following winter, Ludwig would rescue Erika from the advancing Russian Army. Their clothes are homemade from tablecloths. Ludwig had an admin job in the Wehrmacht; *as he wore glasses, the SS did not draft him.*

was engaged to a fellow university student, so Hans started to go on walks with Erika instead. Before long, he popped the question, "Will you marry me?"

On December 23, 1954, on a windy, cold day, two emotionally scarred war children embarked on a path of married adulthood, struggling for normalcy with a strong craving for stability. They had the desire to give their own children what they never had themselves: a carefree, secure childhood. But it was not that easy.

Their small, white, semidetached, 1960s house was built in a country that had to rebuild itself from the ground up. The modest structure had a fenced-in back yard, with my mother's vegetable and flower beds and the luxury of a one-car garage. It was important to both of my parents that the solid brick walls would keep us children safe from a world they had perceived as hostile. Outwardly, the house, in a good neighborhood, provided us with a respectable place amongst the middle class of the small town of Rheinbach. But the walls that were meant to protect were imprisoning us three children, as our parents' unresolved childhood traumas resurfaced in times of peace. The screaming matches of their unhappy marriage resonated off the paper-hung walls.

In later years, I never much enjoyed going back for visits. But when my widowed mother sold the house fifty years later, I cried at the last walk through.

THE GLASS CABINET

My father chose a career in the foreign service. In old age, he had told us about his motivation: "I tried to do my share to repair Germany's tarnished image in the world." His career started in the 1950s, and his first overseas assignment as a young attaché was to the Embassy of the Federal Republic of Germany in Rio de Janeiro, Brazil. He saw his parents again, this time with a family of his own. His next assignment as Chargé D'affaires to the Embassy in Monrovia, Liberia, was a hardship post. All of us contracted malaria, but the extra money he earned was enough for the down payment on a small house back in Germany. Later assignments, interspersed with stays in Bonn, brought him to London as First Secretary, to New York as Consul General, to Luanda in Angola as Ambassador, and finally back to Rio. The Embassy had moved to the new capital Brasilia, and as Consul General he inhabited the former Ambassador's residence overlooking Sugarloaf Mountain.

After my father's retirement from the German Foreign Office in 1992, my parents moved back to the small town of Rheinbach just outside Bonn, by now the former capital. Berlin, having risen from being a Cold War backwater, had once again taken over that role and slowly but surely was rebuilding its center, still devasted by a war fifty years ago and the communist sloth that followed. But

Rheinbach was where my parents had raised their kids, owned a house, and knew the neighbors.

The borrowed glamour of the diplomatic life was gone; it became quiet. My mother took to singing in the church choir and joined a group of birders. My father bought a bicycle, spending days and sometimes weeks biking to near and far destinations. At age seventy-five, he was part of a crew that crossed the Atlantic on a sailing boat.

When he was at home, he would lead anybody who came to visit to a tall cabinet with glass panels that occupied a central position in the entrance hall with the joy of a small boy. It contained all his medals that he had collected during his long diplomatic career. Among them was the large medal from Argentina that he had once worn to the royal court in England. There was also the Order of Rio Branco, the highest medal bestowed by the Federal Government of Brazil. The city of Rio de Janeiro had given him a document declaring him an honorary citizen. He had been very happy as Consul General in Rio, where he helped to plan the important and groundbreaking environmental conference Eco-92. A medal from Senegal was a souvenir from the days when he had acted as a liaison to the embassies of the sub-Saharan countries while serving in Bonn. But the most important medal had a red cross with a black eagle in the center, the *Bundesverdienstkreuz* (the Order of Merit of the Federal Republic of Germany). It was the proof that his efforts had been recognized in his own country as well. Those items bore

Hans being awarded the highest order of Brazil, Rio Branco, Brazil, 1989.

witness to what had been important to him when he had joined the diplomatic service.

On the lower shelves were various mementos from completed bicycle rallies. They showed that the old Feldafing spirit of staying fit had stayed with him. He had completed his last bicycle tour from Berlin to Copenhagen two days before he had been taken to the hospital, where he was diagnosed with the cancer that would kill him within two months.

Two objects were very different from the rest. A menorah and a yarmulke were displayed conspicuously at the center of the cabinet. The small candelabra was technically a hanukkiah and had an engraved plaque at its base from the *Amigos da Comunidade Judaica do Rio de Janeiro* (Friends of the Jewish Community of Rio de Janeiro).

Shortly after he arrived in Rio de Janeiro as the new Consul General for the Federal Republic of Germany, a media campaign was launched against him, labeling him a Nazi. An American journalist had started it with an article written for *O Globo*, the largest Brazilian newspaper. Rumor had it that the publication coincided with Brazil trying to decide whether to buy airplanes from an American or a German company. But that was beside the point. Fifty years after the end of the war, my father had to face his youth again.

Ironically, the claim of being a Nazi was not based on him having attended a top Nazi school or his military service. The questionnaires the Americans had made the boys fill out right after the war had a long list of questions, but Franz told me that none had asked about attending an elite NS school. The Allies had not known enough about the educational system to ask detailed questions, and the Germans had not been eager to enlighten them. The problem for my father was that NSDAP membership lists, under lock and key in American archives for forty years, had been released. They included my father's name and the thousands of other names of schoolchildren who were underage at the time. In 1944, as a special gift for Hitler's fifty-fifth birthday, collective lists had been issued to the schools for the pupils to sign up for party membership. My father had told me:

> Our teacher handed out membership cards. We were told to sign them. Nobody would have objected. It was our duty to make the Führer happy, who had done so much for us. Legally this was more than questionable. We were pressured into joining a party for which we could not vote for another five years, as twenty-one was the age of majority. Our parents and guardians were not asked for their consent.

Hans was not the only target. In 2007, several prominent German personalities, such as the writers Martin Walser and Siegfried Lenz, were attacked by the German media. It turned out that not all of those party membership cards had even been signed by the children themselves. But the damage was done. As a consequence, there was a renewed interest in which German boys had fought in SS units and which ones had merely served in the Flak. The writer Günter Grass and Pope Benedict XVI, the former German Cardinal Joseph Ratzinger, who, like my father, had been born in 1927, were confronted with a media storm. Luckily, my father did not have to relive the past once more; he had already died.

When the campaign against him started in Rio de Janeiro, I was there for a short vacation from New York, where I was living. My father was on a business trip, and I went to the consulate to pick up some mail. I saw several posters and banners displayed just across the building on a traffic island, stating that the German Consul General was a Nazi. I felt deeply ashamed. I went into the consulate asking why nobody had taken down those posters. One of my father's subordinates smiled with schadenfreude—malicious joy—the kind of gloating that seems unique to Germans, directed at his absent boss. He said, "After all, Brazil is a free country, and everybody can voice their opinion."

In rage, I went outside and tore down the posters. I was not there for the events that followed, but I remember that my father went to his friend Hans Stern, the famous German Jewish jeweler. Stern had fled Germany and had lived in Brazil since the 1940s. Subsequently, he built an empire, trading Brazilian colored gemstones. He suggested seeking the help of the Rio Jewish community. Gerhard Katz de Castro, another friend and longtime German Jewish immigrant in Brazil, vouched for him. Soon the fuss died down.

In December 2012, I phoned Gerhard Katz de Castro after my cousin in Rio de Janeiro got a hold of his phone number for me. He was in his early nineties but delighted to talk to me. I asked him, "What made you support my father when he was accused of being a Nazi?"

He explained, "I got in touch with the B'nai B'rith, the clandestine international Jewish organization. The feedback was positive. The intelligence unit of the B'nai B'rith also reported that during his time as consul general in New York, he supported the German Jewish dialogue whenever he could."

I asked him, "Can I quote you?"

"Yes, by all means. I found your father to be a fine man," he replied.

"Are you not concerned that my father was involved with the Nazis as a juvenile?" I asked.

He responded, "It does not matter anymore. My family had to convert to Protestantism to avoid prosecution, and I was in the Hitler Youth myself. Times were difficult for everybody, and what matters is what your father did with his life since."

It was a great relief to hear him say that. But more importantly, I was impressed with his honesty of admitting to the moral compromises made by his own family just to stay alive.

My father had also approached Rabbi Grätz and pleaded his case. He was the rabbi who had given him the yarmulke. It took me longer to track him down. By 2012, he was at a synagogue in California. When I finally reached him by phone, he recounted, "Under my tutelage, your parents discovered Jewish culture. They came to the temple on Shabbat."

It had touched my father deeply that the Jewish community had included him and my mother. The victims were willing to reach out to him and had treated him in the finest Yiddish tradition of being a mensch, a human being of integrity. After my father's retirement, my parents took several trips to Israel, organized by the Lutheran church in Rheinbach. Finally, they had the time and opportunity to explore a religion and a culture that they had learned to hate before they had known anything about it.

When I dismantled the glass cabinet and its contents after his death, I realized that it did not contain any memento of what my father had considered his single most important accomplishment in his career. I was going to find it ten years later in Namibia when I visited the Independence Memorial Museum in Windhoek.

The impressive oversize tube-shaped structure of the Namibian museum was visible from afar, overpowering the surrounding brick buildings built in colonial times. In front of the national museum, an equally oversize sculpture of Sam Nujoma, Namibia's first president after independence, had replaced the *Reiterdenkmal* (the Equestrian Monument), a statue that symbolized Germany's short but brutal colonial reign that ended in 1918. After the Second World War, the country once called Southwest Africa had become a South African protectorate.

The third-floor exhibits focused on the history of the South West Africa People's Organization (SWAPO) and UN Security Council Resolution 435, which had given Namibia its independence in 1991. And there it was! A large, black-and-white photo mounted on the wall of German Foreign Minister Hans-Dietrich Genscher, accompanying the soon-to-be first Namibian President, Sam Nujoma, to the UN. Germany had been the first

Western country to officially recognize Namibian independence, paving the road to the UN resolution.

Speaking fluent Portuguese from his days in Brazil, Hans had been posted as the first German Ambassador in neighboring Angola after its independence. It was at a time when the country had been in a deadly civil war after the Portuguese colonial forces left. Angola had become another Cold War casualty as outside powers were fueling tribal conflicts to get their grip on the country's substantial natural resources. Amid this turmoil, German farmers—who had come to the country as Second World War refugees and had settled to rebuild their already once shattered lives—were brutally murdered.

When I came to visit my parents in Luanda, Angola, at an event for the German expat community in 1981, an older, tall German man attracted my attention. He was handsome with dark, graying hair and massive hands, maybe in his late fifties, looking sad. I asked my mother who he was. She replied:

> I was told that his family lost everything at the end of the Second World War in Eastern Pomerania when the Russians came. The family came here to start a new life and built up a flourishing avocado farm in the interior of the country. When the revolution happened, the soldiers of the MPLA [the Popular Movement for the Liberation of Angola] came to his farm and massacred his wife and children in front of him. Only he managed to escape.

What my father saw in Angola must have brought back memories of his flight through the Russian zone in 1945, where he had witnessed such terrible hardships put on the local population. He had been unable to help the Sudetendeutschen, nor the Angola Germans, but there was still hope for the large settlements of Germans in Namibia.

By assisting the SWAPO, Namibia's independence party that was in exile in Angola, it was possible for him to help negotiate a peaceful transition in the country, acting on behalf of Genscher's Foreign Office.[1] Although, later, some farm killings happened in Namibia, a practice that had spilled over from South Africa, the transition from South African protectorate to self-governed country happened peacefully. It was a win-win situation for everybody. Bloodshed was avoided, and the food supply chain had not collapsed as in Angola. My father's role was to broker the communication, impressing on the German Foreign Office the urgency of offering support to Namibia's liberating forces while convincing Nujoma's SWAPO that it would be more sustainable to protect German farmers from massacres and gradually phase out their land ownership by legal mechanisms. It has been said that the example of Namibia inspired Nelson Mandela when he became president of South Africa.

Hans had done his best so that Germans would no longer be seen exclusively in the role of warmongers the world over. But as a family man, he had been difficult to grow up with. Maybe it was because he had not come across any parenting role models in his own youth that he cared to emulate. His generation had secured our comfortable childhoods and given us a new standing in the world, but they had failed to exorcise the dark spirits of their own childhoods.

While alive, my father had asked me more than once, "My generation has rebuilt this country from its ashes. What is your generation going to do with it?"

At the time, I did not know the answer. Nor did I understand the complexities of the question. It was twofold, involving our parents and their legacy.

My generation, the children of Hitler's war children, were still coming to terms with accepting what had been lacking from our own upbringings. Material comforts could not compensate for emotional shortcomings. Our parents, for all their accomplishments, had been difficult to relate to. In a culture of silence concerning everything surrounding the Third Reich, they did not have the opportunity to talk openly about what had happened to them in a first step toward healing. But we did not know that.

Sometimes it had been as though my father had been reliving those last hours of the Battle of Zawada throughout his adulthood. Again, and again, he was the seventeen-year-old *Gruppenführer* in charge of the lives of nine comrades, and this time he would not fail to save them. Except that he was not; he was the head of a household with three children and a wife who had her own trauma to deal with. In the German Federal Republic of the 1960s and '70s, there was no emergency. So, he had to create them. He could turn anything into a disaster with the potential for high drama. For my father, me coming home late as a teenager was not something that caused him to worry; it was a disaster that was threatening to break up the whole family. How could I be so selfish?

To understand my parents' generation, I watched so many eyewitness reports on German TV and YouTube that I had to stop. Each was more tragic than the next, and the flashing, historical black-and-white film clips were giving me nightmares. Germany's children were truly the last forgotten group of Nazi victims. Unable to talk about it, they had carried their heavy load into old age.

Toward the end of his life, my father had tried to unburden himself of this legacy, but the time for a public debate for openly discussing the subject had not come yet, and I had not been ready to face his story. He missed it by a few years.

Ten years later, I discovered that I was not alone in having perceived my parents as difficult. The author Sabine Bode wrote several books about the trauma of Germany's war children and its transmission to my generation. She called us *Kriegsenkel* (the grandchildren of war).[2] The term stuck; other German authors wrote about it. Self-help organizations and forums to share experiences sprung up. I wrote to Anne, one of the organizers:

My father was eternally engaged in a hopeless fight. Without me knowing it, I spent part of my childhood on the battlefields of Zawada. The other part consisted of coming up against my mother's self-protective wall. My life was tied into the unspeakable past of my parents' own upbringing. In search of their stolen childhoods, they inadvertently made us into their parents. It seemed unfair. But nowhere in the world is it fair when children suffer the consequences of adult conflicts and totalitarian regimes, not in the concentration camps, not on the battlefield. It is not fair to the war children of today in Syria, Congo, or Kosovo; the list is long!

I concluded in my letter to Anne, "That realization does not alleviate the pain. But rather than dwelling on what never was, we need to heal ourselves and thank our parents for what they did do for us."

My mother once said to me, "I am doing the best I can and cannot give you what I do not have." That just about summed it up.

When I read the accounts of other war children of that generation, it seemed absurd that my parents had, once again, been among the lucky ones. Both had experienced what children go through in wars the world over, escaping bombing raids, being shot at, and going hungry. But they had not been among the German refugee children coming from the east in 1945. The eyewitness reports of the children who survived those death treks were among the most heartbreaking of all. Thousands had walked across the frozen Baltic Sea in the bitter cold winter months of 1945 while under constant Soviet fire, their dark figures against the white ice presenting them as easy targets.

Herlind Kasner, née Jentzsch, a war child born in 1928 in Danzig, was fortunate enough to have left the region prior to the war. But she and her daughter Angela, born in 1954, could not have been indifferent to the heartbreaking stories of what had happened to those who the Jentzsch family had left behind in their old hometown. In 2015, Chancellor Angela Merkel, a *Kriegsenkel* herself, invited 1.5 million refugees, who had crossed the Mediterranean with nothing but the shirts on their backs, to settle in Germany. It was a gutsy and brave decision and not without problems, as the following years would show. Integration of those traumatized people was a challenge, and conflicts between locals and newcomers flared up.

But to me, it was the right decision. Nobody could undo the past, or bring back the dead. But the past could be remembered as a warning to the future, and extending humanitarian aid to the disenfranchised today was a step in the right direction.

When I called my mother in 2019, the phone was picked up by a young man who identified himself as Gulkhan, who told me that my mother was having a nap. He was an Afghan refugee whom my mother had invited to live in her spare bedroom while he was learning German and training as an apprentice in the hospitality industry. The initiative to place refugees in the homes of seniors had been organized by Mrs. Doris Kübler, my former teacher and a Presbyterian alderwoman of the Lutheran church in Rheinbach. Her parents had also come to West Germany as young Second World War refugees. My mother and the other old ladies had enjoyed some local media attention for setting an example of giving a true welcome.

It was now the summer of 2020. After many years of research and writing, my work was complete. I was sitting outside my house overlooking the creek. I remembered that it had been, almost exactly to the day, fifteen years since my father had died. I was sorry he never stayed at my house; he would have taken his bicycle and explored the bucolic surroundings.

Had he been sitting beside me, I would have told him that I was ready to answer his question of what my generation would do with the country that his generation had rebuilt for us. My answer would have been:

Your generation removed the physical rubble and destruction that shaped your youth. You went on to apply what you had learned in such painful lessons, by raising us children in an open, democratic society. My generation had to clear away the lingering psychological wreckage of your childhoods. But now we are ready to show the world the importance of living in a democracy that welcomes everyone, because we have to stop amplifying our perceived differences and embrace our shared humanity.

LIST OF LOCATIONS

Listed below, the pre–Second World War German names of places mentioned in the diary have been translated into their contemporary Czech or Polish ones. Locations that remained German after the war were divided into the former Russian zone that became the German Democratic Republic (1945-91), commonly referred to as East Germany, or if they were in the former British, American, and French zones, became the Federal Republic of Germany (1945-present), referred to as West Germany. At the time, Hans was deployed to an area of Czechoslovakia that became part of the Czech Republic in 1993.

- Aussig (German)/Ústí nad Labem (Czech)

- Berlin (German, Capital of East Germany 1949-91 and a Western Sector)

- Bilin (German)/Bilina (Czech)

- Bonn (German, Capital of West Germany 1949-90)

- Bremen (German, West)

- Brüx (German)/Most (Czech)

- Burg Schreckenstein (German)/Hrad Střckov (Czech)/Danzig (German)/Gdańsk (Polish)

- Dresden (German, East)

- Duderstadt (German, East)

- Eger (German)/Cheb (Czech)

- Elbsandsteingebirge (German)/Českosaské Švýcarsko (Czech)

- Falkenberg (German)/Niemodlin (Polish)

- Fulnek (German)/Fulnek (Czech)

- Bad Gottleuba (German, East)

- Hannover (German, West)

- Hultschiner Ländchen (German)/Hlučínsko (Czech)/Kraik hulczyński (Polish)

- Jägerndorf (German)/Krnov (Czech)

- Karlsbad (German)/Karlovy Vary (Czech)

- Karlsbrunn (German)/Karlova Studanka (Czech)

- Komotau (German)/Chomutov (Czech)

- Magdeburg (German, East)

- Mardorf (German, West)

- Olmütz (German)/Olomouc (Czech)

- Ostrau (German)/Ostrava (Czech)

- Rheinbach (German, West)

- Rosslau (German, East)

- Saatz (German)/Žatec (Czech)

- Salzwedel (German, East)

- Schönbrunn (German, East)

- Troppau (German)/Opava (Czech)

- Tyrn (German)/Děrné (Czech)

- Wretschin (German)/Vresina (Czech)

- Zawada (German)/Závada (Czech)

LIST OF ABBREVIATIONS
AND GLOSSARY

Abitur: German high-school diploma, encompasses thirteen years of schooling.

Ahnenpass: "ancestor passport," also called Aryan certificate, used by the Third Reich to establish Aryan German lineage. There was a lesser and a greater certificate, the latter requiring family pedigree back to 1800.

AHS: abbreviation for *Adolf Hitler Schule* (Adolf Hitler School).

Albrecht Dürer: Renaissance painter from the town of Nuremberg, home of Karl.

Auslandsdeutsche: ethnic Germans living overseas.

Bundeswehr: federal defense, the army of present-day Germany.

Der Führer: "The Leader," a title frequently used for Hitler.

Doctor Ulebuhle: children's book character invented by the popular early twentieth-century German author Bruno Bürgel.

Flak: abbreviation for *Flugabwehrkanone* (air defense cannon).

Freiwilliger Arbeitsdienst: Reich Labor Service, voluntary until 1939, afterward compulsory, when it became the *Reichsarbeitsdienst* (Reich Labor Service).

Frundsberg: late fifteenth- and early sixteenth-century mercenary and war leader, celebrated during the Third Reich, and name of the SS unit in which Günter Grass served.

Gau: an administrative territorial unit of the NSDAP.

Gauleiter: regional party leader of the NSDAP.

Germanski: Russian term for a German.

"Heil Hitler!": "Hail Hitler!" Nazi greeting among German citizens required by law.

Herrenmensch: member of the "master race"; racist term coined by the Nazis.

HJ: abbreviation for Hitler Youth (*Hitler Jugend*).

HKL: abbreviation for *Hauptkampflinie* ("main combat line"), the front line.

Jungmann: male student from a Nazi elite school.

Jungvolk: organization for children aged ten to fourteen years before joining the Hitler Youth.

Kampfgruppe: ad hoc formed combat units of varying strength.

KLV: abbreviation for *Kinderlandverschickung* (a Nazi program where all children had to leave the cities and live in the countryside, usually separated from their parents).

Landser: infantryman.

Machorka: brand of Russian tobacco also called "peasant tobacco."

Maskenball: masquerade, arbitrary educational measure at Nazi elite schools.

Mephisto: character of a demon or the devil in the play *Faust* by J. W. von Goethe.

Napola: common name for *Nationalpolitische Erziehungsanstalt der NSDAP*, officially abbreviated NPEA (a type of Nazi elite school).

NS: abbreviation for National Socialist.

NSDAP: abbreviation for *Nationalsozialistische Deutsche Arbeiter Partei* (National Socialist German Workers Party).

Pak: abbreviation for *Panzer Abwehr Kanone* (tank deterrent canon).

Panje **wagon:** a simple Eastern European horse-drawn cart.

Pervitin: brand name of methamphetamine tablets given to German soldiers during the Second World War to keep them alert and pain resistant.

SA: abbreviation for *Sturmabteilung*. It was the Nazi Party's first major paramilitary wing and was eventually superseded by the SS.

Schnaps: a clear German liquor with a high alcohol content.

SS: abbreviation for *Schutzstaffel* (protection squad). It was a paramilitary organization in the Third Reich involved in the majority of atrocities.

Stalinorgel: Russian multiple rocket launcher nicknamed *Katyusha*.

Sturmbannführer: a Nazi paramilitary rank equivalent to major.

Sudetendeutsche: ethnic Germans who had been living in Czechoslovakia since the Middle Ages.

Volkssturm: home guard, militia established by the Nazis during the last months of the war consisting of teenagers who had not previously been conscripted and men over sixty years old.

Walter Flex: German author who wrote about humanity, friendship, and suffering based on his First World War experience.

Wehrmacht: Germany's army before the Second World War.

NOTES

THE VANISHED BOARDING SCHOOL

1. Johannes Leeb, *Wir waren Hitler's Eliteschüler: Ehemalige Zöglinge der NS-Ausleseschulen brechen ihr Schweigen* (München: Wilhelm Heyne Verlag, 1999), 39–53.

2. Ibid., 71–75.

3. Ibid., 101–10.

NOT A NAPOLA

1. Leeb, *Wir waren Hitler's Eliteschüler*, 233–39.

2. Reinhard Siegmund-Schultze, "Nazi Rule and Teaching of Mathematics in the Third Reich, Particularly School Mathematics" (oral presentation: University of Agder, Faculty of Engineering and Science, Kristiansand, Norway), www.numerisation.univ-irem.fr/ACF/ACF08076/ACF08076.pdf (accessed March 23, 2020).

3. Leeb, *Wir waren Hitler's Eliteschüler*, 23–37.

4. Gedenkstätte Sonnenstein, Heft 7.

5. UKEssays, Nazi Elite Schools.

6. Ibid.

7. Stefan Wunsch, email, 24 February 2021.

8. H.E.A.R.T., "Sonnenstein Euthanasia Centre," 2007.

9. Topographie des Terrors, www.topographie.de.

CASTLE BIRDSONG

1. Klaus Ring and Stefan Wunsch (eds.), *Bestimmung: Herrenmensch* (Dresden: Sandstein Verlag, 2016).

2. G. Dennis Gansel, *Napola—Elite für den Führer* (Karlovy Vary: Constantin Film, 2004).

3. "Artur Axmann—Einziges Interview mit dem Reichsjugendführer," 1995 (Teil 1 und 2), Chronos History, www.youtube.com/watch?v=IbIaCd4PqR0; www.youtube.com/watch?v=zBpcycxLKYM (accessed 2 January 2019).

4. "Herrenkinder—Das System der NS-Eliteschulen / Doku 28.05.13," Online Doku Channel (2013), www.youtube.com/watch?v=0dCPnCCVOTs (accessed 13 April 2020).

5. Kai Schlenkermann, "Grass, Günter-Sein Leben und seine größten Werke" (Grin, 2001), www.grin.com/document/102039.

6. Museum Vogelsang, "Destiny: Master Race" Exhibition, www.vogelsang-ip.de/en/ leitmarken/nazi-documentation-vogelsang/destiny-masterrace.html.

SCHOOLED BY BARBARIANS

1. Erika Mann, *School for Barbarians: Education under the Nazis* (New York: Dover Edition, 2014, a replication of Modern Age Books Inc., 1938).

2. Taika Waititi, *JoJo Rabbit* (Toronto: Fox Searchlight Pictures, 2019).

3. Marcel Reich-Ranicki (ed.), *Meine Schulzeit im Dritten Reich: Erinnerungen deutscher Schriftsteller* (München: Deutscher Taschenbuch Verlag, 1997), 29.

4. Erinnern für die Zukunft e.V, "Der Roland und die Nazi Propaganda," Spurensuche Bremen 1933–1945, 2010, www.spurensuche-bremen.de/roland-und-die-nazipropaganda/.

THE FLAG IS MORE THAN DEATH

1. Müller-Lüdenscheidt-Verlag. "Es zog ein Hitlermann hinaus," Volksliederarchiv, www.volksliederarchiv.de/es-zog-ein-hitlermann-hinaus/ (accessed 22 March 2021).

2. Anne Schroth, "Hitler's Erziehingsziele," *Das 20. Jahrhundert*, Vol. 4, 79, 1st ed. (Akain, Berhard & Wagener, Elmar, Grin, 2001) www.grin.com/document/101030

3. Familie Tenhumberg, "Als die goldene Abensonne," Kampflied der SA, www.tenhumbergreinhard.de/taeter-und-mitlaeufer/lieder-und-gedichte/kampflied-der-sa.html (accessed March 22, 2021).

4. Hans Scheu and Hans Jentsch, "Wenn die Stürme Leben wecken," Ingmar Burghardt (2012), www.youtube.com/watch?v=NLOT0pgwaZM.

5. Georg Walter Heyer, *Die Fahne ist mehr als der Tod: Lieder aus der Nazizeit* (München: Heyne Verlag, 1980), 25.

6. Ibid., 109.

7. Ibid., 62.

8. Erich Kästner, "Die andere Möglichkeit," Deutsche Lyrik, www.deutschelyrik.de/die-andere-moegkichkeit.html (accessed March 22, 2021).

9. Hans R. Queiser, *Du gehörst dem Führer!" Vom Hitlerjungen zum Kriegsberichter* (Köln: Leske Verlag, 1993), back page.

FRANZ AND THE FLAK

1. Arno Frank, "Wach und heiter und so weiter," Drogen im II, Weltkrieg, *TAZ*, 30 December 2011, taz.de/Drogen-im-II-Weltkrieg/!5104540/.

2. Norman Ohler, *Blitzed: Drugs in the Third Reich* (Boston: Houghton Mifflin Harcourt, 2017), 67.

3. Simon Schulze, "Nazidroge Pervitin" (original source: *Schlaflos im Krieg* documentary), February 9, 2014, www.drogenguide.blogspot.com/2014/02/nazidroge-pervitin.html.

GLASSES AND MINERAL WATER

1. Omar Bartov, *Hitler's Army: Soldiers, Nazis and War in the Third Reich* (Oxford: Oxford University Press, 1992), 78–90.

2. Wilhelm Tieke and Friedrich Rebstock, *Im letzten Aufgebot 1944–1945: Die Geschichte der 18. SS-Freiwilligen-Panzergrenadier-Division Horst Wessel* (Nation Europa Verlag, Band I & II: Coburg 1994/1995), 15.

3. Ibid., 30.

BARRACK BLUES

1. Hans Robert Jauss, "Jugend, Krieg und Internierung," Göppingen Wissenschaftliche Dokumentation (Online-Resource, Bibliothek der Universität Konstanz, Konstanz 2015), kops.uni-konstanz.de/handle/123456789/30994.

DRESDEN AND DEPARTURES

1. Josef Ossadnik, *Land zwischen den Mächten* (Bissendorf: Biblio Verlag, 2003), 139.

2. Anthony Beever, "They Raped Every German Female from Eight to 80," *The Guardian*, May 1, 2002, www.theguardian.com/books/2002/may/01/news.features11.

3. Anonyma, *Eine Frau in Berlin:Tagebuchaufzeichnungen vom 20 April bis 22 Juni 1945* (Frankfurt: Eichborn Verlag, 2003).

ARRIVING IN SUDETENLAND

1. Tieke and Rebstock, *Im letzten Aufgebot 1944–1945*, 138.

2. Ibid., 110.

THE BATTLE FOR ZAWADA

1. Ossadnik, *Land zwischen den Mächten*, 69.

2. Ibid., 223.

3. Florian Huber, *Kind, versprich mir, dass du dich erschießt. Der Untergang der kleinen Leute 1945* (Berlin: Piper Verlag, 2015), 234.

4. Ossadnik, *Land zwischen den Mächten*, 232.

5. Tieke and Rebstock, *Im letzten Aufgerbot 1944–1945*, 145.

GERMANSKIS ON THE RUN

1. A. Axmann, interview, 1995.

2. Liezel Lentz, "Das Kriegsende 1945 in Karlsbad," LEMO (Lebendiges Museum Online), May 31, 2002, www.dhm.de/lemo/zeitzeugen/liesel-lentz-das-kriegsende-1945-in-karlsbad.html.

3. Heimkehr/Schörner, "Der laute Kamerad," originally published in *Der Spiegel*, February 9, 1955, www.spiegel.de/spiegel/print/d-31969169.html.

4. Rick Ostermann, *Wolfskinder* (Venice: Port au Prince Pictures, 2013).

5. Anthony Beevor, *Berlin: The Downfall 1945* (London: Viking, 2002), 334–36.

6. Dan Bar-On, *Legacy of Silence: Encounters with Children of the Third Reich* (Cambridge, MA: Harvard University Press, 1989), 321–34.

7. Ibid., 322.

A LONG WAY HOME

1. Beevor, *Berlin: The Downfall 1945*, 78.

EPILOGUE 2: A GLASS CABINET

1. *Akten zur Auswärtigen Politik der Bundesrepublik Deutschland* (Munich: Oldenburg Verlag, 1990), books.google.je/books/about/Akten_zur_ausw%C3%A4rtigen_Politik_der_Bunde.html?hl=de&id=k44-AQAAIAAJ, 169.

2. Sabine Bode, *Kriegsenkel: Die Erben der Vergessenen Generation* (Stuttgart: Klett-Cotta Verlag, 2015).

BIBLIOGRAPHY

BOOKS

Anonyma. *Eine Frau in Berlin: Tagebuchaufzeichnungen vom 20. April bis 22. Juni 1945* (Frankfurt: Eichborn Verlag, 2003).

Bar-On, Dan. *Legacy of Silence: Encounters with Children of the Third Reich* (Cambridge, MA: Harvard University Press, 1989).

Bartov, Omar. *Hitler's Army: Soldiers, Nazis and War in the Third Reich* (Oxford: Oxford University Press, 1992).

Beevor, Anthony. *Berlin: The Downfall 1945* (London: Viking, 2002).

Bode, Sabine. *Kriegsenkel: Die Erben der Vergessenen Generation* (Stuttgart: Klett-Cotta Verlag, 2015).

Burger, Horst. *Warum warst du in der Hitler-Jugend? Vier Fragen an meinen Vater* (Hamburg: Rowohlt Verlag, 1980).

Cigaretten-Bilderdienst Altona Bahrenfeld. *Deutschland erwacht: Werden, Kampf und Sieg der NSDAP* (Hamburg: Cigaretten Bilderdienst, 1933).

Gebhardt, Miriam and Nick Somers. *Crimes Unspoken: The Rape of German Women at the End of the Second World War* (Boston and New York: Polity Press, 2020).

Haupert, Bernhard and Franz Josef Schäfer. *Jugend zwischen Kreuz und Hakenkreuz* (Frankfurt: Suhrkamp Verlag, 1991).

Heyer, Georg Walter. *Die Fahne ist mehr als der Tod: Lieder aus der Nazizeit* (München: Heyne Verlag, 1980).

Huber, Florian. *Kind, versprich mir, dass du dich erschießt. Der Untergang der kleinen Leute 1945* (Berlin: Piper Verlag, 2015).

Huber, Karl-Heinz. *Jugend unterm Hakenkreuz* (Frankfurt/M-Berlin: Ullstein Verlag, 1986).

Klönne, Arno. *Jugend im Dritten Reich: Die Hitlerjugend und ihre Gegner* (Köln: PapyRossa Verlag, 2003).

Klüver, Max. *Die Adolf-Hitler-Schulen* (Beltheim-Schnellbach: Verlag S. Bublies, 2007)

Knopp, Guido, *Hitlers Kinder* (München: C. Bertelsmann GmbH, 2000).

Leeb, Johannes. *Wir waren Hitler's Eliteschüler: Ehemalige Zöglinge der NS-Ausleseschulen brechen ihr Schweigen* (München: Wilhelm Heyne Verlag, 1999).

Leunens, Christine. *Caging Skies* (New York: Harry N. Abrams, 2019).

Mann, Erika. *School for Barbarians: Education under the Nazis* (New York: Dover Edition 2014, a replication of Modern Age Books Inc., 1938).

Ohler, Norman. *Blitzed: Drugs in the Third Reich* (Boston: Houghton Mifflin Harcourt, 2017).

Ossadnik, Josef. *Land zwischen den Mächten* (Bissendorf: Biblio Verlag, 2003).

Queiser, Hans R. *Du gehörst dem Führer!" Vom Hitlerjungen zum Kriegsberichter* (Köln: Leske Verlag, 1993).

Radebold, H., W. Bohleber, and J. Zinnecker (eds.). *Transgenerationale Weitergabe kriegsbe- lasteter Kindheiten* (Weinheim and München: Juventa Verlag, 2008).

Ralph Lewis, Brenda. *Illustrierte Geschichte der HitlerJugend 1922–1945, die verlorene Kindheit* (Wien: Tosa Verlag, 2000).

Reich-Ranicki, Marcel (ed.). *Meine Schulzeit im Dritten Reich: Erinnerungen deutscher Schriftsteller* (München: Deutscher Taschenbuch Verlag, 1997).

Ring, Klaus and Stefan Wunsch (eds.). *Bestimmung: Herrenmensch* (Dresden: Sandstein Verlag, 2016).

Rüdiger, Jutta (ed.). *Die Hitler-Jugend: Und Ihr Selbstverständnis im Spiegel Ihrer Aufgabengebiete* (Koblenz: Verlag S. Bublies, 1998).

Schmidt, Helmut, Loki Schmidt, Willi and Willfriede Berkhan, Ruth Loah, Ursula Philipp, and Dietrich Strothmann. *Kindheit und Jugend unter Hitler* (Berlin: Goldmann Wilhelm GmbH, 1994).

Schneider, Michael and Joachim Süss (eds.). *Nebelkinder: Kriegsenkel treten aus dem Traumaschatten der Geschichte.* (Berlin: Europa Verlag, 2015).

Seidler, Hans. *Images of War: Hitler's Boy Soldiers, the Hitler Jugend Story* (Barnsley: Pen & Sword Military, 2013).

Sichrovsky, Peter. *Schuldig geboren: Kinder aus Nazifamilien* (Köln: Kiepenheuer & Witsch, 1987).

Simoneit, Ferdinand. . . . *mehr als der Tod": Die geopferte Jugend* (München: Universitas Verlag, 1989).

Tieke, Wilhelm and Friedrich Rebstock. *Im letzten Aufgebot 1944–1945: Die Geschichte der 18. SS-Freiwilligen-Panzergrenadier-Division Horst Wessel* (Coburg: Nation Europa Verlag, 1994/1995).

von der Grün, Max. *Wie war das eigentlich? Kindheit und Jugend im Dritten Reich* (Darmstadt: Luchterhand Verlag, 1979).

Wagner, Günter. *Die Fahne ist mehr als der Tod: Roman einer Generation* (Hamburg: Claasen Verlag, 1958).

OTHER PUBLICATIONS/NEWSPAPERS

Akten zur Auswärtigen Politik der Bundesrepublik Deutschland (Munich: Oldenburg Verlag, 1990), books.google.je/books/about/ Akten_zur_ausw%C3%A4rtigen_Politik_der_Bunde .html?hl=de&id=k44-AQAAIAAJ, 69-756.

Beever, Anthony. "They raped every German female from eight to 80," *The Guardian*, May 1, 2002, www.theguardian.com/books/2002/ may/01/news.features11.

Frank, Arno, "Wach und heiter und so weiter," Drogen im II, Weltkrieg, *TAZ*, December 30, 2011, www.taz.de/ Drogen-im-II-Weltkrieg/!5104540.

Kuratorium Gedenkstätte Sonnenstein e.V., "Es war eine Welt von Befehl und Gehorsam," *Pirna* 7 (2008).

Kuratorium Gedenkstätte Sonnenstein e.V., "Durchgangsstation Sonnenstein," *Pirna* 6 (2007).

Siegmund-Schultze, Reinhard. "Nazi Rule and Teaching of Mathematics in the Third Reich, particularly School Mathematics" (oral presentation: University of Agder, Faculty of Engineering and Science, Kristiansand, Norway), www.numerisation.univ-irem.fr/ACF/ ACF08076/ACF08076.pdf.

MUSEUMS

Areál čs.opevnění Hlučín-Darkovičky, www.szm.cz/rubrika/41/ expozicni-arealy/areal-cs-opevneni-hlucin-darkovicky.html.

Bücher und Bunkerstadt Wünsdorf, www.buecherstadt.com.

Gedenkstätte/Museum Seelower Höhen, www.seelowerhoehen.de/cms.

Kochi Paradesi Jewish Synagogue, www.keralatourism.org/kochi/ paradeso-synagogue-mattancherry.php.

Muzeum Hlučínska, www.muzeum.hlucin.com.

Ordensburg Vogelsang: "Destiny: Master Race" exhibition, www.vogelsang-ip.de/en/leitmarken/nazi-documentation-vogelsang/ destiny-masterrace.html.

Topographie des Terrors, www.topographie.de.

FILMS/VIDEOS AND INTERVIEWS

"Artur Axmann—Einziges Interview mit dem Reichsjugendführer," 1995 (Teil 1 und 2), Chronos History, www.youtube.comwatch?v=IbIaCd4PqR0; www.youtube.com/ watch?v=zBpcycxLKYM.

Dennis Gansel, *Napola—Elite für den Führer* (Karlovy Vary: Constantin Film, 2004).

"Der Nürnberger Prozess: Baldur von Schirach," Histoclips (2019), www.youtube.com/watch?v=UOVrBYFqXv0.

"Hans-Jürgen Massaquoi: Rekrutierung für die HJ," Zeitzeugen-Portal (2011), www.youtube.com/watch?v=eQxUjhrDZu0.

Hans Scheu and Hans Jentsch, "Wenn die Stürme Leben wecken," Ingmar Burghardt (2012), www.youtube.com/watch?v=NLOT0pgwaZM.

"Harry Valérien: Jugend und Freizeit in der NS-Zeit," Zeitzeugen-Portal (2011), www.youtube.com/watch?v=KwUDYMbiaN0.

"Herrenkinder—Das System der NS-Eliteschulen / Doku 28.05.13," Online Doku Channel (2013), www.youtube.com/watch?v=0dCPnCCVOTs.

"Klaus Schikore: Napola auf Rügen," Zeitzeugen-Portal (2013), www.youtube.com/watch?v=tpUWeR1eHxI.

Rick Ostermann, *Wolfskinder* (Venice: Port au Prince Pictures, 2013).

Taika Waititi, *JoJo Rabbit* (Toronto: Fox Searchlight Pictures, 2019).

WEBSITES

Baker, Kevin. "Hitler's Army: Soldiers, Nazis, and War in the Third Reich (1991)," Not Even Past, 2013, www.notevenpast.org/hitlers-army-soldiers-nazis-and-war-third-reich-1991.

Erinnern für die Zukunft e.V. "Der Roland und die Nazi Propaganda," Spurensuche Bremen 1933-1945, 2010, www.spurensuche-bremen.de/roland-und-die-nazipropaganda.

Familie Tenhumberg. "Als die goldene Abendsonne," Kampflied der SA, www.tenhum-bergreinhard.de/taeter-und-mitlaeufer/lieder-und-gedichte/kampflied-der-sa.html.

Heimkehr/Schörner. "Der laute Kamerad," originally published in *Der Spiegel*, February 9, 1955, www.spiegel.de/spiegel/print/d-31969169.html.

Holocaust Education & Archive Research Team (H.E.A.R.T). "Sonnenstein Euthanasia Centre," 2007, www.holocaustresearchproject .org/euthan/sonnenstein.html.

Jauss, Hans Robert. "Jugend, Krieg und Internierung," Göppingen Wissenschaftliche Dokumentation (Online-Resource, Bibliothek der Universität Konstanz, Konstanz, 2015), kops.uni-konstanz.de/ handle/123456789/30994.

Kästner, Erich. "Die andere Möglichkeit," Deutsche Lyrik, www.deutschelyrik.de/die-andere-moegkichkeit.html (accessed March 22, 2021).

Lentz, Liezel. "Das Kriegsende 1945 in Karlsbad," LEMO (Lebendiges Museum Online), May 31, 2002, www.dhm.de/lemo/zeitzeugen/liesel-lentz-das-kriegsende-1945-in-karlsbad.html.

Müller-Lüdenscheidt-Verlag. "Es zog ein Hitlermann hinaus," Volksliederarchiv, www.volksliederarchiv.de/es-zog-ein-hitlermann-hinaus.

Schlenkermann, Kai. "Grass, Günter—Sein Leben und seine größten Werke" (Grin, 2001), www.grin.com/document/102039.

Schnitzler, Mathias. *Körbe voller Zyankali*, "Der größte Selbstmord der deutschen Geschichte," Deutschlandfunk, April 9, 2015, www.deutschlandfunk.de/koerbe-voller-zyankali-der-groesste-selbstmord-der. 700.de.html?dram:article_id=316610.

Schroth, Anne. *Hitler's Erziehingsziele*, Grin, 2001, www.grin.com/ document/101030.

Schulze, Simon. "Nazidroge Pervitin" (original source: *Schlaflos im Krieg* documentary), February 9, 2014, www.drogenguide.blogspot.com/ 2014/02/nazidroge-pervitin.html.

UKEssays. "Nazi Elite Schools" (2015), www.ukessays.com/essays/ history/the-nazi-elite-schools-successful-history-essay.php.

IMAGE CREDITS

All photographs courtesy of Helene Munson, unless otherwise noted.

Pages 6, 185, 190, 193, courtesy of the mayor of Závada

Pages 27, 41, 53, 56, 95, 121, Cigaretten-Bilderdienst Altona Bahrenfeld, *Deutschland erwacht: Werden, Kampf und Sieg der NSDAP* (Hamburg: Cigaretten Bilderdienst, 1933)

Pages 45, 114, 118, courtesy of Franz Mannhart

Page 70, Archiv Vogelsang IP, Sawinski Collection/Photographer: unknown

Page 68, Archiv Vogelsang IP/Photographer: Foto-Atelier Mertens, Gemünd/Eifel

ACKNOWLEDGMENTS

This book would have never happened were it not for the kindness of Siobhan Fraser and her husband, Alyn Shipton, who both saw potential in my project. Alyn agreed to help me with editing, giving thoughtful input and pulling it all together. I would also like to thank my talented and dedicated editors, Amy Rigg and Alex Boulton. Thank you to Anette Fuhrmeister and Jennifer Hergenroeder for taking my story out into the world. My gratitude also goes to the whole team at The History Press for courageously taking on a book project on a so-far mostly unexplored and forgotten aspect of German history. Until I met them, writing had been a lonely pursuit, as I encountered negative feedback, especially from my German compatriots, who felt that the dead should be left dead and let sleeping dogs lie. But they reinforced my resolve to bring the story of Hitler's forgotten victims, Germany's own children, to life.

I am indebted to the support of Stefan Wunsch, academic director of Vogelsang IP | NS-Dokumentation Vogelsang, who kindly fact-checked the chapters relating to National Socialist (NS) elite education. Many smart suggestions to improve the manuscript were made by Dave Porteous, Joyce de Cordova, Suzi Rosenstreich, Kit Storjohann, and Andrea Rhude from my beloved North Fork Writers Group. Andrea Lorkova, the current mayor of Závada, and my avid reader Gonzalo Tellez never lost confidence in my project. Thank you to friends and family for critiquing early drafts. My gratitude goes to all of you whom I met along the way, who put up with me passionately talking about the subject and who encouraged me to keep writing, when at times the research took a toll on me, questioning my belief in a world that is capable of such monstrosities.

I pay special homage to the writers who came before me, especially Erika Mann with her visionary book *School for Barbarians*, published in 1938. With frightening accuracy, she foretold the terrible things that my father and ten million other German children would be going through in the following years. I hope that my book, the tragic illustration of the exactness of her predictions and its sad aftermath, will serve as a warning to today's world, where radical regimes still send ideologically brainwashed children into war.

INDEX

NOTE: Page references in *italics* refer to photos.

A

Abiture (high school diploma), 113, 250–51
Adenauer, Konrad, 233
Adolf Hitler Schools (AHS), *58*, 58–63, *63*, 67–68
Ahnenpass (Aryan lineage proof), 40, 69
Aktion T4 (Action T4) Program, 57, 60–63
Albert (schoolmate/soldier), 8, 151, 192, 201
Alfieri, Dino, 212
All of Life Is a Fight! (film), 102
Angola, Cold War effect on, 265
Anne (self-help group organizer), 267–68
Anonyma (film), 232–33
antiaircraft gunners. *See Flakhelfer* (auxiliary antiaircraft gunners)
Apollinaris, 126
Army Group Center (*Heeresgruppe Mitte*), 120, 127, 181, 224
August (Hans Dunker's paternal grandfather), *18*, 155
Axmann, Artur, 70, 73, 212–13

B

Bar-On, Dan, 228–29
Bartov, Omer, 129
Basic training, 135–50
  barracks of, 135–38
  defectors from, 148
  food scarcity during, 137–38, 142
  Führereid (oath to the leader), 140
  punishment in, 142–43, 146, 148
  recruitment of soldiers, 147, 149–50
  sleep deprivation during, 138, 148–49
  unhygienic conditions of, 143
Beer Hall Putsch (1923), 140
Beethoven, Ludwig van, 157
Beever, Anthony, 235
Believe and Beauty (youth group), 89
Benedict XVI (Pope/Joseph Ratzinger), 75, 77–78, 126
Bergau, Martin, 150
Bergh, Hertha von, 54
Berlin, as post–Cold War capital, 259

Berlin, battle of, 108, 110
Berlin Alexanderplatz (Döblin), 22
Berlin Wall, fall of (1989), 61, 93–97, 162
Black people, Nazi views of, 90
Black Tulip operation, 211
Blitzed (Ohler), 117
Blockwart (building caretaker), 82
Blutfahne (blood flag), 140
B'nai B'rith, 29, 263
Bode, Sabine, 267
Böll, Heinrich, 85, 116
Bormann, Gerda, 226
Bormann, Martin, Sr., 71–72, 113, 226
Bormann, Martin Adolf, Jr., 71, 226, 228, 251
The Boy from the Amber Coast (Bergau), 150
Brazil
  Hans Dunker's Foreign Service posting in, 29, 259, *260*, 261–64
  Hans Dunker's postwar travel to, 253–54
  internment camps of, 249
  students recruited from, 39–41
Brecht, Berthold, 172
Bruno D. (concentration camp guard), 149–50
Buba, Kazimir, 10–11
Bublies (publisher), 97
Bund Deutscher Mädchen (BDM), 54–55, 88–89, 227
Bundesverdienstkreuz (Order of Merit of the Federal Republic of Germany), 260–61
Bunkers, 185–86, *186, 202*
Bürgel, Bruno, 43
Burg Vogelsang. See Castle Birdsong

C

Captain of Köpenick incident, 86–87

Caspari Barracks, 137
Castle Birdsong
  Adolf Hitler Schools as feeder for, 67–68
  Allied occupation of, 66
  curriculum of, 67
  as modern-day museum, 59, 65–66, 69, 78–79
  ordensburgen (order castles), defined, 67 (*See also Ordensburgen* [order castles])
  roll-call square of, *68, 70*
  SS role of, 68–70, 75–77
"Castle Horror Stone" (*Hrad Střekov*), 162
Castle Sonnenstein, 59, 60
Cat and Mouse (Grass), 76
Catholic League, 75
Chaim (tourist in India), 34–36
Children of War (Pirna museum exhibit, 2020), 223
Children's Crusade of 1212, 97
child soldiers
  age of, 212
  basic training of, 135–50 (*See also* Basic training)
  conscription of students, 109–11, 113–23, *114, 118* (*See also* Nazi educational system)
  departure to Eastern Front, 151–59 (*See also* Sudetenland; Závada, battle for)
  legacy of, 269–70
  parents' knowledge and financial arrangements, 40, 57, 115
  post-traumatic stress disorder (PTSD) of, 33
  in SS, 126–27 (*See also* SS [*Schutzstaffel*])
  statistics of children's deaths, 152, 228–29
  substance use by, 116–17, 148–49, 154
  weapons training at Feldafing, 33, *47*, 47–49, *49*

Chile, Dunker family in, 14–15, 119, 249
Civilian population of Nazi Germany
during battle for Závada, 195
Berlin defended by, 153
civil servants' oath to Hitler, 140
mass suicide (April 12, 1945), 188
rapes of, 232–35
substance use by, 116–17, 148–49, 154
of Sudetenland, 185, *185*
Trümmerfrauen (rubble women), 233
Coca-Cola, 126
Cold War
Angola and effect of, 265
end of, 3, 61, 93–97, 108, 129, 162
German Democratic Republic of East Germany (GDR), 61, 94–97
German education about Holocaust during, 31
inception of, 239
Red Army (RAF) faction and bombing (1989), 74
concentration camps. *See also* Holocaust
camp guards of, 149–50
Gestapo role in, 126
SS–Junkerschulen and, 70
used for displaced persons, 249
Viennese Jews in, 212
convicts, as SS soldiers, 131–32
curriculum of schools. *See* Nazi ideology
Czechoslovakia. *See also* Sudetenland; Závada, battle for
Germany's defeat and, 215–16
Munich Agreement (1938) and, 6
Russian influence (1948), 9
Závada name and, 3
Czech Republic (modern-day), Závada and, 132–33

D

defeat of Germany. *See* Nazi Germany's defeat
Der Spiegel (magazine), 74, 103
Desting: Master Race (Castle Vogelsang museum exhibit), 59, 65–66, 69, 78–79
Deutsche Bank, 73
Deutsche Welle (German broadcast company), 148
Deutschlandfunk German Radio, 55
Dierk (Erika Dunker's brother), *256*
Dieter (schoolmate/soldier), 8, 151, 178
Die Zeit (German newspaper), 74
displaced persons (DPs), 248–49
Dittler (soldier), *102*
Döblin, Alfred, 22
Donohue, Bill, 75
Dostoevsky, Fyodor, 157
Dresden bombing (February 1945), 151–59
Dunker, Erika (Hans Dunker's wife)
at Castle Birdsong, 65–66
characterization of, 267–68
childhood photos, *83, 256*
on Feldafing School, 40–41
on Germany's defeat, 235–36
on "Heil Hitler" salute, 83
on Kristallnacht, 33
marriage of, 257
on Napolas, 51–54
wartime/immediate postwar life of, 251, 254–57
Dunker, Hans. *See also* Feldafing School; Grandparents of Hans Dunker; Sudetenland; Závada, battle for; *individual names of family members*
at camp for displaced persons, 248–49
characterization of, 74–75, 266–68
college/graduate school education of, 251–54
diary entries (*See individual events*)
diary kept by, 1–2, 13–23, 135–38, 193

Dunker, Hans (*continued*)
  discharge and travel home, 231–34, 236–45, 247
  Dittler (soldier) photo by, *102*
  early childhood of, 14–15
  Feldafing enrollment of, *16*, 16–20, *18*, 37–49, *47*, *49*, *51*, *52*, 253 (*See also* Feldafing School)
  final illness/death of, 1, 13–23, 261
  first engagement of marriage, 253–54
  Foreign Office (Germany) career of, 20, 74, 90–91, 108, 259–66, *260*
  grenade injury of, 208–9, 213–24
  legacy of, 269–70
  marriage of, 257 (*See also* Dunker, Erika)
  Nazi party application of, 28, 29
  photos of, *15*, *16*, *18*, *47*, *49*, *51*, *52*, *255*, *260*
  postwar mental health of, 203–4, *255*
  as prisoner of war, 137, 218–21, 239, 241
  school journal kept by, 44, 46, 48, *110*
  in South America, postwar, 249–51, 253–54
  writing style of, 10, 44, 72, 135–38
Dunker, Heinz (Hans Dunker's father), 14–16, *15*, 39–40, *87*, 247–50, 253, 254
Dunker, Helmut (Hans Dunker's brother), *253*, 254
Dunker, Hilde (Hans Dunker's mother), *2*, 14–16, *15*, 17, 39–40, 247–49, 254
Dunker, Tali (Hans Dunker's aunt)
  Ahnenpass (Aryan lineage) of, 69
  characterization of, 84
  death of, 23, 138
  nephew's diary entries addressed to, 28

  nephew's Feldafing enrollment and, 16, 17, 38–40, 43–44, 52, 87
  nephew's post–World War II stay with, 247, 249, 254
  nephew's wartime correspondence with, *138*, 138–43
Dürer, Albrecht, 43

E

Ebony (magazine), 90
Eifel region. *See* Castle Birdsong
Eine Frau in Berlin (*A Woman in Berlin*, anonymous), 154
Elisabeth (empress of Austria), 37
Ellie (landlady, family friend), 252–53
Eschenbach, Wolfram von, 21–22
Esser, Ernst, 45
Esser, Hermann, 45
eugenics (physically/mentally handicapped victims), 57, 60–63, 78
Eyken, Dierk van, 254

F

Faust (Goethe), 4, 242–43, 254
Feldafing School, 37–49
  closure of, 48–49, 250
  conscription of instructors, 42, 60
  conscription of students, 42, 48–49, 109–11, 113–23, *114*, *118*
  deaths of students, 8–11 (*See also* Závada, battle for)
  Dunker's enrollment in, 2
  hierarchy of schools, 45–46, 53
  modern-day use of, 37–39
  name of, 37, 38
  Nazi indoctrination at, 39, 40, 42–48
  NSDAP and, 103–4
  photos of, *41*, *45*, *47*, *48*, *49*
  South American students recruited for, 39–41
  Wagner at, 103

"Fighter for the Third Reich" from
Deutschland erwacht, 27
Fischach, Hans, 44–45, 47
Fitzgerald, F. Scott, 43
*The Flag Is More Than Death: Novel
of a Betrayed Generation* (Wagner),
94–95, 104, 108
*The Flag Is More Than Death: Songs
from the Times of the Nazis* (Heyer),
94–95, 98, 100–102
*The Flag Is More Than Death: the
Sacrificed Youth* (Simoneit), 94–95,
104
Flakhelfer (auxiliary antiaircraft
gunners)
Dittler (soldier) and, *102*
girls as Flaks, 114
Mannhart and, 113–19, *114*, *118*,
121–23
Ratzinger and, 75, 77–78, 126, 262
SS role of, 125–27
Flex, Walter, 43, 98, 197, 213
Foreign Office (Germany), 20, 74,
90–91, 108, 259–66, *260*
Franz Josef (emperor of Austria-
Hungary), 37
Frederick the Great (king of Prussia),
43, 98
Freiwilliger Arbeitsdienst (Volunteer
Labor Service), 85, 132
Fritz (Erika Dunker's father),
250–51, 256
Führereid (oath to the leader), 140

G
Gehlen, Reinhard, 93
Geneva Convention, 214
Genscher, Hans-Dietrich, 107–9,
264, 266
Georg (schoolmate/soldier), 8, 119,
151, 156, 190–96, 201, 205–6
Gerd (schoolmate/soldier)
in combat, 8, 119, 183–84, 191,
192, 194

departure to Eastern Front, 151, 158
in Sudetenland, 171, 177, 178, 179
Gerlach (soldier), 194, 201
German Democratic Republic of
East Germany (GDR), 61, 94–97
Germany, interwar years (Weimar
Republic), 143–44
Germany, Nazi. *See* Girls and women
of Nazi Germany; Nazi educational
system; Nazi Germany's defeat;
Nazi Germany's military; Nazi
ideology; Propaganda; *individual
names of Nazi leaders; individual
names of Nazi organizations*
Germany (modern-day)
Bundeswehr (Army), 39
Burg Vogelsang museum, 59,
65–66, 69, 78–79
Foreign Office of, 20, 74, 90–91,
108, 259–66, *260*
Pirna, *222*, 222–24
Rheinbach, 32, 259–60
Wachtberg, 107–9
Wünsdorf ("Book and Bunker
Town"), 93–94, *94*
Gestapo
concentration camp role of, 126
night raids by, 159
youth groups outlawed by, 99
girls and women of Nazi Germany
anonymous peasant woman, *235*
Berlin bombing and, 153, 154
Bund Deutscher Mädchen (BDM),
54–55, 88–89, 227
child-bearing role of women,
54–55, 102, 144
girls as Flaks, 114
Napolas for girls, 54
National Socialist Women's
League, 225
rapes of, 232–35
Wandervogel (Wandering Birds),
98–99, *99*
youth group propaganda and social
pressure, 88–89, 98–102, *99*

Goebbels, Joseph, 27, 128, 154, 214, 217, 225–26. *See also* Propaganda
Goebbels, Magda, 225
Goering, Hermann, 57, 85, 113, 116, 118, 205
Goethe, Johann Wolfgang von, 4, 242–43, 254
Görlitz, Julius, 49, 71
grandchildren of war (*Kriegsenkel*), 267, 269
grandparents of Hans Dunker
  August (paternal grandfather), *18*, 155
  Johann (maternal grandfather), 17, 86, *86*, 155, 249
  Marie (maternal grandmother), 17, 86, *86*, 155, 243
  Martha (paternal grandmother), *18*, 155, *155*
Grass, Günter, 75–78, 262
Grätz, Rabbi, 263–64
Grundmann, Harald, 59
Gulkhan (Afghan refugee), 269

H

Hacker, Karl
  in combat, 119, 184, 194, 196–99
  death of, 131, 136–37, 167–68, 196–99, 204, 205
  travel to front by, 26, 151, 156
  Závada battle and, 8, 10
Hannah (Erika Dunker's aunt), 256
Hannover bombing (October 1943), 153
Hansen, Dagmar, 111
Hans (shepherd/soldier)
  in combat, 192, 195, 196, 201
  in Sudetenland, 171, 173, 177
  Závada battle and, 8
Harvard Book Store, 81–82
Hay, Louise L., 109
Heeresgruppe Mitte (Army Group Center), 120, 127, 181, 224
Heil Dir im Siegerkranz ("Hail you in the victor's crown") hymn, 85

"Heil Hitler!" salute, 82–85
Heinz, Karl, 184
Heissmeyer, August, 225
Hermann (Erika Dunker's grandfather), 251
Herrhausen, Alfred, 73–74
Der Herr Kortüm (Kluge), 145–46
Heyer, Georg Walter, 94–95, 98, 100–102
higher education system. *See Ordensburgen* (order castles)
Hildegard (Erika Dunker's mother), 99, *99*, 251, 255
Himmler, Heinrich
  arrest of, 205
  children ordered into combat by, 104
  Nazi higher education system and, 70
  SS structure and, 125–26, 128, 133
  Stauffenberg group retribution by, 112
Hitler, Adolf. *See also* National Socialist German Workers' Party (NSDAP); Nazi educational system; Nazi Germany's military; Nazi ideology
  April 20 significance, 59
  on Army Group Center conscription, 181
  Feldafing School and, 37–38
  "Heil Hitler!" salute and, 82–85
  in hiding (1945), 205
  imprisonment of, 140
  Mein Kampf, 69, 96
  Munich Agreement (1938) and, 6, 162
  at Nazi higher education institutions, 70, *70*, 71, 73
  Nero Decree, 153
  NSDAP membership lists and, 262
  oaths to, 140
  Schörner and, 120
  scorned as artist, 97
  SS recruitment from different countries, 130

Stauffenberg group's assassination
attempt, 111–13, 120
substance abuse by, 116
suicide of, 212, 217
Hitler's boy soldiers. *See* Child
soldiers
Hitler Youth
age of, 29
Axmann and, 212–13
Berlin defended by, 153
hymn of, 95
Jewish women killed by, 150
Kinderlandverschickung (KLV) and,
255
Nazi higher education system and,
72, 73
roles of, 38
Schirach and, 62, 70, 95, 103
social pressure and propaganda of,
88–89, 98–102
Wandervogel (Wandering Birds)
and, 98–99, *99*
Hoffmann, Ludwig, 13
Hoffmann (platoon leader), 8, 194,
201–2, 206, 208
Hoffmeyer, Wilhelm, 85
Holocaust. *See also* Propaganda
concentration camps, 70, 126,
149–50, 212, 249
German education about, 31
Jewish victims of (*See* Jews)
Kristallnacht, 33
physically and mentally
handicapped victims of, 57,
60–63, 78
Szálasi (Hungarian dictator) and,
133
"Horst Wessel Lied" (Nazi anthem),
82, 103, 133
Hrad Střekov ("Castle Horror
Stone"), 162
Huber, Florian, 188
Hungary, SS soldiers from, 128,
130–33

I
Ibsen, Henrik, 157
Im letzten Aufgebot (*In the Last
Deployment*, Rebstock and Tieke),
164, 168–70, 173, 193
Independence Memorial Museum
(Windhoek, Namibia), 264
India
Kochi synagogue, 32, *32*
SS soldiers from, 130
Ingeborg (Hans Dunker's former
fiancée), 253
intergenerational trauma. *See
Sippenhaft* (kin liability)

J
Jauss, Robert, 146
Jews
excluded from youth groups, 99
of Feldafing (Bavaria), 37, 39
forced hypothermia/drowning
deaths, 150
Hans Dunker's German Foreign
Office work and, 263–64
killed by Hungary, 133
Kristallnacht, 33
propaganda against, 43, 88, 101
Viennese Jews in concentration
camps, 212
Johann (Hans Dunker's maternal
grandfather), 17, 86, *86*, 155, 249
Jojo Rabbit (film), 83
Junge, Traudl, 112
Jungmädelbund (youth group),
88–89

K
Karasek, Hellmuth, 55–56, 74
Karlsbad, Russian sacking of,
218–20
Kasner, Angela, 268–69
Kasner, Herlind Jentzsch, 268–69

Kästner, Erich, 102
Katherine the Great (empress of
    Russia), 130
Katz de Castro, Gerhard, 263
Keitel, Wilhelm, 108
Kevelaer (camp for displaced
    persons), 248–49
Kinderlandverschickung (KLV), 255
Kin liability. *See Sippenhaft* (kin
    liability)
Klepper company, 159
Kluge, Kurt, 145–46
Knopp, Guido, 90, 227
Kolberg (Nazi propaganda film), 27
*Königlich Sächsische Heil-und
    Königlich Sächsische
    Heil-und Verpflegungsanstalt
    erpflegungsanstalt*, 60. *See also* Pirna,
    Adolf Hitler School (AHS) of
König (soldier), 8, 208–9
Konstanz University, 146
Köpenick incident, 86–87
Kotzur, Hans, 11
Kriegsenkel (grandchildren of war),
    267, 269
Kriegsgräberfürsorge (German
    charity), 129
Kristallnacht, 33
Krössinsee order castle, 67
Kübler, Doris, 269
Kugler (leader of company
    headquarters personnel), 186

L

Land Between the Powers (Ossadnik),
    133, 164, 192
Landser (infantry soldiers), 137
The Last Voyage of the Wilhelm
    Gustloff (Knopp, documentary),
    227
Laval, Pierre, 132
Lazarett (military hospital), 231–32
League of German Girls. *See Bund*

Deutscher Mädchen (BDM)
Leeb, Johannes, 42–46, 55
Legacy of Silence (Bar-On), 228–29
Lentz, Liesel, 220–21
Lenz, Siegfried, 262
Lettow-Vorbeck, Paul von, 17
Ley, Robert, 69, *70*
Lobkowitz family, 162
Lodenfrey (Munich fashion house),
    44
London, Jack, 43
Lorkova, Andrea, 3, *7*, 7–11
Ludwig (Hans Dunker's classmate/
    Erika Dunker's brother), 27, *83*,
    250–51, 255, 256, *256*
Lundgren, Hermann, 40–41

M

Magic Mountain (Mann), 38
Maik (bookstore attendant), 97
Mandela, Nelson, 266
Manderbach, Richard, *70*
Mann, Erika, 91
Mann, Thomas, 38, 39, 91
Mannhart, Franz
    on combat, 113–19, *114*, *118*,
        121–23, 192, 214
    as Feldafing School student, 45, *45*,
        46, *48*, 72, 74, 109–11, 119–20
    late life of, 107, *109*, 123
    on Nazi propaganda, 84, 86, 88
    on *Sippenhaft* (kin liability),
        111–12
Mannhart, Karin, 107, 109, 114, 123,
    215–16
Marie (Hans Dunker's maternal
    grandmother), 17, 86, *86*, 155, 243
Marienburg order castle, 67
Marinesko, Alexander Ivanovich,
    227–28
Marlene (Erika Dunker's sister), 118,
    251, 256–57
Marquardt, Fritz, 249–50

Martenson (soldier), 8, 171, 189, 194
Martha (Hans Dunker's paternal grandmother), *18*, 155, *155*
Marx, Karl, 43
masquerade balls, 46, 110, *110*
Massaquoi, Hans-Jürgen, 90–91
May, Karl, 5, 43
McGill University, 254
Merkel, Angela, 269
Michael (soldier), 205–6
mineral water companies, 126
Moravia–Ostrava Offensive Operation, 181–88, *182*, *185*, *186*. *See also* Závada, battle for
Morell, Theodor, 116
Morlok, Helmut, 78
MPLA (Popular Movement for the Liberation of Angola), 265
Munich Agreement (1938), 6, 162
Mussolini, Benito, 212
MV *Wilhelm Gustloff*, 227

N

Namibia, independence of, 20, 264–66
Napolas
All of Life Is a Fight! (film), 102
Napola (film), 73
Napola Spandau, 57
SS–Junkerschulen and, 69
students' eventual careers, 74–75
in Treskau, 104
Napoleon, 27
National Political Educational Institutions (NPEA), 52
National Socialist German Workers' Party (NSDAP)
Brazil's publicity about membership in, 261–64
Feldafing School and, 38, 39, 103–4 (*See also* Feldafing School)
Hans Dunker's party application for, 28, 29
higher education system and, 67, 69–72

Napolas and, 52, 58
National Political Educational Institutions (NPEA), defined, 52
propaganda symbols of, 84, 87
National Socialist Women's League, 225
Nazi educational system. *See also* Feldafing School; Napolas; *Ordensburgen* (order castles)
Abiture (high school diploma), 113, 250–51
Adolf Hitler Schools (AHS), 58, 58–63, *63*
fees/financial arrangements of, 40, 57, 115
Gleichschaltung (synchronization) of, 56
hierarchy of, 45–46, 53
Hitler Youth and, 52, *53*, 54, 56, 59
masquerade balls, 46, 110, *110*
Napolas for girls, 54
propaganda of, 81–91 (*See also* Propaganda)
Prussian influence on, 54–55, 57, 69, 73
recruitment of students, 39–41, 75–76
Reichsjugendakademie (training institute), 72
sleep deprivation tactic, 138
SS–Junkerschulen, 68–70, 75–77, 128
students as victims *vs.* perpetrators, 78–79
students' careers/legacy of, 73–77
uniforms for students, 2, 44, *52*, 52–53, 56, 72, 73
Volksbildung (education for the people), 69
Nazi Germany's defeat, 211–29, 231–45
Black Tulip operation, 211
displaced persons (DPs), 248–49
German refugees, 211–13

Nazi Germany's defeat (*continued*)
German soldiers as prisoners of
war, 128–29, 137, 213–21, 233,
239, 241
Hans Dunker's discharge and
travel home, 231–34, 236–45
high-ranking Nazis' deaths and
escape, 212–13, 225–26
MV *Wilhelm Gustloff*, 227
Pirna during, *222*, 222–24
prisoners of war statistics, 233
rapes of German women and girls,
232–35
statistics of children's deaths,
228–29
Steuben (German ship), 228
Wolfskinder (wolf children), 226
Nazi Germany's military. *See
also* Basic training; *Flakhelfer;*
Nazi Germany's defeat; *SS
(Schutzstaffel); individual names of
battles*
assignments in final stage of war,
121–23, 165–66
basic training in, 135–50 (*See also*
Basic training)
burial of German soldiers, 8–11,
129
deserters from, 75, 104, 108, 112,
148, 188, 207–8, 224
Freiwilliger Arbeitsdienst (Volunteer
Labor Service), 85, 132
Landser (infantry soldiers), 137
Panzer/tank units first, 28, 77,
114, 120, 121, 165
SA (*Sturmabteilung*), 38, 42, 140
75th Infantry Division, 120
78th Sturm Division, 120
substance use as tactic, 116–17,
148–49, 154
Volkssturm (civilian army), 27
Wehrmachtauskunftstelle (*WASt*)
records, 120

Nazi ideology. *See also* Feldafing
School; Holocaust; National
Socialist German Workers' Party
(NSDAP); Nazi educational
system; Propaganda; Third Reich
history books
"a fighter for the Third Reich" from
Deutschland erwacht, 27
Ahnenpass (Aryan lineage proof),
40, 69
Beer Hall Putsch (1923), 140
censorship and book burning, 43
on eugenics, 57, 60–63, 78
Feldafing School and Nazi
indoctrination, 39, 40, 42–48
Kinderlandverschickung (KLV), 255
Middle Ages and symbolism to,
22, 67
on Protestantism, 251
on race, 41, 90
swastika, 87, 234
Nazi Party. *See* National Socialist
German Workers' Party (NSDAP)
Nehring, Walter, 120
Nero Decree, 153
Nietzsche, Friedrich, 102
Night of the Long Knives, 71
Nobel Prize controversy, 75–78
NSDAP. *See* National Socialist
German Workers' Party (NSDAP)
Nujoma, Sam, 264, 266
Nuremberg trials, 212

O

"Ode to Joy" (Beethoven), 157
O Globo (Brazilian newspaper), 261
Ohler, Norman, 117
Ordensburgen (order castles), 65–79
administration of, 67
Adolf Hitler Schools as feeder
system for, 67–68
Castle Birdsong as modern-day
museum, 59, 65–66, 69, 78–79

curriculum of, 67
defined, 67
Feldafing School and, 71–73
roll-call square of, *68, 70*
SS role of, 68–70, 75–77, 128
students' careers/legacy of school
    system, 73–77
Order of Merit of the Federal
    Republic of Germany
    (Bundesverdienstkreuz), 260–61
Ossadnik, Josef, 133, 164, 192
"Ossies," 94–97
Ottokar (king of Bohemia), 162
Oxford Brookes University, 1

P

Panje wagons, 172, *172*, 184
Panzer/tank units
    1st Panzer Army, 120
    Hitler Youth in Panzer Tank
        Divisions, 114
    96th Tank Division, 121
    SS Tank Grenadier Regiment 39,
        165
    tank grenadier training, 28
    10th SS Panzer Division
        Frundsberg, 77
Parsifal (Eschenbach), 21–22
Peru, students recruited from, 39–41
Pervitin, 116–17, 149, 154
Pfadfinder (Germany's Boy Scouts),
    99
physically/mentally handicapped
    victims, 57, 60–63, 78
"The Pied Piper," 97
Pirna (Germany)
    Adolf Hitler School (AHS) of, *58,*
        58–63, *63*
    end of war and, *222*, 222–24
Popular Movement for the
    Liberation of Angola (MPLA),
    265
Porath (soldier), 189, 191
Postulka, Alois, 11

Potsdam Conference (1945), 162,
    235
Přemyslovci (Czech royal dynasty),
    97
Prien, Günther, 58
propaganda, 81–91
    All of Life Is a Fight! (film), 102–3
    Blutfahne (blood flag), 140
    books about Third Reich and,
        93–105
    "Heil Hitler!" salute, 82–85
    against Jews, 43, 88, 101 (*See also*
        Holocaust; Jews)
    of NSDAP, 84, 87
    recruitment propaganda, 147,
        149–50
    against Russians, 88
    *School for Barbarians/Ten Million
        Children* (Mann) on, 81–84, 87
    songs and music, 82, 95–96,
        98–103
    SS image and, 126–27, 128
    swastika, 87, 234
    uniforms as, *83, 85*, 85–87, *86, 87*
    youth groups as, 88–91 (*See also*
        Bund Deutscher Mädchen [BDM];
        Hitler Youth)

R

race, Nazi ideology on, 41, 90
Ranke, Otto, 117
Der Rattenfänger von Hameln, 97
Ratzinger, Joseph, 75, 77–78, 126,
    262
Rebstock, Friedrich, 164, 168–70,
    173, 193
Red Army (RAF) faction bombing
    (1989), 74
Red Cross, 226, 233
Reichsjugendakademie (Nazi youth
    training institute), 72
Reich Specialist Medical Group, *68*
Reichsschule der NSDAP Feldafing, 38.
    See also Feldafing School

Rheinbach (Germany)
post–World War II, 259–60
synagogue of, 32
Riefenstahl, Leni, 137, 142
"right to be forgotten" court ruling, 78
Röhm, Ernst, 38, 71
Röhrs, Dr., 130
"Roland" (statue), 87–88
Romani people, killed by Hungary, 133
Rommel, Erwin, 58
Rudel, Hans-Ulrich, 58
Rudolf (Hans Dunker's second cousin), 119
Rudolf Virchow Hospital, 13
Rüffer (soldier), 26
Russians. *See also* Stalin, Joseph; Stalingrad, battle of; Závada, battle for
propaganda against, 88
Wehrmacht maps, 93
Rust, Bernhard, 69

S

SA *(Sturmabteilung)*
Beer Hall Putsch (1923), 140
Feldafing School and, 38, 42
Schirach, Baldur von, 62, 70, 95, 103, 141, 212
Schleef, Werner, 148
Schmidt (Hungarian soldier in Germany military), 205, 213, 217–18
Schmundt, Rudolf, 119–20
Scholtz, Harald, 69–70
Scholtz-Klink, Gertrud, 225
School for Barbarians/Ten Million Children (Mann), 81–84, 87
Schörner, Ferdinand, 108, 120, 148, 181, 224–25
Schrimpf, "Tiddy," 250, 253
Schumacher, Josef, 165, 175
Schuster, Otto, 46, 47–48

Scriba, Mrs. (author's neighbor), 84
Sethe, Paul, 105
75th Infantry Division (Nazi Germany), 120
78th Sturm Division (Nazi Germany), 120
Seydlitz, Walther von, 207–8
Simoneit, Ferdinand, 94–95, 104
Sippenhaft (kin liability)
intergenerational trauma, 77–79, 267–70
Kriegsenkel (grandchildren of war), 267, 269
Legacy of Silence (Bar-On) on, 228–29
post-traumatic stress disorder (PTSD) of child soldiers and, 33
transgenerational guilt and, 111–12
Sommer, Theo, 74
Sonthofen order castle, 67
South West Africa People's Organization (SWAPO), 264–66
Speer, Albert, 153
SS *(Schutzstaffel)*, 125–34. *See also* Basic training
basic training of (*See* Basic training)
battle of Stalingrad and German prisoners of war, 128–29
child soldiers of, 126–27
Feldafing School and, 45, 49
Fischach and, 45
Geneva Convention violations, 214
Gestapo and, 126
Grass and, 75–78
Heeresgruppe Mitte (Army Group Center), 120, 127, 181, 224
Himmler and, 125–26, 128, 133
Horst Wessel Division of, 133–34, 164, 165, 187
internal units of, 126
mineral water companies of, 126
multiple nationalities of soldiers, 128, 130–33

Napolas and, 55, 57
physical attributes of soldiers, 128
prisoners of war from, 233
propaganda image of, 126–27, 128
recruits of, 128–32
SS–Junkerschulen and higher
    education, 68–70, 75–77, 128
uniforms as propaganda of, 85
Waffen-SS, 76, 121–23, 126, 130,
    132, 170, 187
Wehrmacht role of, 127–28
St. Stephani church, 155, *155*
Stacha, Jan, *7*, 7–10, 132–33, 164,
    175, 193, 195
Stalin, Joseph, 130, 240
Stalingrad, battle of, 128–29, 182,
    207–8
Stalin Organs, *182*, 182–83
Stauffenberg, Nina, 111
Stauffenberg group, 111–13, 120
Steinheil, E. Forel, 247
Stern, Hans, 263
Steuben (German ship), 228
Stevenson, Robert Louis, 43
Stutthof concentration camp, 149–50
Sudetenland, 161–79
    Germany's defeat and, 215–16
    HKL (front line) conditions,
        168–79, *170*, *172*
    modern-day, 161–62
    Moravia–Ostrava Offensive
        Operation and, 181–88, *182*, *185*,
        186
    soldiers' travel conditions, 161–68,
        167
swastika, 87, 234
Szálasi, Ferenc, 133

T

Tall One (soldier), 195, 202
tank units. *See* Panzer/tank units
Tannhäuser (Wagner), 162
10th SS Panzer Division Frundsberg,
    77

Third Reich. *See* Nazi educational
    system; Nazi Germany's defeat;
    Nazi Germany's military; Nazi
    ideology; Propaganda; *individual
    names of Nazi leaders; individual
    names of Nazi organizations*
Third Reich history books, 93–105
    "Book and Bunker Town" of
        Wünsdorf and, 93–94, *94*
    *The Flag Is More Than Death:
        Novel of a Betrayed Generation*
        (Wagner), 94–95, 104, 108
    *The Flag Is More Than Death:
        Songs from the Times of the Nazis*
        (Heyer), 94–95, 98, 100–102
    *The Flag Is More Than Death: the
        Sacrificed Youth* (Simoneit),
        94–95, 104
Tieke, Wilhelm, 164, 168–70, 173,
    193
Tillman (Hans Dunker's landlady's
    son), 252
Topographie des Terrors (Topography
    of Terror), 62
T4 Program, 57, 60–63
Triumph of the Will (Riefenstahl,
    film), 137, 142
Trümmerfrauen (rubble women),
    233

U

uniforms, *83*, *85*, 85–87, *86*, *87*
United Nations
    Namibia independence and,
        264–66
    Relief and Rehabilitation
        Administration (UNRRA),
        248–49
University of Göttingen, 251–53

V

Vergangenheitsbewältigug (coming to
    terms with one's past), 245

Vichy France, as SS soldiers, 132
Villino (Mann family's house), 39
Vogelsang order castle. *See* Castle
  Birdsong
Volksbildung (education for
  the people), 69. *See also* Nazi
  educational system
Volksdeutsche (ethnic expatriate
  Germans), 128, 131
Voltaire, 98

W

Wachtberg (Germany), post–World
  War II, 107–9
Waffen-SS, 76, 121–23, 126,
  130, 132, 170, 187. *See also* SS
  (*Schutzstaffel*)
Wagner, Günter, 103–4, 110
Wagner, Richard, 162
Waititi, Taika, 83
Walser, Martin, 262
Wandervogel (Wandering Birds),
  98–99, *99*
Wechmar, Rüdiger von, 57–58, 74
Wehrmacht
  Hans Dunker's records, 120
  prisoners of war from, 233
  Russian map collection of, 93
  Schörner pension paid by, 225
  uniforms as propaganda of, 85
Weimar Republic, 143–44
Weizsäcker, Richard von, 35
Wenck, Walther, 108
Wenzel (soldier), 8, 194, 196, 206,
  208
Wessel, Horst, 39, 82, 133
"Wessies," 94–97
"Wild Geese Are Flying through the
  Night" (Flex), 98
Wilhelm Gustloff, 227
Wilhelm I (emperor), 85
Wilhelm II (emperor), 13, 84–85,
  86

Wir waren Hitlers Eliteschüler (*We
  Were Hitler's Elite Students*, Leeb),
  42–46
Wolfskinder (wolf children), 226
A Woman in Berlin (*Eine Frau in
  Berlin*, anonymous), 154
World War II. *See also* Cold
  War; Hitler, Adolf; Holocaust;
  Nazi educational system;
  Nazi Germany's defeat; Nazi
  Germany's military; Závada,
  battle for
  artifacts of, *5*
  battle of Berlin, 108, 110
  battle of Stalingrad, 128–29, 182,
    207–8
  Bremen air raid, 155
  Castle Birdsong and Allied
    occupation, 66
  desertion of German soldiers,
    108
  Dresden bombing (February 1945),
    4, 151–59
  Hannover bombing (October
    1943), 153
  list of locations, 271–73
  Munich Agreement (1938) and,
    6, 162
  Nuremberg trials, 212
  Potsdam Conference (1945), 162,
    235
  Wehrmachtauskunftstelle (*WASt*)
    records, 120
Wunsch, Stefan, 59
Wünsdorf ("Book and Bunker
  Town"), 93–94, *94*

Y

youth groups. *See* Girls and
  women of Nazi Germany; Hitler
  Youth; Nazi educational system;
  Propaganda

Z

Závada, battle for, 181–99
  burials following, 8–11
  church in, *6*, *7*, 10–11
  Dunker's injury in, 8, 9
  events of, 188–99, *190*, *193*, 201–9,
    202
  German and Czech names for, 3
  German landmines and, 206, 208
  modern-day Závada, 1–11, 175
  Moravia–Ostrava Offensive
    Operation and, 181–88, *182*, *185*,
    186

ABOUT THE AUTHOR

HELENE MUNSON grew up in Brazil, Liberia, and Germany. She spent most of her adult life in New York City and Berlin. She studied at University of London, earning a degree concentrated in modern world history, and at Oxford, earning a master's degree that focused on armed conflicts. Learning about today's child soldiers gave her insight into her father's ordeal. When she is not traveling, Helene lives with her grey rescue cat, Trotsky, on eastern Long Island, where she spends her time swimming, reading, and writing.

helenemunson.com | helenemunson helene_storyteller